PUTTING THE FACT IN FANTASY

Expert Advice to Bring Authenticity
to Your Fantasy Writing

EDITED BY

Dan Koboldt

Foreword by Scott Lynch

WRITER'S
DIGEST
BOOKS

WRITER'S
DIGEST
BOOKS

An imprint of Penguin Random House LLC
penguinrandomhouse.com

Copyright © 2022 by Daniel C. Koboldt

Trade paperback ISBN: 9780593331996
Ebook ISBN: 9780593332009

Printed in the United States of America

Book design by Ashley Tucker

CONTENTS

PART 3
HOW TO MAKE IT UP: WORLD-BUILDING

PART 4
WEAPONS AND WARFARE: WHEN IN DOUBT, ADD THESE

THE POINT IS
TO SCREW UP BETTER

A PEP TALK ABOUT RESEARCH
AND WORLD-BUILDING

As a boy in the 1980s I was fascinated by a television miniseries called *North and South*, which told a story of the American Civil War and seemed, to my young eyes, an infinitely vast epic starring every actor in the known universe. Duly inspired, at the ripe age of ten I set out to write my own multivolume narrative masterpiece concerning the War Between the States. Most of my previous (incomplete) attempts to write books had been based on cartoons or games, but with this project I entered a new phase. This would be a real novel, for big people. It had to be full of big ideas! It would have battles on water and on land! It would detail the triumphs and tragedies of families on both sides of the struggle! In my head I imagined I might need six or seven volumes to cover the whole grand story. A thousand pages a volume, at least! The covers would be great, too, with lots of explosions! Big explosions for the biggest bigness ever dreamed up by a guy with a whole decade of life experience—*Men of Blue, Men of Gray!*

(I'm not kidding; that's absolutely what I was going to call it.)

Dizzy with excitement, I sat down to commence the great work. Ballpoint pen met notebook paper.

Exactly one and a half pages later, I gave up.

In that page and a half, a plucky Alabama boy on the cusp of manhood woke, ate breakfast, shaved, hitched up his trusty plow horse, and started a day's work on his farm. That's it, the complete summary of *Men of Blue, Men of Gray*: A guy ate breakfast. In the middle of that second page I discovered an invisible wall, and my eager little brain slammed into it at the figurative equivalent of two hundred miles per hour. Although I was not a child that anyone would have called "rich in self-awareness," my work was halted by a sudden shocking insight— I had no idea, not even a tiny fraction of any idea, what the hell I was writing about.

I knew nothing about living in the American South, I was a complete stranger to being on the cusp of manhood, and I was still years away from shaving. I didn't know what someone in 1861 would have eaten for breakfast, I had no clue how to hitch a horse, and while I was loosely aware that fields were plowed, I was nonetheless innocent of all procedural knowledge. There wasn't a single thing in my feverishly scrawled page and a half that I was capable of describing any further, and the realization paralyzed me. Everything I had ever previously conjured, all my childhood drawings and stories, were predicated on magic and science fantasy and cartoon logic. I could do anything I wanted! There was no possible way to be wrong in those circumstances. But now I was trying to negotiate with reality, and reality came with a long list of demands already prepared.

It was probably the first time in my life I consciously grappled with the idea that not knowing something could damage the thing I was trying to make.

Now, that sounds dramatic. Damage what, exactly, and damage it how, and damage it by whose standards? One's credibility, certainly, and one's self-respect (more on that later). However, what we're talking most urgently about here is damaging the audience's greatest possession—their suspension of disbelief. When disbelief is suspended, it means that someone has fought past all the myriad responsibilities, anxieties, discomforts, and distractions life has to offer, and is experiencing your work with some degree of concentration and acceptance. They have bought into your premise. They have consented to the notion that a magic ring must be thrown into a volcano, or that faster-than-light travel is possible, or that a man in a locked room could be murdered without a sound in the middle of a garden party. Suspension of disbelief is a precious commodity, a sensation to be cherished. It's a little taste of awe and wonder that can make memories for life, leaving us convinced we have shared the experiences of someone who has breathed the air or walked the fields or fought the battles of a completely different world.

Naturally, the audience (whether that audience be reader, watcher, listener, player, or something yet undreamed of) resents it when this pleasing sensation of immersion is damaged, and nothing pokes a hole in suspension of disbelief faster than contradicting what the audience knows, with absolute personal certainty, to be true. A glaring inaccuracy in a work of fiction has a corrosive effect on the audience's trust, and leads to reconsideration of assertions or story elements that had previously been glibly accepted. After all, if you could be wrong about one clear and obvious thing, what else might you have been wrong about along the way?

I have a bit of news that will seem absolutely dire, but if you'll trust and bear with me for a moment, I'll try to explain that it's actually a good thing. Ready for the hard part? Here it is: Whenever you create a piece of fiction, you're guaranteed to screw something up. Guaranteed. You can't avoid it. You will, inevitably, misunderstand something, or fail to research something, or experience one of those simple misfirings of understimulated neurons that will leave you scratching your head years later, wondering how you could have ever been so careless. The answer is simple—like me, you're mortal! We can't help ourselves. The more things we create, the more opportunities we'll have to make fools of ourselves, and that will never change even if we both work very, very hard and live to be one hundred and ninety. We can't make perfect things.

"Oh great," you're now saying. "I'm considering an investment in this lovely book, which is absolutely thick with facts and rules and guidelines and essays on everything from crafts to culture to religion, and this jerk Lynch is telling me it won't matter, can't possibly matter, even if I somehow double my natural life span!"

But ahhhh—it absolutely will matter. The fact that errors are inevitable ought to be a freeing notion rather than a dreadful one. It means that every successful work of art in human history, every famous painting, every great novel, every blockbuster film, has met with success and earned its legacy despite having something wrong with it. Even Leonardo da Vinci scuffed his lines now and then. Even Shakespeare tried too hard. Even Ursula K. Le Guin contradicted herself on occasion. The point of our research, all this mental sweat and tears, all these studies and exercises in world-building, is not to live in anxiety about screwing up. Since that's inevitable, it has to be about screwing up *better*. Suspension of disbelief is something that can be repaired. Even glaring errors fade when submerged in a nice warm broth of better work. I think of it as a friendly transaction between creator and audience; suspension of disbelief can be purchased. Hand me a fantasy novel and show me a series of solid things—good depictions of the fantasy landscape, well-reasoned economics, thoughtful treatment of spirituality, gritty and medically accurate depictions of injury and death—and if the next thing you show me is a wild flight of fancy with no basis in fact, or even an outright mistake, I'm inclined to shrug and say, "What the hell, you've earned it." I might well remember the weaker points of the work, but if they are sufficiently outweighed by the good parts, the care and attention to other details, my forgiveness has no bounds.

Arthur Conan Doyle, justly celebrated for his Sherlock Holmes stories, was also noted for fumbling small details in a body of work wherein small details are critically important. In the story "The Adventure of Silver Blaze," a racing horse is kidnapped, disguised, and returned to the track just in time to gallop to a triumphant victory . . . which was completely against all standard procedures and would have ensured that Blaze and all of his associated humans were barred for life. When we first meet John Watson in *A Study in Scarlet*, he describes a wound from a musket ball in his shoulder, but by the time we reach *The Sign of Four*, the injury has somehow migrated to one of his legs. A neat trick, especially for an unguided nineteenth-century weapon. Do errors like these ruin the stories? My personal answer would be that I own three different copies of the complete Holmes canon. My broader answer would be that Holmes has been more popular than some of the world's major religions for nearly 140 years now. The asset column of the Holmes ledger is so rich that even a stack of memorable errors has never made any real dent in it.

My own debut novel, *The Lies of Locke Lamora*, contains an impressive number of goofs, and I'm happy to enumerate some of them here (because, I hope, the exercise is an educational one, and because I don't want the angry ghosts of da Vinci, Shakespeare, Le Guin, and Doyle teaming up to put me in my place). There is an embarrassing bit in which a character grasps white-hot metal with a thin wet towel, which is actually a bad idea despite the fact that I wrote him as knowing what he was doing. A dry towel would have served him better. I had not started training as a firefighter when that scene was written, and I did not yet have the understanding of certain thermal matters that I do now. There is a cavalier attitude toward the idea of knocking human beings unconscious by thumping them on their skulls as though it were harmless and easy (again, my emergency-responder training eventually corrected this misunderstanding and replaced it with a comprehension of grimmer reality). I had to add a waterfall to the story at the last minute because I drew my city map so carelessly that I had a river just sort of vanishing into nowhere. Indeed, I have a river called the Angevine, which was not actually an homage to the real-world Angevin dynasty but an act of completely forgetting that it existed, and then completely neglecting that words can be googled.

In the same vein, *The Lies of Locke Lamora* features a minor character called Conte, who was named in a deliberate homage to Richard Conte, an actor who appeared in *The Godfather* and the original *Ocean's 11*, two films that were major influences on my work. However, the word "conte" is also the Italian version of "count," and in a world filled with made-up Franco-Italianate words, it was certainly out of place. Poor Conte was especially puzzling to my Italian publishers and their translators. I received several notes to the effect of "What the hell do you mean, his name is just 'Count'? That doesn't make any sense—he works for the equivalent of a baron and a baroness, he guards their door, why would his name be Count?" The question was not unfair. *The Lies of Locke Lamora* is riddled with little moments of exuberant carelessness and outright error. It has also sold more than a million copies around the world, so I hope it serves as an exemplar of how other qualities might continue to outweigh a book's deficiencies for most of its readers.

We can't unwrite our mistakes—we can only move forward and strive to screw up better. This book is a fantastic resource to aid you in doing so. I would certainly have loved to have had a copy about fifteen years ago . . . might have saved me some trouble. May it do just that for you, and help you build deeper, wilder, more charming worlds for your audience to suspend their disbelief in.

—SCOTT LYNCH

HOW TO ASK AN EXPERT

ᕲᕲ

BY ERIC PRIMM

Fantasy is often judged by its world-building. Fair or not, the setting makes or breaks the story as much as the characters. The world of the story influences character and plot by its very mechanics. The mundane, everyday parts of a world—politics, language, even exercise habits—affect the character's development throughout their life. Try to picture Harry Dresden from the Dresden Files living on Roshar from the Stormlight Archive. While Harry could probably survive, he'd stand out like a sore thumb. Building worlds requires a range of knowledge to make a coherent, consistent setting, but the story needs only the information necessary to advance the plot. Building worlds requires research to make that setting believable, and part of any research process is to seek out experts. The following tips will help you seek out experts and get the right information from them.

Part of seeking out a source is knowing how to define an expert. Expertise is often, but not always, marked with some sort of credential. Often degrees confer an air of capability, but certificates don't equate to knowledge. Doctors must graduate from medical school, but the degree doesn't mean they're ready to practice. They are required to undergo an apprenticeship through the internship and residency programs. It's this apprenticeship time that builds expertise. The credential doesn't make the expert; time in the field, working with others in the field, and building practical knowledge are all ingredients in the recipe of expertise. Seek out those involved in the debates and conversations taking place in their chosen vocation. This indicates that the person is up to date on their field. Time spent working builds upon the knowledge gained from study. Therefore, don't just seek out credentials, seek out experience.

Next, make sure the expert is the appropriate one to answer your question. Knowledge becomes more complex as one researches a subject, and specialized information requires specialized knowledge. Just as the average person would be able to tell the difference between the author's cooking, a hobbyist's meal, and a chef's feast, the reader will be able to tell if an author has an average, hobbyist, or expert approach to world-building. The deeper the author wishes to go into detail, the deeper the author has to go into research. For example, there are many kinds of martial arts in the world. When writing a fight scene, an author may keep the fighting general. In that case, any martial artist from a boxer to a sumo wrestler would be able to discuss fighting. However, if the author calls out a specific martial art, like Brazilian jiu-jitsu or Filipino arnis, the author needs to seek out practitioners who train in that martial art. Each contains motions, concepts, and strategies that are shared across different disciplines. A punch is a punch is a punch. But each martial art also has unique traditions, language, motions, concepts, and strategies. So, a savate boxer will understand the mechanics of kicks in Muay Thai, but the details of the wai khru ritual will be missing. It's those same details that will make the author's fantasy martial art believable.

How an author asks a question matters as much as the information being sought. This goes beyond mere politeness. Please, be polite, but also be specific. For example, let's say you decided to base part of your fantasy world on the Cold War between the US and the Soviet Union. If you ask a historian to explain the Cold War, they're going to give you book or documentary recommendations. There's too much history that falls under the banner of the Cold War because it spanned the entire globe. A high-level overview is going to be too vague and won't provide the details necessary for a good setting. Even breaking down the Cold War into regional areas—Europe, Russia, the Korean Peninsula, Africa, or China—is still too vague. Books abound that discuss generalities and specifics, but you must drill down into the exciting passages. Maybe your Cold War fantasy could be inspired by Project Bluebird, a CIA-funded research project designed to fend off communist mind-control techniques based on the trial of Hungarian cardinal József Mindszenty. With these details, you can ask about narcotics and mind-control techniques or the show trial of a priest in a supposedly atheistic nation. Not only is this a more interesting question because it gives a specific starting point for a discussion, but it also shows the expert that you're willing to do a little work. Asking a vague question is also akin to asking someone to teach you a subject. Focused questions indicate a familiarity with the topic that fosters discussion instead of lecturing.

When the expert answers your question, expect more information than you actually need. The expert doesn't know exactly what piece of information will make your story work. You may not know until you sift through the response. Treat the response as you would a book. Read it. Read it again while taking notes. If it's a conversation, record it. Listen to it a couple times. Take notes. Did the expert answer your question? Does anything need clarification? Did it help? Did any tangents sound more interesting than the main answer? The point of research is to deepen your understanding of the world you're trying to create. Does the expert's response accomplish that goal?

Just as endless revision is a diversion to put off finishing the project, endless research can be as well. It's possible to research too much. Remember the goal is to use details from this world to flesh out your fantasy world. How do you know if you've got enough information? Honestly, this is the wrong question. You don't have to have mounds and piles of information. You have to understand the information. Do you understand it enough to be able to convince someone unfamiliar with the subject that you know what you're talking about? If so, then you've done enough. Your job as an author is to convince a reader unfamiliar with your world that what they're reading works in that setting. Another way to gauge your knowledge is by asking the expert the following question: "If I understand you correctly, you're saying [insert knowledge here]?" This question ensures that you understand the expert's response in the way it was intended.

Finally, when asking an expert for help, you are asking someone to do work for you. Remember that when asking. It helps to acknowledge their work. The expert may say no. After all, everyone is caught up in their own lives. Say thank you anyway because it builds a bridge, and maybe that person can help you in the future. Maybe that person will come to *you* for help in the future. Remember that the person on the other side of your question is a person, not an anthropomorphized Google search.

To put it all together, let's return to the fictional Cold War setting. One society in your world learns that the other has come across a stockpile of magical weapons. To understand how a society might react, you begin researching the so-called missile gap during the Cold War. After a little bit of reading, you come to find out that the missile gap was political propaganda based on bad intelligence. Instead of asking a historian who specializes in the Cold War or a political scientist who studies propaganda what the missile gap was, you can ask how the politicians used the missile gap to their advantage. How quickly did the US learn that the missile gap wasn't real? Did politicians use the fear generated by the missile gap to stockpile their own weapons or initiate negotiations? Both? By understanding how people responded, you can choose how your society responds. Do they follow our history, or do they branch off on their own? Either way, with that research, you can add details to make the character choices consistent with how people react.

Fictional stories are an author's reactions to their own time. Stories are born out of an author's experiences and dreams. But even fantasies require a certain amount of verisimilitude with the human experience. The more true the author can make details the reader is familiar with, the more willing the reader will be to trust the author's fictional elements like magic, dragons, and faster-than-light travel. By getting the details right, the author immerses the reader in their world, and asking an expert is a good way to get the details right.

PART 1

❧

IT ALREADY HAPPENED: HISTORY AS INSPIRATION

WORLD-BUILDING WITH THE SPANISH INQUISITION

ॐ

BY JAY S. WILLIS

Both Monty Python's and Mel Brooks's modern portrayals of red-robed men with funny accents exploit the brutality and hatred derived from the Spanish Inquisition for laughs. All joking aside, this powerful medieval and Renaissance institution born of antisemitism and over-zealous religious fervor offers an invaluable resource for any fantasy, alt-history, or sci-fi author in world-building. Want a disturbing way to torture your characters and/or build an oppressive regime? Look no further than the Spanish Inquisition.

The first inquisitor general to receive a royal appointment was Tomás de Torquemada, who had been one of the seven inquisitors commissioned by papal letter in 1482. He was made inquisitor of Aragon, Catalonia, and Valencia by Pope Sixtus IV on October 17, 1483. The appointment of Torquemada was a crucially important event in the development of the Spanish Inquisition.

Rigid and unbending, he would listen to no compromise of what he
deemed to be his duty, and in his sphere he personified the union of the

spiritual and temporal swords which was the ideal of all true church-men. Under his guidance the Inquisition rapidly took shape and extended its organization throughout Spain and was untiring and remorseless in the pursuit and punishment of the apostates. —Henry Charles Lea, A History of the Inquisition of Spain, *vol. I, 174*

As the Spanish Inquisition gradually gained independence from the crown, it rose in power and influence to become an institution virtually equal with the Spanish crown, with supremacy over all other governmental bodies.

The Spanish Inquisition dealt with heretics in many disturbing ways. Under the Inquisitorial Process,

the accused was assumed to be guilty and . . . the object of the tribunal was to induce or coerce him to confess his guilt; that, for this purpose, he was substantially deprived of facilities for defence and that the result, for the most part, depended on his powers of endurance which the judges, at discretion, could test to the utmost. —Lea, History, *vol. II, 465*

The accused was virtually helpless. The individual was taken to a secret prison, confined to a cell and excluded from all outside contacts for days, weeks, or even months, and left wondering about their fate. Inquisitors were not only attempting to punish the body; their holy mission of saving souls, though the means were quite questionable, was of the utmost importance. An Inquisitional Procedure was to be based on the ideal of the inquisitors being able to judge all cases based on truth, justice, and impartiality.

The evidence of witnesses is scrutinized in the light of their character and quality and those who are found to bear false witness are most severely punished. The accused, while detained in the prisons, are treated kindly and liberally, according to their condition; the poor and the sick are abundantly furnished with food and medicines . . . and are favored in every way . . . and . . . as Time is the revealer of truth, cases are not hurriedly finished but are prudently prolonged, as is requisite when there is such peril of the life, fame and property, not only of the accused but of his kindred. —Lea, History, *vol. II, 483*

The inquisitorial ideal remained only that, an ideal that was never truly attained. The holy mission of saving souls was attempted by inhumanely harsh methods, including the extraction of confessions by torture and various punishments for recompense.

The crime of heresy was exceptionally hard to prove, and the Inquisition's most effective means of ascertaining the truth was through confessions brought about by torture.

The conditions held to justify torture were that the offence charged was of sufficient gravity, and that the evidence, while not wholly decisive, was such that the accused should have the opportunity of "purging" it, by endurance proportionate to its strength. From the inquisitor's point of view, it was a favor to the accused, as it gave him a chance which was denied to those whose condemnation was resolved upon. —Lea, History, *vol. III, 7*

Certain limitations were supposed to be placed on torture. No torture was allowed to intentionally put life or limb in peril. Technically, torture was allowed only to be applied once. However, it was often stopped, suspended for a time, and resumed later.

Without going into their gory details, the varieties of torture employed by the Inquisition can often be judged solely by name: water torture, the pear, the heretics' fork, the rack, and the saw and the pendulum were all methods employed, ranging greatly in severity. The meticulous reports maintained by the Inquisition reveal the stark reality of their tactics.

> *The secretary faithfully recorded all that passed, even to the shrieks of the victim, his despairing ejaculations and his piteous appeals for mercy or to be put to death, nor would it be easy to conceive anything more fitted to excite the deepest compassion than their cold-blooded, matter-of-fact reports.* —*Lea*, History, *vol. III, 18*

The punishment system utilized by the Inquisition was as harsh as the torture system used in gaining confessions. There were several minor penalties implemented by the Inquisition. Reprimands, sometimes verbal, other times as severe as lashings, were used often. Those accused of even minor offenses were also exiled at times. The more peculiar of such lesser punishments included the razing of the house of a heretic, and such spiritual penance as requiring fasting and pilgrimages.

The harsher penalties usually resulted in severe wounds or death. Lesser penalties, if they can truly be called such, were imposed with great zeal. Scourging, when a public lashing took place while the victim's charges were read aloud, was common. Some of the unfortunates who were convicted by the Inquisition were sentenced to man the oars of the Spanish fleet's galleys. Others were imprisoned permanently.

The harshest of all punishments were the burning at the stake and the auto-da-fé. Those who were burned at the stake were the heretics who were turned out by the Church and handed over to the secular authorities to take over the criminal's punishment.

The auto-da-fé became the Spanish Inquisition's largest show of authority, and it generally spared no expense to ensure impressiveness and vast amounts of public attendance. Most, but not all, auto-da-fé ceremonies were held as public exhibitions. Some private ceremonies were held in churches, away from the public. During the auto-da-fé, the sentences of those heretics to be punished were read to the public after a procession of those condemned, the inquisitors, and all officials involved into the public square. The inquisitors preached a sermon followed by a general celebration. The burning of the condemned took place at the end of the day, after all the minor penalties had been administered.

The Spanish Inquisition gradually came to an end due to European political factors, internal corruption, and general public hatred. It was officially abolished on July 15, 1834. Yes, it lasted that long.

The Inquisition's fanaticism grew in Spain out of the enmity between Christians and Jews. However, during its operation, it gradually became a completely independent body, functioning not to oppress the Jews but to finish the holy quest of saving the world from heretics of all sorts. It was efficiently organized and became quite effective in accomplishing its purpose.

The memories of the horrid accomplishments of the Spanish Inquisition are often selectively forgotten. Such atrocities should never be justified or allowed to continue by society, whether committed in the name of religious fanaticism, politics, or individual prejudices. Alas, we all need to learn from the past so as not to repeat it. That doesn't mean fiction writers can't or shouldn't utilize the dark and insidious institution to forge meaningful and powerful conflicts in their stories. Substituting fantasy, or alien races, or practitioners of magic or other forbidden arts as the driving forces behind an Inquisition in fiction offers an untapped wealth of conflict for any author and opens wide meaningful opportunities to memorialize and learn from man's extensive inhumanity against man. Your characters will never see it coming. After all, "Nobody expects the Spanish Inquisition!"

REFERENCES

Henry Charles Lea, *A History of the Inquisition of Spain*, vols. I–IV (London: Macmillan Company, 1907).

FIVE FACTS ABOUT
THE AMERICAN OLD WEST

୧∾ଡ଼

BY HAYLEY STONE

I have a confession to make.

I haven't seen many Westerns. Maybe only a handful.

I know what you're thinking: *But, Hayley! You've written a novel set
in the Old West! And now you're writing this chapter about it! You fraud!
You no-good, dirty rotten scoundrel!*

Yes, yes. Let it all out.

Y'see, while both my dad and grandfather are enormous Western
film fans, I was never taken with them much myself growing up.
Maybe it was the harmful racial stereotypes that made villains or side-
kicks nonwhite (it's estimated one in four cowboys was actually Black,
but you'd hardly know it from the predominantly white casts), or the
scarcity of compelling female characters who didn't ultimately suc-
cumb to damseling by the end of the film. It wasn't until I began researching the actual history that I developed a deep love for the period.

What's more, with the growing popularity of flintlock fantasy
and weird west, the Western setting is seeing a delightful revival. Yet,

like those classic Westerns of yesteryear, there is a danger of falling into those same tropes. Which is a darn shame, because truth is stranger than fiction, and the real Old West might boast the strangest tales of all.

That said, here are a few interesting facts about the *real* Old West in all its wacky, frontier glory.

1. It Was Customary to Photograph Dead Outlaws

Being an outlaw was a rough gig, and most criminals' careers ended in a dust grave. Even so, it was sometimes difficult to convince a nervous public that the bad men were, in fact, dead. One solution was photography. Not only was photographing dead outlaws necessary for legal purposes (confirming the kill for a reward, if one was being offered), but it also helped settle locals.

Even more disturbing, the dead outlaws were posed for the photos in an upright position, usually propped against a wall. Photographers had to move quickly, while the outlaws were still "wet," in order to get them fixed before rigor mortis set in.

Sometimes the mythology of an outlaw survived his own death, making the photographic evidence even more crucial. In the case of the outlaw Bill Dalton's death, one newspaper—fed up with their doubting readership—responded with a snarky headline that could be ripped right from *The Onion*: "Mr. Dalton Continues Dead."

Yes, Westerners may have been accused of a lot of things, but being gullible wasn't one of them. They were the original "pics or it didn't happen" crowd.

2. People Took Their Cows Very Seriously

Often more detrimental than outlaws, range wars were a constant source of violence on the frontier, particularly in Montana, Wyoming, and Texas. Few things were as important to a man out West as land and cattle; fortunes rose and died on these cows. In fact, many wars stemmed from conflicts between great cattle empires (some managed by British or Scottish companies) and homesteaders. They're your typical "mom 'n' pop versus corporate" stories—but with more cows.

Whether a feud or a range war, when a dispute turned bloody—as they did frequently—it was just as likely to stay contentious for a long time. These Western "blood feuds" passed from generation to generation, kept alive by kin and a mean, stubborn spirit.

Arguments over cattle or horses could often be simply an excuse for fighting, too. The Civil War left a lot of sore losers on the side of the South, and the conflict experienced its dying throes in many of these feuds and wars.

Examples include: the Sutton-Taylor feud, the Graham-Tewksbury feud (also known as the Pleasant Valley War), and the Horrell-Higgins feud.

3. Not All Women Worked as Prostitutes

This should go without saying—but apparently not, if you judge by the amount of female characters practicing the world's oldest profession in Western fiction.

In reality, frontier women lived diverse lives. They worked as physicians, ranchers, businesswomen, and brothel owners. Many were wives and mothers. Others even became outlaws themselves. And contrary to popular belief, saloon girls and hurdy-gurdy girls—German immigrant girls who played an instrument of the same name and worked as paid dance partners out West to lonely prospectors—were not interchangeable names for a prostitute but separate careers altogether.

Prostitution was not a one-size-fits-all business, either. It had its own caste system, strictly enforced by the women themselves, beginning at the top with those working in high-end parlor houses, and ending with crib girls at the bottom who had to see multiple men a night just to survive. Unfortunately, given the unforgiving nature of the business, there was almost no possibility for upward mobility. Instead, women who aged badly or women who contracted a venereal disease had only one way to go—down. The idea of a prostitute marrying her john and escaping the life has been romanticized as well; when it did happen, it often ended badly due to suspicions of infidelity.

4. Alcohol Was Prohibited in Indian Territory

The sale of alcohol to Native Americans had been prohibited since 1802, but it was not until 1832 that Congress passed a law banning it entirely from Indian Territory. One judge later explained its purpose as being for "the preservation of order in the Indian tribes, and peace between them and the frontier settlers . . . and the preservation of the existence of these savages." The United States government *clearly* had the Native people's best interests at heart. Right.

Much as Prohibition in the twentieth century led to the rise of the mob, prohibition in Indian Territory led to all kinds of smuggling efforts, particularly on its Kansas border. Natives who wanted to drink or purchase liquor were required to come over the border to do it; yet any Native who wanted to conduct trade business could not do so if they were so much as judged to be inebriated. The law was also nearly impossible to enforce, especially given that the various tribes were not consulted on it beforehand.

Far from being the protective measure judges claimed it to be, evidence suggests prohibition caused a whole slew of other problems, ultimately doing more harm to the Midwestern tribes than good.

And last, but not least . . .

5. Express Agents Were Badass

Many US Marshals have gone down in history as tough as nails, and rightfully so, but those brave men who guarded express cars were no shrinking violets, either.

Following the Civil War, train robbery became a profitable industry for many outlaws, and the most valuable target was a train's express car. At least one express agent was situated inside, along with a substantial amount of money. His job was straightforward: If the train was held up, he was to defend the express car at all costs. That meant everything from barricading the door to ventilating any robber who made it inside.

Unfortunately, outlaws would try and blow up the barricaded door, maiming or sometimes even killing the agent inside. In one instance, to avoid such a fate, an express agent let an outlaw inside, giving the appearance of surrender—only to then take an ice maul to the misled bandit's head. Not such a pacific fellow, after all.

In Summary

The West was a unique culture all its own, where outlaws prowled the open ranges, and feuds drew whole families into conflict. Women were as present as men, and made of just the same mettle. Prohibition in Indian Territory caused more problems than it solved, leading to smuggling operations on the part of white settlers in particular, while express agents were the first and often last line of defense against greedy killers.

As a setting, the Old West offers a gold mine of potential story lines and characters—certainly more than the stereotypical lone ranger tale! If you're going to tackle the Old West, consider drawing from its bottomless well of real-life history rather than decades-old film classics. In addition to inspiration, you'll discover diversity and details necessary to making your readers feel like they've just stepped outside for a show-down beneath a hot, Western sun.

FURTHER READING

Dee Brown, *The Gentle Tamers: Women of the Old Wild West* (Lincoln, NE: Bison Books, 1981).

Bat Masterson, *Famous Gunfighters of the Western Frontier* (1907).

Joseph G. Rosa, *Age of the Gunfighter: Men and Weapons on the Frontier, 1840–1900* (New York: Smithmark, 1993).

Robert Barr Smith, *Tough Towns: True Tales from the Gritty Streets of the Old West* (Guilford, CT: TwoDot, 2006).

FEMALE PROFESSIONS IN MEDIEVAL EUROPE

‿❧

BY TAHEREH SAFAVI

Homemaker, midwife, prostitute. Sometimes it seems like those are the only female archetypes in medieval fantasy, and the occasional chain-mail-bikini-clad "warrior" wielding a sword that weighs more than she does.

So what exactly did women in medieval Europe do? As with all things fantasy, an author doesn't need to stick strictly to history, but a bit of logic in your world-building goes a long way. To help you extrapolate the role of women in your fantasy world, this chapter aims to give you a fundamental understanding of the reasons why things often panned out as they did.

Limitations of Premodern Childbirth

Childbirth is really, really hard. Ask your mother. Ask any mother. Then ask them how it would have gone without an epidural.

Thanks to modern medicine, childbirth today has drastically lower chances of infection and hemorrhaging, not to mention those lovely painkillers. Relatively, it's a cakewalk. And any mother will tell you it's still no cakewalk.

In addition to the difficulty of childbirth itself, it's important to remember that widely available effective birth control (such as the Pill in the 1960s) made a huge difference in the lives of women. Suddenly, they could choose not to reproduce. Before that, the work a woman took on was often limited by what she could do while pregnant or with a nursing infant in tow. One need only ask a modern stay-at-home parent how much else they get done during the day, and remember that before widespread, affordable infant formula (1950s), that parent had to be the mother, as she was the only one who could feed the child.

Wet nurses did exist, but in a small hamlet of only a few hundred people, the odds were low that there was another woman who'd just weaned her own child but was still producing milk. It's important to realize that milk production demands a lot of calories, and in the pre-industrial world, food availability was always in question. A woman forced to wet-nurse a second child, when her own child still needed milk, might see her own child starve. If you create a character who has use of a wet nurse, you must be prepared to write her as extremely wealthy, extremely lucky, or extremely cruel.

Exceptions to the Rule

The infertile, the postmenopausal, and the celibate were all free to pursue professional callings. But remember, when populating your fantasy world without available birth control, those women were exceptions. If your female character's time is not taken up largely by the continuation of the species, stop to think of a specific reason why.

Living in a convent is a fantastic reason. In addition to those with genuine religious callings, convents provided a refuge for female non-conformists and intellectuals. Nearly 10 percent of women in medieval France and England never married, and "marriage to the church" provided many of them with a livelihood and education not otherwise available. Female writers, artists, and religious scholars were nurtured by the church, as well as botanists, healers, and educators. The medieval church was a major economic enterprise, and the abbess of a large convent was a force to be reckoned with.

According to the CDC, around 10 percent of women in modern America are infertile. Assuming an average menopausal age of fifty, another 15 percent of the medieval female population were too old to become pregnant, based on skeletal analysis of archaeological sites. This adds up to 35 percent of the female population without children—although some of those women surviving to menopause likely never had children, given the not-insubstantial odds of dying in childbirth. Reducing the total a little to account for women in two groups, e.g., those who were both older and also nuns, this means roughly 30 percent of your female population is realistically free to pursue occupations that would be hampered by having a small child in tow.

For the other 70 percent of women, childbirth and childcare figures prominently into their daily lives.

Running the Family Business

Most businesses were family-owned, and women with children participated in nearly every economic aspect of medieval life. In most cases, only a man was allowed to own property or a business, but his wife, daughters, mother, and sisters were invaluable to operating it. Frequently, women ran the entire show as proxy to absent male relatives.

As stated by Christine de Pizan (1363–c. 1430), a famously competent widow from Venice:

Because that knights, squires and gentlemen go upon journeys and follow the wars, it beseemeth wives to be wise in all they do, for that most often they dwell at home without their husbands who are at court or in diverse lands. . . . The lady who lives on her estates must be wise and must have the courage of a man. She should not oppress her tenants and workers but should be just and consistent. She should follow the advice of her husband and of wise counsellors so that people will not think she is merely following her own will. She must know the laws of warfare so that she can command her men and defend her lands if they are attacked. She should know everything pertaining to her husband's business affairs so that she can act as his agent in his absence or for herself if she should become a widow. She must be a good manager of workers. To supervise her workers, she needs a good knowledge of farming. She will be sure to have adequate supplies for the spinning and weaving of cloth for the wise housekeeper can sometimes bring in more profit than the revenue from the land.

Managing an estate is no mean task, similar to managing a large hotel, if that hotel might also have to mobilize as a military unit. If your political system is feudal, any man with an estate is away, either at war or schmoozing his superiors, a good portion of the year. The character who consents to let your adventurers sleep in the barn is almost certainly the lady of the manor, not the lord.

In towns, the wives of merchants or artisans could assist their husbands in their trades or pursue their own. Evidence of multiple proficiencies is shown in a 1363 parliamentary ordinance specifying that men had to keep one trade, while women might pursue as many as they pleased.

That exemption, however, speaks to the fact that although women could learn trades, they were rarely permitted to master them. Medieval guild records list many women, but rarely in positions of power or supervision, and often limited to lower levels of production by bizarrely specific laws. A female dyer, for example, was not permitted to lift cloth from the vats, and a female pastry maker was permitted to carry only one box of biscuits around town at a time.

Your female townswoman likely worked multiple odd jobs to make ends meet, possibly while carrying a baby on her back. It would also be entirely reasonable to see a competent baker's, cooper's, or wheelwright's wife practically running the whole business for him. Everyone in town might know she was the one to ask if you wanted something done, even though he was officially speaking for the family at guild meetings.

The textile industry was full of women. Medieval silk weavers were a notable exception among guilds, with women controlling every aspect of production, and predominantly female supervisors and guild masters. In other trades, the best legal loophole was if a woman's husband died. Many notable widows inherited property or businesses in their own right, often to huge financial success. The famous champagne house Veuve Clicquot literally translates as "Widow Clicquot." The eponymous widow was a far more formidable businesswoman than her late husband, and the house's best product is called, fittingly, La Grande Dame.

Other Unexpected Female Trades

Although it's easy to picture women working as midwives, in textile production, or as cooks and washerwomen, for some inspiration, the following is a list of unexpected trades from the Paris guild records of the 1300s. In all cases, there were fewer women than men, and some trades were later restricted to men only, but there are at least some historical precedents for women working in the following male-dominated fields:

- Apothecary
- Armorer
- Barber-surgeon
- Brewer
- Carpenter
- Shipwright
- Door maker
- Gravel digger
- Mason
- Spurrier
- Tailor

Although English universities barred female medical practitioners (the Holy Roman Empire, it should be noted, did not, and there were German female doctors), men have historically been terrified of child-birth. Midwives attended to birth and general female health, making them effectively OB/GYNs of the Middle Ages.

Famous twelfth-century women who contributed significantly to medieval medicine included the Benedictine abbess Hildegard of Bingen, who published the treatise *Causae et Curae*, and the Salerno midwife Trota of Salerno, whose *De Passionibus Mulierum* is still praised by modern obstetricians for its thoroughness and relative knowledge.

Women in Warfare

Pope Urban II's call to the First Crusade in 1095 used explicitly masculine language, and an account of the Third Crusade stated, "A great many men sent each other wool and distaff, hinting that if anyone failed to join this military expedition, they were only fit for women's work." Muslim records, however, make note of the active involvement of Christian women, not only as camp followers, but also as strategic advisers and active combatants.

It's important not to overlook the importance of camp followers. Historically, the domestic needs of an army (everything from cooking and washing to nursing the wounded) heavily depended on the informal services of camp followers. The camp followers weren't necessarily prostitutes; often the wives and children of soldiers simply moved around with them.

Camp followers were also extremely likely to pick up whatever make-shift weapons were available and enter the line of battle with their men. While female knights were certainly rare, so were knights in general. It's important to remember that medieval armies were a mixed lot, and only a small percentage were full-time professionals. A large portion of the forces were levied from the poorer classes, and among those, an untrained woman armed with a pointed stick was just as useful as a man in the same position. Period paintings show women fighting alongside men in besieged cities. Although not outfitted with armor as their professional male counterparts are, they are shown swinging weapons and clearly not passive.

Formal military supply infrastructure did not become thorough enough to eliminate the need for camp followers until the late nineteenth century, so a fantasy world modeled on any period before that would have had a large and ragtag secondary army of camp followers along for the journey.

On the other end of the spectrum, highborn women often prominently rallied and directed their own troops. In the early twelfth century, Empress Matilda was the first woman to pursue a claim to the post-conquest English throne in her own right, and in the later twelfth century, Eleanor D'Aquitaine is famous for accompanying her first husband on crusade, and later rebelling against her second. In the fourteenth century, Marguerite D'Anjou commanded the Lancastrian forces almost exclusively in the name of her mentally incapacitated husband.

It's important to remember when building a fantasy world that there are only as many nobles making waves in a feudal economy as there are billionaires making waves in ours—less than 1 percent—but among this small set, it's realistic to have at least one dauntless highborn woman flying in the face of expectation.

Conclusions

Although faced with the much steeper challenges of childbirth and childcare before the availability of modern birth control, modern medicine, and infant formula, women participated widely in every level of the medieval economy. The wives of farmers, craftsmen, and soldiers worked alongside them, often inheriting the businesses on their husbands' deaths. Highborn women managed everything from estates to kingdoms in proxy to their husbands, and "marriage to the church" allowed women to pursue art, literature, and medicine.

SOME FURTHER READING

An excellent primary source is the original text by Trota of Salerno, first published in the late 1100s: *The Trotula: An English Translation of the Medieval Compendium of Women's Medicine.* Christine de Pizan's spectacular feminist writings can be found (along with lots of other cool stuff) in *The Lady in the Tower: Medieval Courtesy Literature for Women* by Diane Bornstein.

For more about townswomen and merchants' wives, check out *From Workshop to Warfare: The Lives of Medieval Women* by Carol Adams, Paula Bartley, Hilary Bourdillon, and Cathy Loxton; *Women in the Middle Ages: The Lives of Real Women in a Vibrant Age of Transition* by Joseph Gies and Frances Gies; and

Women and Work in Preindustrial Europe by Barbara
Hanawal, which also contains excellent material on midwifery.

For more information on women in battle, search online for the
academic papers "Women on the Third Crusade" by Helen
Nicholson and "The Woman Warrior: Gender, Warfare and Society
in Medieval Europe" by Megan McLaughlin.

HISTORICALLY ACCURATE WAYS TO DIE

ᶜᵛᵒ

BY WANDA S. HENRY

Our society often imagines people in the past as having lived and died as we do today, yet those nostalgic ideas rarely include men and women covered with lice and vermin and living near waterways clogged with human and animal waste. The stench alone would kill someone today, and back then, the prevalence of raw sewage did our ancestors no good. From 500 to 1500, the typical life expectancy was about thirty-five years of age, and nineteenth-century Europeans did not live much longer. Infant mortality skews these averages, and some lucky few, 5 to 10 percent of the population worldwide, lived beyond sixty years of age in that time period.[1]

Any historical overview of causes of death runs into the problem of sources. Advances in bio-archaeology have helped identify fatal injuries caused by battle wounds and trauma, but there are limitations due to the osteological paradox, meaning that causes of death, particularly diseases, rarely leave evidence on skeletal remains.[2] Textual evidence continues to offer an essential window on death in the past, although records about causes of death present their own challenges, since individuals in earlier times had different conceptions of the human body and typically attributed cause of death to symptoms like fever rather than identifying the underlying cause. For this reason, medical historians exercise caution in retro-diagnosis based upon contemporary evaluations.

The available evidence suggests that, during prehistoric times, hunter-gatherers died before twenty years of age primarily from trauma. Accidents, such as falls or attacks by animals or other humans, proved lethal even if the individual survived the event; few measures existed to stop bleeding, infection, or other complications. Also, for their own survival, companions often abandoned the sick and injured.[3] Only after humans settled into communities, sustained by agriculture, did the average life expectancy rise to the mid- to late twenties. While death by accident continued to occur, infectious disease represented the most common cause of death, as farmers and peasants lived alongside domesticated animals in unsanitary circumstances. Simply put, poop was everywhere, and disease vectors, including those animals and other people, shared bacteria and viruses, such as chicken pox and measles, which killed humans.[4]

The migration of people from rural areas to towns made economic sense and allowed for advantages in communal living, but urban living held its own dangers. Overcrowding and poor sanitation meant that city dwellers had shorter life expectancies than country folk. Infectious disease was again the top killer.[5] In biblical times, epidemics threatened to wipe out entire communities. Plagues came in the form of typhus, smallpox, sweating sickness, and other illnesses. Infections spread along trade networks with ports as focal points for merchandise, travelers, and vector-borne diseases. Once contagion arrived, high-density populations accelerated pestilence, which radiated to locations farther afield. The Black Death lasted from 1346 to 1353. *Yersinia pestis*, in its manifestations as bubonic, septicemic, and pneumonic plagues, killed 75–200 million people in Africa and Eurasia and lingered for nearly four hundred years, causing a series of recurring epidemics in Europe until 1722. Smallpox occurred in ancient times, but earned its name only after syphilis appeared in the 1490s.[6] Syphilis was known as the French Pox or the Italian Pox—one's prejudice determined the name. Smallpox killed about one-third of its victims, and all communities were vulnerable until the introduction of a vaccine at the end of the eighteenth century. Perhaps as many as 300 million died of smallpox worldwide in the twentieth century; only in 1977 was smallpox eradicated.[7]

The nineteenth-century sanitary movement, improved nutrition, and modern medicine made for measurable declines in death by infectious diseases. A series of worldwide cholera epidemics, starting in 1817, renewed focus on public health. A waterborne bacterium, cholera causes severe diarrhea, leading to dehydration—the cadaverous victims sometimes appeared blue, and their infected feces spread disease in neighborhoods with poor sanitation and inadequate water supplies. By the end of the nineteenth century, physicians recognized germ theory as the reason for disease, leading to significant changes in the treatment of illness. However, innovations in public health and medicine could not stop the influenza epidemic of 1918, which killed between 20 and 40 million people worldwide; similar misunderstandings about the transmission of pathogens led to the spread of COVID-19.

What did people in the past imagine about causes of death? For thousands of years, Jews, Christians, and Muslims believed that God sent sickness and death as a scourge for sin, although Europeans concurrently understood miasma and contagion caused disease. Prayer was a widely accepted remedy for sickness, but heaven help the poor sinner who sought treatment from a medieval or early modern medical practitioner. Indeed, the cure was often worse than the disease. From classical times until the nineteenth century, Europeans accepted the idea that the humoral system determined one's health and temperament.

The four bodily fluids, or humors, were phlegm, blood, black bile, and yellow bile. Humoral theory involved a holistic approach with consideration of one's virtue and situations that today's medical experts would find trivial if not completely irrelevant. Above all, good health depended upon balanced humors, and physicians prescribed purgatives to expel toxins and balance the humors. Bloodletting as a common response developed from the notion that digestion transformed food into blood through concoction or cooking. That view led to the aphorism "Feed a cold and starve a fever." Humoral theory led physicians to advocate topical applications of mercury as a treatment for syphilis because the resultant perspiration, vomiting, and diarrhea would restore balance. Arsenic and antimony were other remedies. Bloodletting often appeared to help, although, of course, loss of blood was dangerous, and invasive surgery was often lethal from shock or infection. Surgeons began using anesthesia in the late nineteenth century and antibiotics from the early twentieth century.

Bills of mortality, published weekly in London from 1603 to the 1840s, listed causes of death. Symptoms, such as fever and convulsions, frequently were listed. Medical historians have only reasonable assumptions for listed causes.[8] "Gripping of the guts" could have been used for any number of abdominal pains, while "rising of the lights" was likely a lung infection. "Quinsy" seemed to be an abscess on the tonsils. "Chincough" was probably whooping cough. "Horseshoe head" could have described infants with hydrocephalus. Some women died of "mother" or "fit of the mother," which was apparently caused by a "wandering womb," since many believed the uterus could travel about the body. "Overlaid" meant that an infant was smothered in bed by accident or on purpose. "Teeth" was a common cause of death, typically listed for babies, which suggests that the child died at teething age, perhaps from a mouth infection. During the nineteenth century, families used laudanum to soothe babies' sore gums. Laudanum overdoses certainly occurred among adults and might have killed thousands of babies. "Strangury" and "stone" seemed to refer to a blocked urinary tract. "Tympany" meant bloating or swelling in the abdomen, and "dropsy" meant edema or swelling in a limb. "Flux" and "bloody flux" were terms for diarrhea. A glandular swelling in the neck was often called "scrofula" or "king's evil," and a purported cure involved the "royal touch" of the French or English monarch. "Old age" and "decay of nature" appeared regularly for the elderly, while both young and old could die by "decline," which involved failing vitality from an undiagnosed cause.[9]

Up until World War I, most people died at home. While the Byzantine Empire and the Islamic world tended to the sick in hospitals from the early Middle Ages, western European hospitals initially served travelers or worked as almshouses before catering to the sick poor by the sixteenth century. The presence of contagion made hospitals hazardous places. Death by bacterial infection, often streptococcal, called puerperal fever or childbed fever, occurred more frequently when women delivered babies in birthing hospitals than if they stayed at home. From the twentieth century onward in developed countries, people generally died from chronic diseases, typically cancer or organ failure, as long lives exhaust hearts, livers, and brains.[10]

Always and everywhere, people have their own theories about causes of death. In 1841 in England, death registers showed that one man and two women died of "broken heart," and several died of "grief." That same year, a coroner's jury determined that a man died "suddenly by a visitation of God." When challenged by the registrar, the coroner refused to change that verdict. "He was happy to say he had not yet outlived his belief in God, and he hoped it would be long before an English jury could be found that had done so."[11]

REFERENCES

1. Alan Kellehear, *A Social History of Dying* (Cambridge: Cambridge University Press, 2007), 87–104.

2. Robin Fleming, "Bones for Historians: Putting the Body Back in Biography," in *Writing Medieval Biography: Essays in Honour of Frank Barlow*, ed. David Bates (Woodbridge, UK: Boydell Press, 2006), 34.

3. Kellehear, *Social History*, 28–46.

4. Kellehear, *Social History*, 69–86.

5. Fleming, "Bones for Historians," 41–45.

6. Donald R. Hopkins, *The Greatest Killer: Smallpox in History* (Chicago: University of Chicago Press, 2002), 29.

7. D. A. Henderson, "The Eradication of Smallpox—An Overview of the Past, Present, and Future," *Vaccine* 29, no. 4 (2011): D7–D9.

8. Wanda Henry, "Women Searchers of the Dead in Eighteenth- and Nineteenth-Century London," *Journal for the Social History of Medicine* 29, no. 3 (2016): 447, 459–60.

9. Joan E. Grundy, *A Dictionary of Medical & Related Terms for the Family Historian* (Rotherham, UK: Swansong, 2006), 84–88.

10. Kellehear, *Social History*, 213–33.

11. Thomas Forbes, "Crowner's Quest," *Transactions of the American Philosophical Society* 68, no. 1 (1978): 32.

A QUICK AND DIRTY GUIDE TO FEUDAL NOBILITY

୶

BY TAHEREH SAFAVI

One of the most common mistakes that fantasy authors—and patrons at Renaissance faires—make is addressing everyone and everything as "m'lord." Not everyone was a lord; that notion defies the most basic grasp of economics. There were different kinds of lords, especially in different periods—the system was constantly evolving—and there were specific ways to address each type.

Detailing every type of feudal lord that ever existed is a Herculean task already undertaken by numerous (very dry) textbooks, so this article aims to break down the underlying reasoning behind the system. As fantasy authors, you do not need to cleave to any existing real-world system as long as yours is created with a reasonable, self-consistent logic. For this chapter, we'll focus primarily on European systems and touch a little bit on the medieval Muslim world as well.

Not Everyone Was a Lord

Let's start with the fundamentals of feudalism. The basic premise was that *those who could take something, did*. The Norman Conquest was exactly what it sounded like: William, Duc de Normandie, trumped up a claim to England, sailed over from France, and took it. That wasn't the first time, either; William wasn't French. "Norman" is a contraction of "Norseman" or "Nordmann" (what modern Norwegians still call themselves). It's the French word for the Vikings who sailed down from Scandinavia and took half of France, thus starting a long tradition—as Eddie Izzard quipped—of taking whatever they wanted via the clever use of flags.

Of course, if a conqueror spent all his time taking things, he was too busy to grow his own food. He had to convince farmers to give him a share of their crops. How to accomplish that? Show up at their houses with all his sword-toting buddies and take it. By now, you're hopefully starting to picture the king and all his peers a lot less like dandies in frilly lace collars and a lot more like heavily armed thugs.

This is where we get the concept of a "landlord": all land belongs to the lord who conquered it. He permits farmers ("villeins") to live there in exchange for tithes. There are also freeholders who own their own farms, but if you're not packing enough heat to kill the lord and his thugs, it's best to enter his protection racket instead.

As these protection rackets grow, the lord can't manage it all directly, so he taps some of his favorite armed thug buddies to run parts of it for him. He "creates" them (appoints them in the newly created title of) comté, jarl, etc. of a given area. The newly promoted muscle gets to live large in exchange for managing, taxing, and defending his new turf. The lord is essentially a cartel boss. The don, el jefe, what have you.

By nature, there aren't very many cartel bosses.

In 1307 England, there was still only one type of lord below the king—an earl—and there were only eleven of them. England may not look very big on a map, but try walking from London to York with only the clothes on your back and as much food as you can carry. To the average person of the era, it was a serious undertaking to get beyond the borders of the earldom in which they were born. They knew they had a lord, theoretically, and a king somewhere, but they knew nothing about either of them.

Here's a comparison for modern Americans: unless you live in DC and work in a relevant sector, have you ever actually met a US president in person? Perhaps you saw one of them once in your life at some official event, like if they came to visit your school to make an endowment and pose for a photo op. Have you met the governor of your home state? Do you even know your governor's name? There are five times as many American governors now as there were British earls in the thirteenth century, but the average American doesn't walk around seriously expecting to bump into one on the street.

That's how many lords versus nonlords you should have in your fantasy world.

The System Keeps Changing

The fun part about systems made up at the whim of a single mob boss is that the rules keep changing. During the reign of William I, there were exactly three types of nobility: king, earl, and baron. The first English duke was created in 1337, when Edward II made the Black Prince Duke of Cornwall. An English duke was below the king but above an earl. This had nothing to do with the continental system, where over the tenth and eleventh centuries various Frankish comtés (counts) and Norse jarls (earls) began arbitrarily styling themselves "Duc" (duke) as a matter of personal aggrandizement, and many times the effective power of a duc or a comté in terms of land held and troops commanded surpassed that of the nominal king. Remember: heavily armed thugs. If one wanted to move up the hierarchy or obtain land belonging to one's neighbor, one could always accomplish that by bigger army diplomacy.

Titles were sometimes refused. In 1385, Richard II of England made Robert de Vere (already the ninth earl of Oxford) the first marquis of Dublin. "Marquis" is a reference to the "marches," or borders, as he was defending a border territory. The next marquis, created in 1397, refused to use the title because he felt a made-up honor carried no weight. It went unused until Henry VI revived it in 1442.

As a loose guide, the British hierarchy as of 1611 went:

- King
- Duke
- Marquis
- Earl (equivalent to a count)
- Viscount
- Baron
- Baronet

Variations are fairly obvious in their implication: a grand duke would be above a regular duke, a baronet below a baron. The female styles in English are mostly related, e.g., duke/duchess and baron/baroness, though earl's wives were still called countess (probably because *earless* sounds like something that happened to Van Gogh).

It's important to realize that kings were not the only type of sovereign (a ruler with no one above them), nor were they necessarily king of a large area. There were—and still are—some sovereign duchies, in which the duke is the top of the line. Pre-conquest England was divided up into dozens of small kingdoms, such as Mercia, East Anglia, and Wessex, which were eventually consolidated by the usual means of one of the kings beating up his neighbor and taking the land. This is true throughout most of history. The *Iliad* speaks of a "coalition of Greek Kings" of which Agamemnon was high king. Ramses the Great described himself as "King of Kings," as did many Persian shahanshahs.

"Prince" was not always a word for a king's son, either; in its broadest sense, "prince" is a generic term for a top-level ruler. One might refer to a collection of "foreign princes": a general mishmash of approximately ruling-class men who might have a reasonable claim to an independent rule of some territory, including dukes, emirs, shahs, and what have you. For an exhaustive list of examples from which to create your fantasy hierarchy, Wikipedia has an excellent page on royal and noble ranks.

Specific Forms of Address

The rules vary by time period and country, but, in general, a top-of-the-line ruler such as a king or queen is addressed as "his/her/your majesty" or "his/her/your grace," and the king may be called "sire." An emperor or equivalent—a king of kings—would be "his/her/your imperial majesty," to specify that they have conquered other smaller kings. A prince or princess is "his/her/your highness." Everything below that is "his/her/your lordship/ladyship." "His/your excellency" came much later, and was used for a chancellor or prime minister.

The Arabic word "emir" (literally "commander") refers very broadly to all princes, both sovereign rulers and their sons. You address an emir as "Sayyidi-al-Emir." "Sultan" ("power" or "authority") is largely interchangeable. Both have political authority but do not have religious authority: that's the "caliph" or "khalifa," the successor to the Prophet. Who exactly that successor should be, and whether he holds more power than local emirs and sultans, has historically been a big argument. Using these words with nuance can be a great way to show entwined religious and political struggles in your fantasy novel. You can address your caliphs as "Emir al-Mu'mineen" ("Commander of the Faithful").

"Shah" is a uniquely Persian term for a king, and also used in Persian-adjacent cultures like the Ottomans, Mughals, and Bengals, with "shahanshah" ("king of kings") or "padishah" ("master king") for the emperor, "shahbanu" ("lady king") for the queen consort or empress consort, and "shahzadeh" ("descended from") for their children.

"Bahnbishin" ("queen") denotes sisters, daughters, and lesser wives of the shah, and miscellaneous noblewomen can be called "khonum" ("lady"). After the seventh-century Arabic conquest of Iran, lesser princes also came to be called by the Arabic word "emir," but the title is not from the same language family and can be kept apart in your fantasy world unless you purposely want to show a religion-forward culture conquering and intermixing with a more secular one. "Shah" is not a religious term, although from the Safavid dynasty onward it was used by Muslim rulers.

Jumping back to European conventions, it's common to refer to someone by the name of the land they own, because if you pick a fight with that man, you've picked a fight with his whole country. To use an example from our forthcoming novel *Berserker Queen*: Gilbert, Duc de Lorraine, can be referred to simply as "Lorraine." If you pick a fight with Gilbert—say, by hurting his daughter—the entire country of Lorraine is about to open a can of whoop-ass on you. He can also be called "my Lord of Lorraine," and most people, even his relatives, will refer to him in some version of that in public. His daughter might say, "My father of Lorraine will not tolerate that behavior," or his brother, the Comté de Hainut, might say, "I stand with my brother of Lorraine." He would be addressed by his personal name only in private, by people he's very close to and whom he has specifically invited to do so.

The prefix "sir" denotes knighthood. It's a job qualification and goes with a man's first name. Being a knight means you get to be called "sir," just as finishing a doctorate means you get to be called "doctor." Being a knight does not make you lord of a country, just as having a PhD does not make you the governor of a state. By the tenth century, every heavily armed cavalryman was called a knight. It was dead obvious that the lord could fight, too—Richard III was the last English king to die in combat at the battle of Bosworth Field in 1485, "fighting manfully in the thickest press of his enemies"—and it was much more important to mention that he was in charge. "Lord of [wherever]" is for the big boss; "Sir [so-and-so]" is for all his muscle.

"Master," "mistress," "goodman," and "goodwife" are polite forms of address if someone is landless and not a knight, likely a younger son of petty gentry, or a tradesman. In general, use the most flattering/ important title available, unless the character is purposely being familiar or rude.

Examples

The following are fictional characters for a hypothetical fantasy novel based on real-world titles, consistent with all the rules above.

Teagan Chambrer, knight commander general, youngest (non-inheriting) son of the Thegn of Duck's Crossing, could be addressed as:

- Sir Teagan
- General Teagan
- Master Chambrer (But this would be insulting, as it ignores the fact that he is an officer.)

But NOT:

- Lord Anything (He's not.)
- Sir Chambrer (He, Teagan, personally, is the knight, not his entire family.)

William "Shortpate" Huntley, first earl of Greenford, knight of the realm, could be addressed as:

- Lord Greenford
- Greenford (with no preamble)
- Sir William (But it's a bit familiar/pretentious to use his personal name, as it implies that his person is more relevant to you than his

status as an earl. Sir William might be used by a friend or by a woman flirting with him. If someone has a rank or title, use of their first name or pet name alone is extremely personal; you must be invited to use it, and you would probably only use it in private. No one, regardless of comparable rank, addresses someone by a pet name uninvited, unless they are purposely being rude or overly familiar.)

- Master Huntley (but again, insulting)
- William Shortpate (History has a surfeit of Williams, and epithets are nicknames used to tell them apart. The same applies for Henrys, Johns, Richards, and so on. Some are aggrandizing, e.g., "the Great" or "the Fearless," and some are insulting, e.g., "the Fat" or "the Bald" or "the Stammerer." With a potentially insulting epithet like "Shortpate," it would be a clear character choice whether someone said this to his face or only behind his back.)

But NOT:

- Sir Huntley (He, William, personally, is the knight, not his entire family.)
- Sir Greenford (His property is not a knight.)
- Lord Huntley (owner of his family?)
- Lord William (owner of himself?)

Robert Caenid, second earl of Nor'watch, knight of the realm, and lord treasurer, could be addressed as:

- Lord Nor'watch
- My Lord Treasurer
- Sir Robert (accurate but very personal)
- Master Caenid (accurate but insulting)

But NOT:

- Lord Robert (owner of himself?)
- Master Robert (master of himself?)
- Sir Treasurer (The office of treasurer can fight on horseback?)

Stephen fitz Wheelwright ("fitz" means "son of," and wheelwright is a profession; this is a literal statement that his father is the town wheelwright—fitz Wheelwright is not a family name), captain of the guard, a common infantryman who is not a chevalier, could be addressed as:

- Captain Stephen
- the wheelwright's boy (insulting now that he is an officer, but would have been his form of address formerly)

But NOT:

- Sir Stephen (He is not a qualified heavy cavalry fighter.)
- Master Wheelwright (That's his father.)

Ahmad ibn Rahsin al-Nazir, Khalif of Quo'roba, Defender of God's Faith, and Prince of all the Western Realms, could be addressed as:

- Emir al-Mu'mineen (This would be the most respectful, as his position implies that he prioritizes his religious role.)
- Sayyidi-al-Emir (This is correct but lesser and potentially insulting.)
- Lord of Quo'roba
- Ahmad al-Nazir ("Al-Nazir" means "the Victorious." Arabic is just as full of epithets used to tell apart rulers as European cultures; however, unlike the English and French, Arabic epithets are not commonly insulting.)

But NOT:

- Lord Rahsin ("Ibn" means "son of." Rahsin is his father's first name. Owner of his dead father?)
- Khalif Rahsin (Despite technically being the successor of his father, the term is religious and refers to the line of the Prophet.)
- Khalifat Ahmad ibn Rahsin ("Khalifat" or "caliphate" is the territory held by a khalif/caliph, the same way a kingdom is held by a king. This is like saying "Kingdom Louis VI of France.")

Soltan Esmael Mirza Ashfari, oldest son of Artaxerxes Shahan-shah Ashfari the Magnificent and heir apparent to the Four Corners of the Universe, can be addressed as:

- Esmael Mirza ("Mirza" is the honorific for "prince" and goes after the given name in Persianate titles.)
- Soltan Esmael Mirza ("Soltan" in the Persian case means "captain" or "governor," a job title like "sir." One would still mention that this particular captain is also a hereditary prince.)
- Prince Esmael

But NOT:

- Soltan Ashfari (Ashfari is a dynastic name, "of the dynasty of Ashfar." This implies he's the only one of the family to ever govern a province, which is unlikely.)
- Prince Mirza (Prince-Prince! This is a goofy redundancy.)
- Prince Soltan (Prince-Captain!)

Generally, all women married to a knight or better can be referred to as "my lady," although you would only attach a name if you would do so for her husband. A lady retains her title after being widowed as a courtesy, even if she remarries a man of lesser station. If there is a new woman who can claim the same title, the word "dowager" will be attached to the widow's title.

Eliza Caenid, widow of the former Earl Nor'watch, mother of Robert, the current earl Nor'watch, could be addressed as:

- My Lady Countess
- the Dowager Countess Nor'watch

But NOT:

- Lady Nor'watch (That's her daughter-in-law.)

Leila Ashfari, second wife of Artaxerxes Shahanshah, could be addressed as:

- Leila Banbishin (a term for a lesser queen, not the empress or queen consort)
- Leila Khonum (a generic respectful term for "lady," still used in modern Farsi as "ma'am")
- Lady Leila

But NOT:

- Leila Shahbanu (reserved for the first wife or queen consort)
- Lady Ashfari (She's married into the dynasty, and she is certainly not the only one.)

Conclusion

The biggest thing to remember when designing your own system is that it's all about the land. Feudal lords are like mob bosses: When too many exist in a given area, turf wars occur. Since the land is so important, the form of address almost always makes reference to it, and you certainly wouldn't treat someone like he ran the place if he didn't. Just picture what would happen if the Godfather overheard you calling some other shmuck "boss."

This is only the briefest of overviews, of course, but hopefully it gives you some keywords to plug into Google. Some specific resources include:

A Genealogical History of the Dormant, Abeyant, Forfeited, and Extinct Peerages of the British Empire by Sir Bernard Burke is thorough but very antique.

Dictionnaire de la Noblesse de la France is in French and equally antique, but also thorough and available free online.

The Shannameh by Ferdowsi is the national epic of Iran and the original source text for everything on this topic.

The Persian Empire by Mehrdad Kia is a modern encyclopedia not written in poetry.

Arabs: A 3,000-Year History of Peoples, Tribes and Empires by Tim Mackintosh-Smith is modern and more readable.

God's Shadow by Alan Mikhail is specifically Ottoman.

Good luck with your world-building! Special thanks to Dr. Rachel Schine for verifying the correct usage of Arabic titles.

RELIGIOUS CULTURE OF THE ANCIENT NEAR EAST

BY HAYLEY STONE

To say I love the culture and history of the ancient Near East is an understatement.

My oldest cat's name is Ashurbanipal, I've revisited the goddess Inanna's descent into the Underworld and confrontation with her sister Ereshkigal in poetry, and I own a borderline embarrassing number of books on the subject.

Something about ancient Near Eastern history, with its casual merging of the mythic and mundane, captures my imagination like few other periods and places do. As the fantasy genre expands by welcoming in the voices of marginalized creators and moving away from the familiar setting of the Western medieval world, I believe much can be learned from the religious culture of the ancient Near East and considered by the modern fantasy writer when constructing the complex societies and histories of their own worlds.

Because the history of the ancient Near East is a subject of incredible breadth and depth, I will be narrowing the scope of this chapter to some of the most compelling aspects of the intersection between its culture and religion. Although this is by no means a comprehensive examination, I do hope that it will serve as potential inspiration and a launchpad for further research.

But first . . .

What We're Talking About When We Talk About the "Ancient Near East"

In simplest terms, the ancient Near East primarily refers to two ancient Mediterranean cultures: Mesopotamia—in what is today Iraq, Syria, Iran, Kuwait, and Turkey—and ancient Egypt from roughly 4500 BCE to 539 BCE. In that time, we see an expansion in the understanding of the world through mathematics, art, and engineering. We also see the rise of imperialism through military conquest, more centralized government, and—most crucial to the development of laws and mythic texts—the invention of writing.

Thousands of years of history is a lot to cover, so for the purposes of this chapter, we will be turning our gaze specifically to the Akkadian Empire in the Early Bronze Age (c. 2334 BCE) for concrete examples of the religious culture that pervaded ancient society throughout this era.

Why this period in particular? Well, the Akkadian Empire overtook Mesopotamia's first civilization, Sumer, and became the region's first major empire, paving the way for the states of Assyria and Babylonia (of Hammurabi fame). To me, this period perfectly encapsulates the ancient Near East during a period of strong cultural change while including many elements traditionally associated with the region.

Also, it features one of my favorite historical figures—cited as the world's oldest known author—but we'll get to her in a moment.

A Gift from the Gods: The Invention of Writing

Much has been written about magic systems in fantasy novels, and to the ancient peoples of the Near East, writing must have felt exactly like that—magic. It was an absolute game-changer, allowing the transfer of messages over vast distances and the ability to keep records; kings could now communicate their explicit orders directly to their generals without worrying about the messenger getting it wrong, merchants could keep track of their orders and payments (and complain about one another), oral stories could be recorded, and the list of benefits goes on.

There are two main myths about the invention of writing—one that emphasizes the benevolence of the gods, the other the ingenuity of humanity. In the first, the goddess Bel gives the gift of writing to humans personally; in this tale, writing isn't something invented but an existing knowledge Bel simply bestowed on mankind. In the second tale, King Enmerkar of Uruk develops writing out of the frustration of trying to solve riddles posed to him by another king—and delivered via an unreliable messenger—in the course of their trade agreements.

Both tales are exaggerations, but the latter may offer a hint to the truth. Writing in the ancient Near East developed out of economic need, facilitating more complex trade through better bookkeeping. Yet, in a culture as religious as this one, it makes perfect sense that writing would also be absorbed into the larger mythos and given its own mythical origins.

Hand in Hand: The Union of Religion and Culture in Ancient Society

In the *Epic of Gilgamesh*, the titular hero is harassed by the goddess of love, Ishtar, after refusing to become her lover. She doesn't take his rejection well and, amidst causing Gilgamesh all sorts of other grief, threatens to raise the dead to devour the living. (Zombies!) In another tale, the high god Enlil decides to destroy the world with a massive flood because humans are keeping him awake with all their *noise*.

When mentioning Mesopotamia, the first thing that pops into many people's minds are these stories of humanity's brush with the gods. And it's no wonder, as religion was one of the core foundations of Mesopotamian society, informing almost every aspect of its culture. It was the gods who empowered kings, granting them a divine authority to maintain order, and for much of this era a great deal of wealth and property was also concentrated in the hands of the priests and priestesses who operated the temples, for they were viewed as the gods' chosen servants.

Rather than being a place to congregate for worship, Mesopotamian temples functioned primarily as the symbolic heart of the city. The temple didn't just consist of the highly recognizable ziggurat with its terraced levels but an entire complex serving as the earthly home of a particular deity. Cult statues inside the temple represented the city's patron god or goddess's physical body, and when an enemy wanted to hit a city where it hurt, they might steal this statue, weakening morale by quite literally, in the minds of the people, depriving them of their protective deity. This reportedly happened on multiple occasions to the statue of the patron god of Babylon, Marduk—psychological warfare at its finest!

Away from the levers of power, the average layperson expressed their own religious dedication through personal piety, practicing moral behavior in a reflection of their gods, who they believed longed for goodness and order (despite what their actions in some of the early myths might suggest). They celebrated the greatness of the gods through holy days and festivals dedicated to them, and tried to interpret their will through divination. When ill, it was not uncommon to believe the sickness was caused by having displeased one of the gods, or from being invaded by a bad spirit (or demon) and to seek aid from a priest specialized in a form of spiritual exorcism.

In all ways, the ancient Mesopotamian approach to religion was one of fomenting intimacy with their chosen deity, giving freely of themselves rather than demanding boons.

Lastly, it is impossible, and quite frankly a disservice, to discuss ancient Mesopotamian religion without also crediting the woman to whom it owes one of its most significant evolutions.

Gods by Any Other Name Would Be as Great: Enheduanna and the Syncretization of the Sumerian and Akkadian Religions

Enheduanna (born c. 2285 BCE) was the daughter of King Sargon of Akkad, also known as Sargon the Great, who established the Akkadian dynasty. She was assigned the position of high priestess at the temple of Nanna (the moon god, not to be confused with the goddess Inanna) in the Sumerian city of Ur to help her father control that portion of his vast empire. It was a shrewd political move by Sargon, made more effective by Enheduanna herself, who did well as the first woman to ever hold the powerful position of high priestess in Ur.

In addition to being a princess, Enheduanna was also a poet. She is credited with the invention of the hymnal format later seen in other literary works, such as the Bible, and her poetry was crucial in syncretizing the Sumerian and Akkadian religions, reconciling many of their beliefs into one mythology. For example, the Sumerian goddess Inanna merged with the Akkadian goddess Ishtar, the former's name featuring prominently in many of Enheduanna's temple hymns. Inanna's elevation by Enheduanna consequently reinforced Enheduanna's own authority and helped solidify her father Sargon's rule.

Her life wasn't all sunshine and ziggurats, however. At one point, Enheduanna was forced to flee into exile due to a violent revolt organized by a Sumerian rebel, Lugalanne. She wrote poems capturing this tumultuous time, pleading with her patron goddess to intercede. In her poems and prayers, we see personal devotion, trust, and, yes, sometimes frustration that was emblematic of ancient Near Eastern religious attitudes. The gods had the power to change the direction of a person's life—but would they?

In this case, Inanna must have been firmly on the side of her poet-priestess because Enheduanna ultimately triumphed over Lugalanne and reclaimed her seat as high priestess, serving for approximately forty years and leaving a lasting cultural legacy.

In Summary

The religious culture of the ancient Near East—especially where it concerns ancient Mesopotamia—informed every aspect of its history and society. Myths were woven together with historical events, as in the story of the invention of writing, and the people themselves were contented by divine explanations for aspects of the world they could not otherwise explain.

But the gods were not merely seen as manifestations of weather or misfortune; they were considered to be sentient, physically present more often than not, and fair. While religion could be used to justify a king's desire for war, the general attitude was one of fostering personal bonds with the sacred. Nowhere is this pictured more clearly than in Enheduanna's temple hymns, which not only espouse a genuine love and appreciation of her goddess but also helped govern the transformation of Inanna into a deific icon capable of being embraced by both Akkadian and Sumerian people, ultimately ensuring a survival of belief instead of its destruction.

FURTHER READING

Stephen Bertman, *Handbook to Life in Ancient Mesopotamia* (New York: Oxford University Press, 2005).

Betty De Shong Meador, *Princess, Priestess, Poet: The Sumerian Temple Hymns of Enheduanna* (Austin: University of Texas Press, 2009).

Charles Halton and Saana Svärd, *Women's Writing of Ancient Mesopotamia: An Anthology of the Earliest Female Authors* (Cambridge: Cambridge University Press, 2017).

James B. Pritchard, *The Ancient Near East: An Anthology of Texts and Pictures* (Princeton, NJ: Princeton University Press, 2011).

AFRICAN AND ASIAN EXCHANGES WITH MEDIEVAL EUROPE

༄

BY TAHEREH SAFAVI

One of the most common assumptions of the average reader (and writer) of fantasy novels is that medieval Europe was homogenous and largely white. Not only is that belief erroneous, it is a symptom of deliberate misinformation that has pervaded Western culture for hundreds of years. This chapter is a very brief attempt to help unravel some of that misinformation and introduce aspiring authors to important names that will help start them on their own research journeys.

How Trade Connected the World: All the Cloves in Constantinople

Deeply ironically for those who associate Vikings with insular white supremacy, the fame of the Viking age is based on their ships and far-flung trade routes: their connectivity with the rest of the world. The absolutely stunning map on pages 56–57—*11-12th Century Trade*

Routes by Martin Jan Månsson—gives some perspective on how connected this world was.

In addition to trade, there was a great deal of intermarriage. In Scandinavia, communities may have limited their female children to avoid starvation. If a farm was big enough to feed only one family, they would raise only one girl. The farm passed to her, to feed all her future children: the original concept of a dowry, that with which a girl has been endowed. Male children were not limited and were also expected to find their own way in the world, which led to a surplus of aggressive young bachelors fighting for the very few women. After several centuries, this aggression exploded out of Scandinavia in the form of the Viking age.

More than gold and jewels, those Vikings wanted wives and farmland. Anywhere they could get away with marrying and settling down, they did. Normandy and Sicily are two examples of places where the sheer number of Norse who settled down was so high, they completely changed the population demographics. Even if they couldn't secure farmland, they would still take wives, and their mixed children populated the next generation of Viking crews. Genetic analysis on Viking-era graves indicates a high degree of genetic mixing—the antithesis of the Nazi concept of Vikings as a "pure" race.

Norse trade routes connected with the silk road and trans-Saharan routes. Muslim travelers wrote extensively about Norse they met, and Arabic coins fill buried Norse hoards. So many Norse moved to Constantinople (Istanbul) to enlist in the Varangian Guard—an elite unit of personal bodyguards to the Byzantine emperor—that a medieval Swedish law had to declare no one could inherit while serving in Anatolia.

They had a similar "yes, and . . ." approach to conversion, cheerfully adding Jesus and Muhammad to their own Norse pantheon and portraying them together in artwork. Textiles have been found that were woven in Sweden with a Kufic pattern possibly featuring the word "Allah," implying someone in Sweden was either Muslim themself or at least familiar enough with Muslim designs to copy them.

The word "Viking" means "raider"—a statement of profession, not of ancestry—and genetic analysis further shows that some skeletons buried with Viking equipment and weapons are not Scandinavian. When Viking crews lost a few men to battle or sickness, it was more practical to replace them immediately than to sail home short-staffed. Evidence from sagas and legal codes confirm indifference to ethnic origin so long as the new sailor was willing to uphold their moral standards. In addition to trade, it is likely they employed and intermarried with people of Middle Eastern and North African origin, and possibly even some East Asians and sub-Saharan Africans.

South of the Sahara, the Wagadou Empire was an enormous player on the international scene, thanks to their exceptional gold and salt mines. The Soninke people of Wagadou were Islamized and intermingled with their Arabic trading partners to the north. The later Empire of Mali was even larger and wealthier, and its tenth emperor, Mansa Musa, may have been the wealthiest man in human history. He introduced himself to the medieval world on his legendary pilgrimage to Mecca, accompanied by around sixty thousand attendants clad in brocade and Persian silk, heralds, slaves, a menagerie, and eighty camels carrying three hundred pounds of gold each, which he distributed to the poor along his route. His progression was widely documented by awestruck eyewitnesses and provided the inspiration for the gold-flinging imagery used in Disney's *Aladdin* for the entrance of Prince Ali.

Non-Arabic Muslims were not always accorded equal status, despite the fact that Islam explicitly teaches the equality of all Muslims. The Umayyad Caliphate had four main social classes: Muslim Arabs, Muslim non-Arabs, non-Muslims, and slaves. This caused social unrest as Islam spread and new converts were not given the same social rights. One famous revolt against the Umayyads was led by Umar ibn Hafsun, a sawada (Black sub-Saharan) commander born near Málaga, Spain. He united the disaffected muwallads (Muslim citizens of mixed parentage) and mozarabs (Christians living under Muslim rule). When he was finally defeated in 917, it's plausible that some of his rebels may even have joined mercenary Viking crews to escape Umayyad vengeance. Contrary to modern assumptions, neither the Norse nor the Soninke are recorded as having any concerns about skin color, and they had well-established trade relationships.

Thanks to all this contact, in a fantasy novel based on the Viking age, it would be perfectly plausible to write Middle Eastern and Black Vikings. Darker-skinned people abounded in premodern Europe. From the Roman era to the Renaissance, contemporary color images exist to attest to their presence. The Severan Tondo depicts Lucius Septimius Severus, a third-century Roman emperor born in Libya, as having a much darker complexion than his Syrian wife. Westminster tournament rolls from the sixteenth century depict John Blanke twice as one of six trumpeters on horseback in the royal retinue, with notably dark skin and a turban, indicating likely Black Muslim (possibly Malian) origin. He is listed as "the blacke trumpeter" in Tudor payrolls and has been portrayed in modern television to look exactly as he does in his portrait—much to the chagrin of white supremacists who wish to rewrite history.

Non-European Voyagers

For authors who want to create characters based on non-European traders and explorers who could plausibly have had contact with the West, this section will help kick-start your research.

Ibn Battuta, a fourteenth-century Amazigh historian, traveled more than any other explorer in premodern history, around seventy-two thousand miles, more than triple the journeys of Marco Polo. His account, *The Rihla* (or *A Gift to Those Who Contemplate the Wonders of Cities and the Marvels of Traveling*), covers thirty years of journeys through Iraq, Iran, Arabia, Somalia, the Swahili coast, Anatolia,

Central Asia, India, Southeast Asia, China, Spain, North Africa, Mali, and Timbuktu.

East Asian grave goods have been found as far west as Stockholm, just beyond which a small bronze Buddha figure, likely produced in sixth-century Kashmir, was found in the Helgo treasure. Buddhist and Hindu ideas and artifacts spread along the maritime silk road, which flourished from the second century BCE to the fifteenth century CE. Austronesian-speaking sailors across Indonesia, Malaysia, and the Philippines dominated the southeast Asian corner of the route, working with Tamil sailors from south India, and Persians, Arabs, and Greeks in the Arabian sea and east Africa.

The Majapahit Empire, based in Java, was a Hindu-Buddhist maritime power covering thirteen thousand islands of Indonesia. A contemporary poet described it as the center of a huge mandala extending from New Guinea and Maluku to Sumatra and the Malay Peninsula— a span as wide as London to Istanbul. As the controllers of cloves, camphor, pepper, sandalwood, and, most important, nutmeg—a spice with both medicinal and hallucinogenic properties—the maritime nation established such economic dominance as the famed "spice islands"; the following Muslim empires that conquered them tried to claim descent. Marco Polo described Java as "the largest island in the world, subject to a great king who pays tribute to no one. . . . Its ports throng with merchants and its treasure is beyond telling. . . . The Great Khan could never get control of this island."

Although exaggerated—Sumatra is larger than Java, and the Majapahit kingdom did not grow spice, only controlled the trade routes— Marco Polo was right that the Mongols would never conquer there. At this time, the late thirteenth century, the Mongol empire was at its peak. Two generations after Genghis Khan, his grandson Kublai Khan expanded Mongol power to its largest extent. Although he never conquered the spice islands, under Kublai, the Mongols had contiguous control from Europe to the Japanese sea.

Even more widely traveled than Marco Polo was Zheng He, a Chinese fleet admiral and diplomat. He commanded an immense fleet and armed force on seven major expeditions, now called the Ming treasure voyages, to explore the world on behalf of the Yongle emperor. Using the largest ships in the world at the time, he led China to become the superpower of the Indian ocean.

Zheng He preferred to expand Chinese power through diplomacy, and his abundant army awed most would-be enemies into submission. The ships were laden with gifts to present to foreign rulers—luxury items that China monopolized, like silk, porcelain, and musk—and gold to purchase precious goods at low rates. He brought back spices, sandalwood, camphor, precious stones, ivory, ebony, coral, tortoise shells, rhinoceros horns, ambergris, tin, and cobalt oxide. Many of these items were necessary for China's industry, and the voyages kickstarted an economic boom. The voyages went down the eastern coast of Africa and may have even rounded the Cape of Good Hope. He brought home exotic animals, such as ostriches, elephants, and giraffes, in tribute to the emperor, which were seen as proof of the Yongle emperor's Mandate of Heaven.

Islam spread much farther east than most Western writers realize, and Zheng He is among many medieval East Asian figures to have been Muslim—though by the end of his life the well-traveled mariner embraced multiple beliefs, seeking protection from both the tombs of Muslim saints and the Chinese sea goddess Tianfei. With backing from the Ming Empire, the spice-dominating Majapahit Empire in Indonesia was eventually replaced by the Muslim Malacca Sultanate. An Arabic missionary born in Indonesia named Karim ul-Makhdum finally brought Islam as far east as the Philippines, founding the Sheik Karimol Makhdum Mosque in Tawi-Tawi. From there to the tip of the Emirate of Granada at the Strait of Gibraltar, fourteenth-century Islam had the widest contiguous reach of any organized religion in the medieval world.

REFERENCES AND FURTHER READING

Timothy Brook, *The Troubled Empire: China in the Yuan and Ming Dynasties* (Cambridge, MA: Harvard University Press, 2013).

Tim Hannigan, *A Brief History of Indonesia: Sultans, Spices, and Tsunamis; The Incredible Story of Southeast Asia's Largest Nation* (Clarendon, VT: Tuttle Publishing, 2015).

Homa Katouzian, *The Persians: Ancient, Mediaeval and Modern Iran* (New Haven, CT: Yale University Press, 2009).

Mehrdad Kia, *The Persian Empire: A Historical Encyclopedia* (Santa Barbara, CA: ABC-CLIO, 2016).

Tim Mackintosh-Smith, *Arabs: A 3,000-Year History of Peoples, Tribes and Empires* (New Haven, CT: Yale University Press, 2019).

Patricia McKissack and Fredrick McKissack, *The Royal Kingdoms of Ghana, Mali, and Songhay: Life in Medieval Africa* (New York: Henry Holt, 1993).

P. James Oliver, *Mansa Musa and the Empire of Mali* (self-published, 2013) (children's book)

Susan Wise Bauer, *The History of the Medieval World: From the Conversion of Constantine to the First Crusade* (New York: W. W. Norton, 2007).

RELIGIOUS FUNDAMENTALISM IN FANTASY

୧୬

BY SPENCER ELLSWORTH

Imagine this: you're a medieval lord with a crappy piece of land, stewing on wrongs done you by your more-successful brothers. A mysterious redhead comes to you and promises that you will gain the throne. Just worship her very weird, very not-Catholic god. Oh, and seal the deal with freaky sex.

What would you, Average Medieval Lord, do? Throw in with the weird god and the freaky sex, send her packing, or, since this is the medieval era, let the locals burn her as a witch?

Put a bookmark in that scenario. We'll come back to it.

I was on a panel a few years ago, talking about history, and when the Crusades came up, an audience member declared, "Well, the Crusades were about loot!"

As someone who's read every book about the Crusades that came out in the last ten years, I can authoritatively say: Not quite. Not at all, in some cases. (Although very much so at times.)

There's a dichotomy in our minds when it comes to Crusaders. Modern skepticism and our modern experience of religious fundamentalism paint Crusaders as either gold-crazed looters or frothing religious nutballs. We see them the way we see fringe societal elements today. Weirdos. Vicious murdering lunatics.

It's hard to get one's head around it, but humans being what they are, the Crusaders can have complicated reasons for slaughtering a whole city full of innocent people for . . . complicated reasons.

When Melisandre of Asshai shows up in A Song of Ice and Fire with the aforementioned nudity, virility, and mandate to burn the heathens for R'hllor, or when the Children of the Light roll into town looking for Darkfriends in The Wheel of Time, they're much more ISIS than Crusader.

Fundamentalism is really a modern phenomenon, asserting religion as a societal force in a world that could make religion irrelevant. The self-proclaimed Enlightenment and following liberalization created walls between church, school, bank, and entertainment.

In the medieval world, crusading and other religious violence were as mainstream as Green Day in 1995. Medieval society was saturated with religion. Whether in the Islamic or Christian world, church, school, bank, and entertainment were all the realm of God.

Thus, medievalist society wasn't fundamentalist, but ebbed and flowed with waves of mainstream revivalism.

The First Crusade came about because Pope Urban II had been asked, by the Byzantine emperor, for help in regaining lands he'd lost to Islamic armies, and holding on to the remaining, threatened Byzantine territory. Pope Urban saw this as his chance to deal with a major issue of the day: violence between Christians. For a land that was supposed to be united under Christ and the Roman Church, Europe was a fractious, bloody place.

One infamous sermon later and Urban had created a social movement. Thousands of lords and tens of thousands of pilgrims sold everything they had and hit the road to take Jerusalem back.

Godfrey of Bouillon and his brother, Baldwin, both heroes of the First Crusade, appear to be on the two sides of the looter/devout madman coin. Godfrey stayed with the First Crusade all the way to Jerusalem. Upon the conquest of the city (which involved killing so many Muslims and Jews that "men were wading up to their ankles in enemy blood" and "piles of heads, hands and feet lay in the houses and streets"), Godfrey refused a proffered kingship. He would not be king in the city where Christ was king.[1]

Baldwin had no trouble accepting that kingship after Godfrey died. This after Baldwin had abandoned the First Crusade to run off and acquire the Armenian Christian principality of Edessa by very devious means. So, were they two sides of the looter/devout madman coin?

Yes. And no.

Godfrey was, no doubt, devout, because he had reformed after years fighting the papacy. There was genuine humility in his crusading, but there was also realpolitik. He wanted to leave his family in the papacy's, and God's, good graces.

That was more important than his finances—because, for all the "loot" in the Levant, he had mortgaged his entire estate to go on crusade.

His brother Baldwin couldn't have been entirely mercenary, though. He also sold his considerable holdings in France to go on the First Crusade. He cared about his salvation, but he also cared about his bank account, as his takeover of Edessa shows.

Godfrey and Baldwin saw feudalism and Catholicism as the organizational instruments of God. They believed in God, Heaven and Hell, the pope, and the divine right of the king, all wrapped up in a nice little box.

This is why Dante placed Brutus and Cassius at the same level of

Hell as Judas. For Dante, a betrayal of Caesar was a betrayal of God. (Never mind that Caesar wouldn't have cared for Jesus; he was the founder of the Holy Roman Empire and thus godly by Dante's retcon.) Dante was perfectly willing to call out priestly and papal hypocrisy, but even as incisive a thinker as he never questioned the notion of divine investiture. This is why the reformers in the Renaissance were often as intolerant within their self-established systems as Catholics had been. Most Muslims, for that matter, didn't question the need for a caliph, despite the fact that their own religion never specified a central authority.

When God directs all politics, all politics involve God.

Most fantasy heroes are anachronistic. Given a few hundred years of Enlightenment mindset and democracy, we tend to write heroes who look on kings and popes and claims of godliness with suspicion, who recoil with horror at war and intolerance, who have hot sex without worrying what God would think.

Melisandre might have been able to turn Stannis against the Great Sept of Westeros, but in medieval Europe, all the freaky demon sex in the world wouldn't turn a savvy politician against Jesus. (Told you we'd get back here.) That's not pure politics—any medieval thinker would hedge their bets on the afterlife. And though Robert Jordan based his extensive world on the seventeenth century, just about every governor in the seventeenth century would agree with, and field their own version of, the Children of the Light.

Not that you should go write fanatics. Modern readers need a little anachronism in order to relate to a medieval hero. Godfrey is a sympathetic character until you find out that he mowed down Muslims and Jews from the back of his horse. But there are few quasi-fantasy medieval worlds that show how intricately faith was woven into preindustrial society; the only one that comes to mind is Lois McMaster Bujold's Chalion series, which got this right and collected a slew of awards for it.

Now you, Average Medieval Lord, can do what you choose with the redhead's offer. But if you're truly medieval, you will take this opportunity to remind me: Things shall proceed according to God's will, not ours.

REFERENCES

1. Thomas Asbridge, *The First Crusade: A New History* (Oxford: Oxford University Press, 2005), 316–17.

FOMENTING REBELLIONS IN FANTASY

༄

BY COLLEEN HALVERSON

Rebellions are a staple of science fiction and fantasy, but oftentimes we see uprisings and revolutions pitted in dualistic terms of "good" and "evil," with the brash, brave rebels on one side fighting against the oppressive Empire on the other. I became interested in colonial uprisings when I started working on my dissertation on the early nineteenth-century Irish novel. I found all these great books—primarily by women, interestingly enough—depicting the 1798 Irish Uprising, and I wanted greater context to better understand them.

This uprising was one of the bloodiest in Irish history, the death toll in the tens of thousands. My impressions of this uprising were initially straightforward. On one side, you had the Irish, who wanted to overthrow imperial rule, and on the other side, the English, who wanted to maintain said imperial rule. Simple. But as I began researching, I found a multilayered conflict complicated by politics, religion, geography, new philosophies, and ancient grudges.

My novel *Through the Veil* features a rebellion, and the sequel to my debut will delve into it in more detail. Even though my novel is urban fantasy, I tried to apply what I learned from my research on the 1798 Irish Uprising in order to make it more nuanced and realistic. It would be impossible for me to describe every group involved in this event, and because of my academic background, my research is slanted on the Irish side of things. But I hope that by describing the various factions, it will help fellow world-builders to enrich their revolutions.

The Empire

This includes the ruling class, the state, colonial agents, officials, their families, and the mercantile system catering to them. The empire creates the economic conditions under which everyone in the colony must abide, and to justify their system, they create an entire culture to help validate its existence. In Marxist terms, we would call this "superstructure," the dominant ideology that generally protects the interests of the ruling class. In Ireland, for instance, colonization began with economic interests at heart (but also political and religious interests, but that is a whole other story). The English saw that Ireland has fertile soil and cattle, so they wanted to take it. But over time, the ruling class had to justify its presence; thus, they deemed the Irish "uncivilized," "barbaric," and "too emotional" to rule themselves. We see this ideology perpetuated in the "stage Irish" character in a lot of English theater of the time. So even if you weren't personally oppressing the Irish, if you were living in England at the end of the eighteenth century and buying theater tickets, you might find yourself in a complex cultural system that perpetuated this sort of oppression.

Questions for World-Building: How did the empire come to power? What economic, political, and cultural interests fueled colonization? How does the empire maintain power through ideology, cultural influence, surveillance, and legislation?

The Empire's Dissidents

But every empire has its naysayers within its ranks. Many members of the English intelligentsia spoke out against imperialism. For instance, Romantic poet Percy Bysshe Shelley, inspired by the radical views of liberty circulating at the time, traveled to Ireland in the early years of the nineteenth century to aid in the Irish cause. The Irish resistance also found surprising allies in abolitionists who saw abolishing slavery and Catholic Emancipation as fundamentally linked.

Question for World-Building: What are philosophical, religious, and social narratives within the empire running counter to its claims?

The Allies

Very few rebellions can succeed without the outside help of some wealthier, more powerful ally. In the lead-up to the Irish Uprising, the French saw an opportunity to gain a foothold in the country to aid their ongoing war with England. They planned two invasions, neither of which succeeded because of the weather(!), but this support turned the uprising from a small colonial skirmish to a major international incident.

Questions for World-Building: Who are the allies in your uprising? What do they want? How do those aims overlap with the goals of the rebels? How do they deviate?

The Intermediaries

These citizens were born in the colony but are a part of the genteel upper crust and see themselves as belonging to the Empire. Their hybrid identities are influenced by local culture, even though they might find themselves beholden to the superstructure. In Ireland, this group was the Anglo-Irish, otherwise known as the Ascendancy. These were descendants of invading forces, and for a time they held government positions, enacted laws, served as local justice, and existed as inter-mediaries to the crown. Yet, many members of the Anglo-Irish felt particular affinities toward Irish culture and sometimes sympathized with Irish causes, even if in a paternalistic way. The writer Maria Edgeworth and her father Richard Lovell Edgeworth were great examples of members of the Ascendancy who maintained one foot in English culture and one foot on Irish soil, seeing themselves as "reformers" to a war-torn and impoverished land. In this way, they often found themselves in a nebulous "in-between" space within their social sphere.

Questions for World-Building: What unique, hybrid identities emerge in what Mary Louise Pratt would call your world's "contact zone" (the space where two cultures clash, intermingle, blend, etc.)? What issues are your intermediary characters sympathetic toward? In what way do they mirror the dominant ideology?

The Middle Class

Even the most oppressive colony will have its middle class among the native population. These tend to be low-level clerks in the civil service, merchants, or what was often the case for the Irish, Catholics who were able to live on land rented on extremely long leases. Many scholars point to how, for much of the eighteenth and nineteenth centuries, there existed a "Hidden Ireland," with powerful, wealthy families hiding beneath a façade of poverty to fool the English gentry. Largely centralized in urban areas, these were individuals who had just enough money to seek an education and enough leisure time to read and engage in some degree of intellectual life. This middle class is generally native but can include intermediaries of a lower class. In Ireland, the United Irishmen began as a debate club with both native Irish and Anglo-Irish members, but turned revolutionary as the flames of rebellion took hold in America, France, India, and colonies around the world.

Questions for World-Building: In what capacity does your world allow

for a middle class? What philosophies and ideas fuel their desire for an upris-
ing? Who or what inspires them?

The Native Lower Class

These are generally poor farmers and factory workers with some or very
little education. Because it was illegal for Catholics to pursue an education in Ireland under English rule, ad hoc schools called "hedge schools"
emerged to serve this disenfranchised population. Because these schools
existed in secret and outside of the superstructure, they did not transmit
the dominant ideologies of the empire and often undermined them. In
the late nineteenth century, the Defenders emerged as a "homegrown"
group of discontents serving to assist Catholics against local persecution. While the United Irishmen stood purely for the ideals of Thomas
Paine, the Defenders' position was a complex web of Enlightenment
values, Stuart politics, agrarian protests, and personal grudges. The
United Irishmen and the Defenders would eventually join forces in the
uprising, but they remained uneasy allies, as many of the United Irishmen saw the Defenders as local yokels, and the Defenders viewed the
United Irishmen as bourgeois charlatans.

Questions for World-Building: What localized persecutions are fueling the
feelings of rebellion among the lower classes in your world? How does their
isolation from the dominant culture assist in a strong sense of identity among
them? How do they see the wealthier, more privileged members of the
uprising?

The Subalterns

Subalterns are on the lowest tier in the uprising ladder. These are illiterate, landless individuals living a subsistence existence. In Gayatri Spivak's famous essay "Can the Subaltern Speak?" she discusses how these
shadowy, impoverished individuals are co-opted by the middle class to

shame and belittle their imperial rulers. In other words, subalterns are often spoken *for* but do not speak for themselves. The middle class might imagine the subalterns' desires as uniform, but for Spivak they are heterogeneous, multilayered, contradictory, ambiguous. A conversation between a middle-class member of the rebellion and a subaltern might go as follows:

MIDDLE-CLASS REVOLUTIONARY: *So tell me what you want.*

SUBALTERN 1: *I want a goat and maybe a new pair of shoes. And yeah, the empire is terrible.*

SUBALTERN 2: *I want to kill that guy over there who happens to have a different religion than mine because he shot my brother in a gambling dispute.*

MIDDLE-CLASS REVOLUTIONARY: *Okay, so you guys are saying you want liberty and freedom from religious persecution. Got it.*

SUBALTERN 1: *No.*

SUBALTERN 2: *Did you hear what I said? That guy killed my brother!*

MIDDLE-CLASS REVOLUTIONARY: [Walks off.] *This is great, guys. I'll put this in our next pamphlet. Really good stuff. Cheers.*

Questions for World-Building: Who is on the lowest tier in your uprising? In what ways are their needs "unknowable" within the ideological discourse of the revolution? How are their needs and wants multilayered, localized, personal, and perhaps at odds with the larger movement?

Conclusion

Obviously, this essay can't contain all the complex players within an uprising, but I have found that authors who move beyond dualistic thinking create rich, intricate worlds and characters. These are just some of the questions I asked myself as I crafted the world of *Through the Veil*, and they are constantly on my mind for its sequel, as the tension between various stakeholders in the world intensifies.

ENCHANTED MOURAS AND MIRACLES: PORTUGAL'S MOOR AND CHRISTIAN ANCESTRY

ᕙᕗ

BY DIANA PINGUICHA

Portugal is an old country, and our recorded history goes back for hundreds of years. Our myths and legends vary from region to region, depending on who occupied it. In Alentejo, where I grew up, both Christian and Moor influences remain, from words, to food, to folklore.

A brief history recap: the Umayyad Caliphate expanded to the region of Hispania and ended the Visigothic Kingdom. Many Christian nobles retreated to the north of the peninsula, pushed back by the caliphate's expansion. The caliphate's rule lasted around five hundred years, with their strongest influences being in the south of the Iberian Peninsula, since that's where they ruled the longest. To this day, people from northern Portugal will call us southerners "Moors" as an insult without realizing that they, along with most Portuguese, have Moor ancestry.

My hometown of Estremoz is known for its wine, marble, and being the dying place of Isabel of Aragon, Holy Queen of Portugal and wife to Dinis I. A lot of the city is dedicated to her, and for as long as I can remember, I've heard the story of her miracle, when she turned bread into roses to escape the king's ire. As the story goes, she saw the commoners were starving, and against the king's wishes she sneaked out of the castle every morning to give them bread. One day, when he caught her and demanded to see what she had hidden in her skirts, she proclaimed her burden to be roses, knowing full well that it was bread. When forced to reveal what she carried, it was not bread that tumbled to the ground but roses. Thus, the Miracle of Roses was born, a kind of miracle that can also be found in other countries, such as Hungary, where the same story is attributed to Isabel's great-aunt, Erzsébet.

When I decided to put my own spin on her story, I knew I wanted her to have actual magical powers, and I wanted to reference Erzsébet as having them, too. But aside from the miracle story and some surface-level details I'd learned in school, I knew little about her other than her being an actual saint who built hospitals and care houses for sex workers and who gave food to the poor. I found out she was engaged to Dinis when she was ten and officially married him at twelve, but their marriage wasn't consummated until much later. They were a great ruling couple, possibly one of the best we had.

When I decided that in my version of the story she'd have a gift where she could turn all food into flowers with a touch, I set to investigating more about the problems of the time. I learned of many things that weren't as simple as our history books painted them to be. Namely, we tend to paint the Moors in broad strokes, but archaeological research suggests that the Moors weren't solely Muslim but an amalgamation of Jewish, Muslim, and Christian people who'd sworn vassalage to the caliphate. The same research postulates that the caliphate didn't expand through war but through trade, and that the people chose to align themselves with the Islamic kingdom, since to the common person, it made little difference who was in charge, only how their rulers treated them.

Looking at how the Catholic Church and its followers have mistreated many people throughout the centuries, I don't find it hard to believe that the commoners willingly changed sides and swore vassalage to the one that might treat them better. The caliphate also brought much-needed innovations, such as the use of the astrolabe and irrigation, as well as new crops like sugarcane. It's a misconception that the caliphate demanded conversion—it didn't, and people only converted to Islam if they chose to.

My research led me to another Portuguese myth: that of the enchanted moura. Enchanted mouras are Moor women, usually of significance to the caliphate, who've been enchanted in some form or another. We have many stories about them, and both of my parents' hometowns (one near Sintra, the other near Vila Viçosa) have enchanted moura legends of their own. What all these women have in common is that they were enchanted during the Reconquest, and that they needed a man to break their enchantment. Some of the women were trapped inside stones, others in the form of an animal such as a snake, others inside wells, others in riverbanks. Each enchantment was different, and as such, so was the way to set the moura free. For instance, according to the legend in my dad's hometown, you have to show no fear while a snake climbs up your body and plants a kiss on your lips: Should you be able to do this, a Moor princess will give you the treasure she's guarding.

The story I chose to adapt was that of the moura Salúquia, who supposedly threw herself from a tower when she realized the Portuguese had killed her intended and used his missive to take her town of Al-Manijah. The town really was taken captive, but Salúquia's suicide was likely a fantasy of the time. This led me to think I could change that fantasy into something of my own and rewrite that story to give the Moor princess more agency. I also couldn't find any legend referencing *how* her curse could be broken, so why not with the most fairytale way of all: a kiss?

That's how I ended up taking the facts of Isabel's reign—the things she did, how she was—and blending them with otherworldly abilities that would give way to the miracle she supposedly took part in. The Miracle of Roses is, in itself, already a fabrication, and I saw fit to push it even further into fantastical territory. And with the moura Salúquia, I took the facts of the Reconquest and rewrote her story around those while also giving her supernatural powers.

Portuguese culture has both Christian and Moor ancestry, and the Moor side is more prevalent than most want to see or admit. It lingers in our food, our words, our monuments; it's a disservice to our past and the scientific accomplishments of the Moors that we're never truly taught a lot about them in our schools. It seemed fitting to blend together Christian myths with Moor legends while dismantling many of the wrongful notions we have about the time when they originated.

My ultimate goal was to remain true to the figures I was portraying, and the medieval beliefs and system. To do that, I found I didn't need to stick to all the facts, only to some. And when a book is ultimately fiction, the small deviations from what really happened don't truly matter. Choosing where facts end and fantasy starts is tricky, especially when in a historical setting. And we also have to remember that our own history has been heavily doctored by whoever told the story of that history. You want to be faithful to the facts, but sometimes the facts don't lend themselves to the heart of the story. And in a historical fantasy, you want to use the facts, but don't be afraid to let the fantasy take over when it's what you need to make your story sing.

A BRIEF HISTORY OF
REAL-WORLD MAGIC

ୋ୨

BY JAY S. WILLIS

Authors and readers of modern fiction often believe our modern concepts of magic and mages stem only from Tolkien and the King Arthur
legends. In fact, a study of scholarship from ancient Rome and the
medieval and Renaissance periods reveals modern wizards in fiction
are firmly rooted in much older real-world works and treatises. Writers
of fantasy interested in magic would be well served to look to the works
and thoughts of a collection of real-world medieval and Renaissance
"mages" for inspiration.

Several great scientific minds originated real-world concepts of
magic based in science, medicine, and philosophy. The history of magic
in the medieval and Renaissance periods originates primarily from the
works of four prominent authors in Roman times: Seneca, Ptolemy,
Pliny, and Galen. These thinkers provided a firm foundation for "magic
thought" that further developed in the Middle Ages and into the
Renaissance.

The most dominant ancient magic themes tended to revolve around divination, dream magic, astrology, and natural magic. Sound familiar? Many of the stories told in modern fiction, television, film, comic books, and video games are all variations upon these ancient concepts.

Seneca, an ancient philosopher often cited in the Middle Ages, derived his views on magic from divination and astrology. Seneca viewed the stars as being divine and considered their study as sacred and almost religious. Although he firmly believed in the impact the stars had on future events, his major focus was the divination of the future by thunderbolts, of all things.

The works of Ptolemy mostly concerned math, science, astrology, and astronomy. His most important contributions were in the fields of math and science. However, Ptolemy compiled a great deal of information on astrology and astronomy, considering them very valid sciences, and placed much greater emphasis on the stars than Seneca did. In Ptolemy's study of astrology, he believed each planet, which in turn influenced the entire world, was affected by four basic elemental qualities: heat, cold, dryness, and moisture. Ptolemy said that each of these qualities was either good or evil, with heat and dryness being good, and cold and moisture being evil. Note that Ptolemy's elemental ideas don't correspond directly with earth, air, fire, and water, but there are similarities, and in ancient times there was also a focus on tying each element to a moral judgment. Modern games and literature are firmly rooted in elemental systems of magic, usually without awareness of the origins.

Pliny's *Natural Magic*, an ancient encyclopedia, covers many topics, including magic and astrology. His attitudes toward magic are rather complicated, because his writings contain moral judgments on the times he lived in. However, in discussing magic, Pliny related it to the study of medicine and believed that magicians had advanced medicine the furthest. Pliny believed astrology and magic were closely related, and he briefly mentioned divination by thunder. Most of his criticisms regarding magic focused on an intellectual basis rather than morals, unlike Ptolemy's.

The works of Galen—probably the most prominent physician in Roman times, and often misunderstood, misinterpreted, and neglected—concentrated mostly on medicine. However, he also included his views on magic in his writings.

Galen agreed with Ptolemy's theory on the four elements and believed to some extent in divination. Galen's views included very little on astrology. He was accused of practicing magic in his medical practice, though he denied such accusations. Witch? Necromancer? Heard such indictments in modern genre fiction?

The most important ideas about magic used by the Renaissance magus came from the Hermetic tradition of magic. Works by Hermes Trismegistus concerning magic centered on astrology and the occult sciences. Hermetic magic revolved around the idea of a system of the All, with everything in the universe in relationship. With the proper knowledge of plants, stones, metals, animals, and images relating to the planets and God, one could create a link with this system by means of sympathetic magic. The Hermetic magic was mostly of a talismanic sort, creating talismans in order to link into the power of the All. Sound familiar? Foci, spell components, totems, holy symbols? Modern games (both RPG and video), as well as fantasy fiction, are littered with such derivations grounded in these ideas.

Picatrix, based on Hermetic tradition, is a work on sympathetic and astral magic. It explores the Hermetic ideas of making and using talismans to bring spiritus from the heavens into the material of the talisman, thus harnessing its power.

Perhaps the best synthesis of magic in the Middle Ages and Renaissance was exhibited by Giovanni Pico della Mirandola. In his works, Mirandola not only originated the romantic concept of a soulmate, he gave the Renaissance magus the magic of Cabala, synthesized from the Jewish mystical Kabbalah practices.

European Cabalist magic was an attempt to tap into the higher spiritual powers, placing great importance on angels and divine spirits. Cabala was at its core a concept of gaining knowledge of God. The magic derived from it was to be used mystically to aid in contemplation, or to make use of the power of Hebrew, or to invoke angels to perform feats of magic. Mirandola felt that no magic could be effective without using Cabala to complement and strengthen it. Mirandola created a successful marriage between Hermeticism and Cabala. This synergy in concepts ties in quite nicely for the modern fantasy fiction writer or game designer seeking to build their own system of magic.

The major similarities in magical beliefs from ancient times to the Renaissance were the beliefs in divination, especially by thunder, dream magic, astrology, and natural magic, which came from the Hermetic tradition. Clearly the forces of nature and the heavens played into the magical beliefs of everyone. Whether those of antiquity and the Middle Ages actually had the knowledge and abilities to accomplish the feats they spoke of is irrelevant.

Those of us building worlds and forging new imaginative systems of magic to serve as the engines of our fiction, games, and other media can learn quite a bit by gazing into the minds of the great magic innovators of antiquity. Even a cursory review of the ideas of Galen, Ptolemy, Pliny, Seneca, and Mirandola offers a better understanding of the history of magic created by real-world thinkers and scientists.

The idea of placing strictures on magic derives from ancient real-world beliefs. Sympathetic magic, binding magical powers into talismans, and detailed rules all hearken back to the concepts of magic developed in medieval and Renaissance Europe. From Merlin to Gandalf to the Force to Harry Potter, all our most treasured magic in modern fantasy fiction can trace its roots to the scientists and "magicians" from the medieval and Renaissance periods. A bountiful harvest of rich conflicts and plot points abound for modern authors willing to dig around in the past.

REFERENCES

Much of the information shared here was cultivated from this eight-volume treasure trove of knowledge:

Lynn Thorndike, *A History of Magic and Experimental Science* (New York: Columbia University Press, 1923).

PART 2

❧

SPEAK, FRIEND, AND ENTER: LANGUAGES AND CULTURE

ARCHAEOLOGY IN SCIENCE FICTION AND FANTASY

❧

BY GRAEME K. TALBOYS

It is likely the first "archaeologist" to come to mind when mentioning characters in science fiction and fantasy is Dr. Jones or Lara Croft, depending on your medium of choice. Their exploits—while not considered typical of the actions, behavior, and ethics of genuine archaeologists—certainly color a lot of people's perceptions.

There was a time when antiquarians raided tombs for treasures. They did untold damage and were, in their way, far worse than grave robbers, as they were generally educated gentlemen who should have known better.

The same holds true for a lot of archaeology in written works of fiction. There is, of course, the need for a touch of poetic license, but as someone versed in archaeology (and museums), I often cringe at the way in which it is depicted.

Here are some common misconceptions.

Myth: Archaeology Happens Overnight

Although the television series *Time Team* proved that you can dig a site in three days and extract a lot of useful information, a dig is only a small part of the archaeological process. Planning can take years. Not just the gathering of sufficient manpower, but putting in place finances, gaining legal permission, hiring equipment and operators, arranging accommodation for all those working in the field, and so on. And then comes the analysis of what has been found, which can take decades.

Myth: You Find What You're Looking for About Ten Seconds After You Start Digging

No. Indeed, archaeologists are unlikely to be looking for anything specific in that sense. Sites are chosen because they are likely to yield a wide amount of information about a given period (usually the one in which the dig director is a specialist). It is true that amazing things can turn up on day one. But it is rare. You are just as likely to dig for six weeks and uncover a few stones that may or may not be associated with the foundations of buildings. And if there is anything really interesting to find, it's almost certain to be under the spoil heap or found on the last day.

Myth: Technology Is Taking Over

There is no doubt that technological advances have made archaeology more interesting—ground-penetrating radar and other geophysical applications along with aerial photography, lidar, 3D scanning, and the use of powerful portable computers have added to the mix. They have certainly made it easier to decide where to dig, but there is no substitute for digging a hole and scraping soil while watching with experienced eyes.

Myth: Archaeology Is About Treasure

Treasure is rare, which is why it hits the headlines—most finds are bits of broken pottery and the remains of food, stuff our ancestors threw away. Beware. Saying "Archaeology is rubbish" will not make you many friends in the archaeological community. They've heard it before.

Myth: Archaeology Is About Dinosaurs

No, it's not. Paleontologists do that, and the last thing you want to do is tread on their toes, in case they unleash the reconstituted raptors.

Myth: It's Just About Old Objects and of No Use to the Real World Today

Old objects are just the starting point. Archaeology is more about the story that can be derived from the object and the context in which it was found. Reconstructing this story from the evidence allows archaeologists to uncover patterns of human behavior and the reasons for change, human health and diet, the importance of environment, resource distribution, and, in more recent times, urban planning, as well as the way in which all these elements and more are linked. This information, in turn, is of inestimable value to modern planners, doctors, and any politician worthy of the name. And there are more than a few countries with economies that rely on archaeological tourism (which is why certain groups destroy dig sites after having looted the movable items for sale on the black market).

Myth: An Archaeologist Is an Archaeologist

Yes. And no. When you learn archaeology, you tend to cover all the bases. Eventually, however, you will specialize. The majority of archaeologists are generalists, but you also have:

- Zooarchaeologists, who study ancient fauna.
- Osteoarchaeologists, who study human remains from archaeological sites.
- Experimental archaeologists, who test archaeological hypotheses, usually by trying to replicate how something may have been done in the past.
- Historical archaeologists, who study written and oral records of the past.
- Industrial archaeologists, who study buildings, machinery, and other artifacts of the industrial past.
- Environmental archaeologists, who specialize in the relationship between ancient peoples and the places they lived.
- Geoarchaeologists, who study the natural processes that affect archaeological sites.
- Surveyors, who collect information about the location, distribution, and organization of ancient human cultures across a large area.
- Underwater archaeologists, who study remains found in, around, or under salt or fresh water or buried beneath waterlogged sediment.

I could go on. I expect you want me to stop.

Myth: It's an Easy Profession

Archaeologists are just a bunch of weird layabouts who dig holes, live in tents, and drink lots of beer. Well, that last bit is true. So is the bit about tents during some digs. Being an archaeologist is far from easy, though. Digs are physically and mentally demanding. But digging is just a small part. You then have to analyze your finds, keep up with all the latest finds from elsewhere to make better sense of your own, pub-lish papers, teach, and so on.

Yes, archaeology is usually safe, but then sometimes it isn't. Deep trenches can collapse. Constant rain or sun can sap your health. There are insects and diseases. Industrial sites can be toxic. Battlefields of the twentieth century contain unexploded ordnance. And digs can suddenly find themselves in conflict zones.

The Truth About Archaeology

So how can writers portraying archaeologists and archaeology in their fiction accurately portray the people, their work, and their findings?

Fact: Archaeologists Spend Most of Their Working Day in an Office

They are either typing reports, reading reports, examining artifacts, grading papers, filling in forms to apply for funding, preparing materials for exhibition, attending meetings, or quite possibly sneaking in the odd game of *Angry Birds*. While this doesn't make for an exciting read, some effort should be made to convey the idea that archaeology is pretty much like any other job.

Although . . . that might be the motivation for an archaeologist to do something a bit dangerous or unusual, just to break the routine. Too bad if it starts the countdown on a planetary doomsday machine left there from a warship that crashed five millennia before.

Fact: Most of the People on Digs and Back in the Lab Are Students

They will be youngish, poor, very likely a disappointment to their parents (who probably wanted them to be bankers or doctors), and the majority of them will go on to be something other than archaeologists when they graduate. There just aren't the jobs, and those that exist are poorly paid. They are doing it because they love it.

Which leads nicely to the next point. It is one of the few fields of endeavor where everyone on a team is likely to be there because they want to be there. That doesn't mean everyone gets along, but they have the love of their work in common, which makes a strong bond and creates fertile ground for intense discussions about what they are doing.

Fact: Archaeology Is the Poor Relation

It is at the back of the queue when the funding is given out. Very few people in positions of authority see the worth of it, and quite a few wish the need for funding would go away, as it tends to hold up engineering and building projects. Digs, in particular, are overstretched. There's never enough people and never enough time. What was once a leisurely gentleman's pastime is now usually done against the clock. If it isn't, it means the site under investigation is in some forsaken place subject to poor communication, harsh conditions, and no pub. A lot of archaeologists work in museums.

Fact: It Is Difficult to Predict the Future of Science

Science fiction is littered with failures. Some things can be extrapolated. Advanced geophysical surveys are already undertaken from orbit. One suspects the quality and resolution will increase. In the end, however, it always comes down to trowels in the trench and the human eye. It is why, even with today's technology, you will always find people at a dig and back in the lab drawing artifacts and their contexts. They learn to pick out the detail that is important.

Fact: A Dig Director Is Like the Captain of a Vessel

They need to have an understanding of the principles of everything under their command (surveying, digging, finds, conservation, diplomacy, law, and so on), but they are not expected to be experts in everything. Their greatest role, aside from their own specialization, is being a good leader and organizer.

Archaeology has an ethical dimension that is often neglected in storytelling in favor of the artifact. Digs are often culturally sensitive, especially around the exhumation of human remains and artifacts of religious or spiritual significance (which for some cultures is everything). Any interference with the past raises issues. Most archaeologists work ethically, although there are areas that are highly politicized, such as decolonization archaeology, the repatriation of Indigenous artifacts, and the relationship between community archaeology and heritage. These areas need exploring in fiction and offer the greatest opportunity for gripping narrative.

BOOKS ON ARCHAEOLOGY

Paul Bahn, *Archaeology: A Very Short Introduction* (Oxford: Oxford University Press, 2012) offers a short, inexpensive overview.

Kevin Greene and Tom Moore, *Archaeology: An Introduction*, 5th *Revised Edition* (London: Routledge, 2010) is pricier, but both comprehensive and comprehensible.

SOME SCIENCE FICTION/FANTASY WITH ARCHAEOLOGICAL CONTENT

H. P. Lovecraft, *At the Mountains of Madness* (1936)
A novella in the Cthulhu mythos about an expedition to Antarctica, revolving around the discovery of an ancient, cyclopean, and inhuman city.

Algis Budrys, *Rogue Moon* (1960)
The exploration of an incomprehensible and deadly structure on the moon, which tackles the notion of how you make sense of something that is alien.

Robert Silverberg, *Across a Billion Years* (1969)
Archaeologists explore the remains of an ancient civilization and go in search of the culture that created them.

Arkady Strugatsky and Boris Strugatsky, *Roadside Picnic* (1971)
Though not specifically about archaeology, it does highlight the real
problem of formulating any understanding of an alien culture from
artifacts that are just plain baffling and defy scientific study.

John Brunner, *Total Eclipse* (1974)
An archaeological expedition studies a civilization to determine the
cause of its demise and battles against interference from an Earth in
turmoil.

Jack McDevitt, *Engines of God* (1994)
Archaeologists follow a trail of discoveries across the galaxy to try to
discover what connects a series of vanished civilizations.

Thomas Harlan, *Wasteland of Flint* (2003)
An alternate future where the Aztec empire rules human space,
with an archaeologist as the main character.

THE LINGUISTICS
IN *ARRIVAL*

෴

BY CHRISTINA DALCHER

When I see the word "linguist" in a book blurb or a movie synopsis, my nose starts twitching like a bloodhound on the scent. Most of the time, disappointment lies at the end of the hunting trip:

The linguist is a translator (*The Interpreter*, 2005); the main character is a hyperpolyglot (*The Informationist*, 2011).

The plot turns on the unintelligibility of languages (*Enemy Mine*, 1985; *Windtalkers*, 2002).

The filmmakers employ a clever linguisticky gimmick, like putting all the dialogue in Latin, Hebrew, and reconstructed Aramaic (*The Passion of the Christ*, 2004) or Yucatec Mayan (*Apocalypto*, 2006).

The linguist could easily be replaced by an expert in another field without altering the story's substance (*Still Alice*, 2014).

All are fine films and books, but my inner linguist sulks after watching or reading them. As she did when I watched *Arrival*, the 2016 blockbuster where "linguistics professor Louise Banks is tasked with interpreting the language of the apparent alien visitors."

Okay! Cool! My inner linguist and I poured a glass of wine and sat down, prepared to be amazed. Here's what we came away with.

The Short Answer:

Arrival gets some things right, gets some things wrong, could have done some things better, and isn't about linguistics at all.

In fact, I didn't find nearly as much language science in the flick as I expected.

The Longer Analysis:
What *Arrival* Gets Right

1. The necessity of interaction

Upon hearing the spoken Heptapod language for the first time, linguist Louise Banks immediately informs Colonel Weber that translation based solely on the audio would be impossible; while she already knew the Farsi necessary to translate off-site two years ago, with this unknown language, she needs to be there with the aliens, interacting with them, teaching them English. Sounds good to me.

2. Methodology

Louise's fieldwork method is entirely credible in a situation that requires a monolingual discovery procedure (where there is no shared language between fieldworker and subject). She begins by constructing a Swadesh list of common words and concepts—an excellent start to gathering data on the Heptapods' (or any unknown) language. I don't recall Louise ever mentioning the term "Swadesh list" in the film, which is a shame. The one hundred words in the list, originally chosen for their cultural independence and maximal availability across languages, make for an excellent starting point. Morris Swadesh deserved at least a nod in the screenplay. Still, I'll give the writers credit for Louise's example of a pulaski (a tool used by firefighters) when Colonel Weber asks why she is building a vocabulary list of grade-school words instead of starting with more specific terms.

3. Focus on written communication
   At first, I balked (as did my inner linguist) at the decision to communicate with the Heptapods via the written word. Rereading the script, however, I find this justifiable: Louise insists there is no way she can reproduce their sounds (or study the Heptapods' articulatory mechanisms), so she decides to try writing and visual communication. Points awarded for working with what she's got.

4. Explaining the complexity of language
   A perfect Linguistics 101 lesson occurs when Louise shows the difficulty of asking a question like "What is your purpose on Earth?" before establishing the Heptapods' comprehension of the question's parts: the nature of interrogative structures, the collective "you" versus specific "you," the lexical semantics of each word in a larger phrase, etc. Nice work here rebutting Weber's insistence that the six-word question isn't complicated. It is.

5. A neat twist on a linguistic theory (albeit not a very popular one)
   The plot (and the major twist) in *Arrival* hinges on the infamous Sapir-Whorf Hypothesis: the strongest version of this controversial (and widely disputed) theory of

linguistic relativity poses that all (all!) thought and action is determined and constrained by the language an individual speaks. Indeed, we see this bearing out in *Arrival* when Louise's acquisition of the Heptapod language endows her with the ability to think as the aliens do—seeing both past and future events simultaneously. While this is a gargantuan leap to take, even for those agreeing with Sapir and Whorf, I'm happy to give credit to Ted Chiang (author of "Story of Your Life," on which *Arrival* was based) for incorporating a linguistic theory—even a flawed one—in such an imaginative way.

6. Appropriate details

And speaking of which, the clever use of the Sanskrit word for "war" (*gavisti*) and its literal translation ("desire for more cows") sets up the language-culture interface quite nicely. (Although it would be even nicer if the screenwriters had let us all in on the relevance of Banks's test, rather than using it as a cute device to get her the job.)

I also liked that Louise came clean about the Aboriginal "kangaroo" meaning "I don't know" being a myth. Thanks to linguistic consultant Jessica Coon's input, we've got one fewer apocryphal language tidbit floating around.

What *Arrival* Gets Wrong

I'm referring to notes I took while viewing, plus the script's final shooting draft, and I'll be going into some detail, so hold tight.

1. Unsupported linguistic factoids

What first turned me off (and made my inner linguist choke on her wine) was Louise's classroom claim that Portuguese sounds different from other Romance languages because it was seen as an "expression of art." Here's the quote: "The way it was written and spoken was rooted in aesthetics." First, I've never heard that before. Second, the idea that Portuguese's nasal diphthongs, for instance, were somehow manufactured to sound artistic is preposterous. Third, written Portuguese doesn't look much different than written Spanish or Italian or Romanian. I'm still trying to wrap my head around why the screenwriters—or anyone—would think the inclusion of this tidbit would do anything other than show us how little homework they did.

2. The linguist-as-polyglot/translator/interpreter

Louise is introduced early on as a translator. I wish she hadn't been, as this only perpetuates the misconception that linguists are polyglots whose focus is on learning languages rather than studying their structure. In an interview with Dr. Jessica Coon, one of *Arrival*'s consulting linguists, Coon remarks that the filmmakers told her this: "Theoretical linguists are really not Hollywood's main audience concern." Super.

3. Science versus linguistics

The film seems bent on telling us that linguistics is not science, and Louise stands silent at every opportunity to counter this. In the helicopter, when she first meets Ian the physicist, he tells her, "The cornerstone of civilization isn't language. It's science." I won't disagree that language and science are different creatures, but this would have been a perfect opportunity for our leading lady to mention that linguists *are* scientists. She doesn't. Worse, Ian the Physicist (not Louise the Linguist) is the one who points out the structural ambiguity of the Heptapods' "offer weapon" transmission. Ian says, "You approach language like a mathematician"; Louise takes it as a compliment rather than coming back with something like "Yeah, buddy. That's what we do in truth-conditional model-theoretical semantics." And the scene that made my inner linguist fire spitballs at the television? You got it—that one where young Hannah asks Louise about a technical term (non-zero-sum game), and Louise responds with "You want science, call your father." Whew. Major slam on the entire field of formal linguistics there. To make matters worse, Hannah wasn't asking about science—she posed a *vocabulary* question.

4. Conclusions drawn from writing systems

The Heptapods' "nonlinear orthography" is our first introduction to the Sapir-Whorf Hypothesis and the widely disputed concept of linguistic determinism. Specifically, the Heptapods' language, being written in logographs (as opposed to ordered sequences of sounds or words, as in English), causes Louise to wonder if the aliens might also think in a nonlinear way. Googling "nonlinear orthography" returns top hits that reference *Arrival*, so it's tempting to conclude this aspect of the Heptapod language is unearthly and illustrative of the aliens' ability to live in both past and future simultaneously. But there are problems. First, the Korean Hangul writing system is nonlinear: Letters are not written one after the other; they are grouped together into syllable blocks—yet no one thinks Koreans have some unworldly ability to see future events. Also, the Heptapods' way of conceiving time would be better illustrated with a demonstration of nonlinear *syntactic processing*. Consider this: Suppose my language's writing system involves my first writing all the verbs in a sentence, then the nouns, then prepositions, adjectives, adverbs, articles, and so forth. That would be a nonlinear orthography, but it wouldn't necessarily alter how I interpret the sentence "Jane took the stinky trash to the dump." As much as this non-linear device is necessary to the film's plot twist, I wish it had more to do with language processing and less to do with logographic writing.

5. Pedagogy

Much of Louise's pedagogical method seems to revolve around vocabulary lessons. We see her with the whiteboard that says "human," then her own name, then Ian's name. We watch both of our experts demonstrating "walk," "eat," and "tool." Unfortunately, none of these lessons can get the Heptapods further along the path to interpreting the all-important question the army wants answered—the concept of an interrogative is never taught, nor is the collective/specific "your," nor is the notion of predication ("Your purpose on Earth is _____"). Sure, we're watching a movie, but when that movie is about an expert linguist teaching aliens how to understand her, a line or two about how that requires more than teaching individual vocabulary words is warranted.

What *Arrival* Could Do Better

1. Kill the trope

There's no need to make Louise a polyglot (apparently, she was fluent in seven languages by the time she was sixteen because her father was relocated every year to a new country). This is another of those linguist-as-translator tropes that undermine the real essence of the entire field of linguistics. Plus, one year seems a rather short period of time to acquire a language.

2. Show your work

I would like to see more detail showing exactly how Louise parses the Heptapods' logograms. Not a lot of detail, but enough to make it look as if an actual linguist was at work in these scenes. It's called verisimilitude, and a sprinkling of it wouldn't necessarily turn the flick into a dull linguistics seminar. (Interestingly, it wasn't a linguist at all who worked behind the scenes in the development of the code that analyzed Heptapod B—that job went to *programmer* Christopher Wolfram.)

3. Understand the expert and her limitations

The idea that linguistics is a single field comes through strongly in the film. On the one hand, we see Louise lecturing on historical linguistics near the beginning of the story; later, she's portrayed as translator, acquisition expert, and fieldwork specialist. In one scene, she's studying spectrograms—visual representations of an acoustic signal showing frequency, amplitude, and time—tools that are highly specified to phoneticians and have little to do with Louise's task, since she's already decided to focus on communicating with the Heptapods via written symbols. Which brings to mind my next question:

Why didn't the army have an entire *team* of linguists? I mean, come on, there are a ton of us out here, each with our own subspecialties: syntax, semantics, pragmatics, morphology, phonology, phonetics, acquisition, historical linguistics, comparative linguistics, computational linguistics, sociolinguistics, and so on. I'll bet that if twelve

Heptapod-driving vehicles suddenly show up on Earth tomorrow morning, the people in charge will be looking for more than one linguist.

But—that's really the issue here. There's no need for more than one linguist, because *Arrival* (like Chiang's short story) isn't about linguistics. Nor is it about aliens. Or military tactics. Or the ability to see the future. It's about, as we understand in the final few minutes of the film, one person and what that person chooses to do when she knows what will eventually happen. The Heptapods' gift, while loosely tied to Sapir and Whorf's ideas of linguistic determinism (your language influences your behavior), could have been bestowed on a mathematician or a plumber, and the dramatic impact of exercising free will in the face of total knowledge would have hit me just as hard. My only complaint is this: The impact of Chiang's story—and all of its subtle and timeless beauty—is wrapped up in a movie pretending to be about linguistics, sometimes getting it right, sometimes not.

REALISTIC TRANSLATION IN FICTION

❧

BY MARIE BRENNAN

We've all seen it in the movies. A plucky band of explorers finds an inscription in a forgotten ruin or on a strange artifact. The closest thing the band has to a linguist, an archaeologist, or (in a pinch) a historian will push their glasses up their nose, peer at it, and then read out a nice, coherent, grammatical English sentence, decorated with a few pauses to remind you that they're having to think about it real hard.

This . . . is really not how translation works.

It's fine on the rare occasions when the person doing the translation happens to be working with a well-preserved text in a language they speak and read fluently. But most of the time, the linguist/archaeologist/historian is ranging much further outside their comfort zone to a "related" language (because we all know that speaking Spanish lets you read French with 100 percent fluency, right?) or, in a worst-case scenario, a completely unrelated language that just happens to be from the same continent.

Possibly the most egregious offender I've ever seen is the movie

Alien vs. Predator. I'm fine with buying into the basic premise, ridiculous as it is: A motley band of specialists find themselves exploring an ancient and mysterious pyramid buried in the ice of Antarctica. But when they find a panel of carved stone (and brush it clear of cobwebs, because we all know ancient pyramids need cobwebs, even when they're buried under a mile of ice), the following dialogue ensues between two archaeologists recruited from a dig in Mexico:

THOMAS: *I recognize the Egyptian.*

SEBASTIAN: *The second symbol is Aztec. Pre-Conquest era. The third is Cambodian.*

And then they proceed to read what it says.

There are so many flaws in this, I barely even know where to begin. It might make some vague amount of sense if the panel were trilingual, like the Rosetta Stone: the same text written in Egyptian, Nahuatl (the Aztec language), and Khmer (the main Cambodian language), so that our intrepid archaeologists were only reading the one they actually knew. But there are multiple problems with that. First, the Aztecs didn't have a full writing system, capable of representing complete and grammatically complex sentences. Second, the archaeologists speak of individual *symbols*, not whole blocks of text. And the image doesn't show us three different writing systems; it shows one, which has the overall blocky shape of *Mayan* writing—a different script entirely (but one that, unlike Aztec, *is* a full writing system).

So a couple of archaeologists who work in Mexico are able to read a mash-up of three wildly unrelated languages in the space of a couple of seconds. There's also a later scene where the main archaeologist shines his flashlight over a whole room filled with writing on the floor and walls and ceiling, declares "The hieroglyphs are a little difficult to make out," and then casually infodumps the entire backstory of the

Aliens and the Predators for his companion—because if he couldn't deliver the CliffsNotes translation of an entire room on sight, how would anyone ever know what was going on?

In reality, translation is full of stops and starts, uncertainties and bits you skip in the hope that the next bit will clarify the part that's baffling you. There are verbs with conflicting glosses, differences of dialect, idioms you don't recognize, abbreviations that leave out half the word, scribal errors that turn a whole phrase into gibberish. You mistake the future first-person passive indicative for the present first-person passive subjunctive and think that *numquam vincar* means "May I never be conquered" instead of "I will never be conquered." Many writing systems lack vowels, or punctuation, or even spaces between the words—which means that you have to dissect the text into its constituent parts before you can even begin figuring out what it means.

Some languages make this harder than others. English relies heavily on word order to make sense of a sentence, but in a highly inflected language, where words change form depending on how they're being used, you can rearrange them in all kinds of ways for aesthetic effect. Though I've failed to track down the piece in question, I have a memory of translating a poem in Latin class that started with a verb . . . whose subject was buried down in the second stanza. Translating something like that is more akin to assembling a jigsaw puzzle than following the yellow brick road.

Or take Japanese, a language whose aesthetics tend to prioritize allusion and indirection. In a Japanese poem, it's entirely possible the subject *isn't there at all*. You have to infer it from the surrounding context—which might include a different poem written four hundred years earlier, because the one you're translating is quoting that previous work, and the intended audience of literati was expected to recognize the quote and fill in the subject accordingly. Can you imagine translating an ancient curse only to discover the writers of the curse assumed you understood the oblique mythological reference that tells you what action will unleash the demon?

It gets worse when the language in front of you isn't the one you really speak. My experience with Latin and Spanish means I can figure out *some* French, and the spread of the Chinese writing system means you get a degree of mutual written intelligibility between unrelated Asian languages, but the finer points fall away: verb tenses, prepositions, all the little linking bits that tell you how the big blocks of meaning fit together. That sentence has something about opening a door—is it saying that I *should* do it, or that I should absolutely *not* do it? Are the aliens bringing a gift, or are we the gift being given to the aliens? In the types of stories where translation is important, these distinctions tend to matter rather a lot.

Mind you, having slagged on *Alien vs. Predator* for its characters' magical ability to translate an Egyptian/Nahuatl/Khmer mash-up, I do have to give them props for this exchange:

THOMAS: *"You may . . . choose . . . to enter."* [He pauses.] *"Those who choose may enter."*

SEBASTIAN: *It's not "choose." It's "chosen." "Only the chosen ones may enter."*

This comes closer to the reality of translation than most examples (including the rest of that movie). Thomas shows uncertainty about the subject of the verb, switching from "you" to "those who," and also the verbs themselves, relocating the English modal "may" from the choosing to the entering. Sebastian corrects one of those to a perfect passive participle and adds the limiter "only." The core elements remain the same throughout, but the specifics of meaning shift pretty radically before they arrive at a final translation.

The best way to accurately represent the process of translation in a story is to have actually done some yourself. If you've studied a foreign language, you know what types of errors you've made with that language—mistaking one word for a near homophone, forgetting to pay attention to verb tense, placing modifiers in the wrong order because the sentence structure is different from what you're accustomed to—and you can incorporate those mistakes/errors into the scene to create a sense of realism. If you're monolingual, then it's time to do some research and talk to a person with the appropriate experience. University departments can be great for this if you're writing about a real-world language, but even if the language is invented, using something real as your foundation will ground the moment in concrete detail. English is an SVO language—subject followed by verb followed by object—so an English-speaking person translating an SOV language might initially read out the inscription in a very awkward order, then rearrange it to sound more like proper English.

Or just give your characters a universal translator. They might thank you for it.

DEVELOPING REALISTIC FANTASY CULTURES

❧

BY HANNAH EMERY

Can you describe your fantasy story's dominant culture in one sentence?

That's where many of us start when we're writing, especially those who really love to world-build. We hit on a concept for a race of cat-people, or think about how people would be different if they'd evolved underwater, or decide to tweak how human reproduction works. Concepts like these are fantastic starting places: With a little research and creativity, they can be spun pretty quickly into a full-fledged culture, with elaborate practices, values, stories, and beliefs about how the world works.

And you can stop there. A lot of authors do, including some whose books are runaway bestsellers. But if you want your story to portray a realistic society, building "the culture" won't be enough for three reasons: cultural drift, cultural exchange, and deviance. Let's unpack these a little.

Cultural Drift

How old is your primary culture? And how much territory does it cover?

There's a lot of talk both inside and outside the United States about "American culture." You know, the culture of Big Macs and organic local farmers' markets, of abstinence pledges and the reality show *16 and Pregnant*, of—you get the idea. Even in "the information age," the US still has regional cultures. If you're familiar with those cultures, you might make assumptions about someone from the Bay Area, or the Bible Belt, or Brooklyn, but you'd likely realize there's not much you can assume about someone from "America." The country's just too big.

The same goes for cultural change over time. Even in a relatively young country like the US, there have been dramatic cultural changes since its founding, and modern people get into positively brutal arguments about what the original culture was (just ask someone with an opinion on the issue about what "separation of church and state" means).

Over time and distance, the Vulgar Latin spoken in the Roman Empire fragmented into the very different Romance languages. Culture fragments, too, and it also changes in response to local conditions. The American Revolution changed its people's culture dramatically. So did the slave trade. So did the car.

Failing to take cultural drift into account seems to be particularly common when you're developing nonhuman cultures (centaurs are noble, dwarves are gruff, elves are arrogant, you know the drill). One exercise to help you get around this is to think about which of the cultural traits you've developed are actually rooted in biology: Those are the ones most likely to be universal across cultures. For instance, *almost all* human children are raised in family groups; *almost all* humans subsist on some combination of plant matter and animal protein; *almost all* humans will have sexual partners at some point in their adult lives. But think how many variations exist on those themes if you widen the scope to all human cultures.

Cultural Exchange

Think fast: Where did tomatoes originate?

If you guessed Italy, I can't blame you. Tomato sauces and bruschetta are so strongly associated with Italian food now that it can be hard to believe there were no tomatoes in Europe until the sixteenth century. They originated in southern Mexico and came to Europe with returning Spanish explorers. Same thing with chili peppers, brought first to Europe and then to Asia from the "New World." People traveled, they saw new things, and they adopted those things as their own.

Intelligent creatures are curious. If people from your primary culture have contact with other cultures, whether through war, alliance, or just casual encounters, some parts of those other cultures will trickle home with them. Some American GIs who served in Vietnam came home with a new taste for Southeast Asian cuisine; some sub-Saharan Africans who heard the preaching of European missionaries decided this Jesus stuff might be worth exploring.

Food and religion are particularly good examples of cultural exchange, because they're pretty portable and fairly resistant to extinction. When people travel to a new country, they bring their cuisines and their faiths along, and even when immigrants assimilate, food and faith tend to persist longer than other things. But the longer an export is immersed in a new culture, the further it's likely to drift from its original source material. Christianity in Africa looks quite different from Christianity in Europe; "Chinese food" in the United States is very different from Cantonese or Szechuan cuisine. Blame cultural drift again, along with syncretism (a term most commonly applied to religion): combining new cultural elements with ones that are already working well. East and Southeast Asia are notorious for this, with many people's religious practices incorporating elements of Buddhism, Daoism, Confucianism, and local Indigenous traditions without the practitioners seeing any contradiction.

Cultural exchange is particularly common where two cultures bump up against each other often. This is why "ethnic" food is most prevalent in big cities that are common immigrant destinations, and why there are more Mexican restaurants in the southwestern US (i.e., close to Mexico) than in New England. If your story's set in a border town, it will almost by definition not be monocultural.

Finally, of course, there's cultural exchange in the most direct sense of the word. When two human cultures first meet, there are two things you can almost always count on: they'll try to kill each other, and they'll make babies. Even if there are taboos against intercultural sexual relations—even if it's punishable by death—it'll still happen. And the children who come from those unions will have to be categorized within the societies who could potentially claim them, and decide for themselves what cultural space they're going to occupy.

Which brings me to my final bullet point. I suspect that right now, someone reading this is preparing to protest that their fantasy culture is the exception, that their cultural authorities (king, warlord, high priests, whoever) maintain a policy of strict isolationism, so there are no opportunities for cultural exchange, and they're immortal, so there's limited opportunity for cultural drift because the story coming from the top never changes. To you, I say that even in the most authoritarian societies, there will always be the crazy ones.

Deviance

What was US culture like in the 1950s? (Hint: This is a trick question.)

If you took early American TV as your guide, you could easily believe the America of the '50s was a land of capitalism-loving, comfortably middle-class families, with stay-at-home moms and breadwinning dads. But, of course, some Americans still got divorced in the '50s, some were in same-sex relationships, some were poor, some were Communists. The dominant culture's social norms may have pointed people toward the *Leave It to Beaver* ideal, but the reality was a little different.

Whatever norms, beliefs, and values your society has, there will be people who stray from them. People who don't believe God created the universe, or don't believe that the Big Bang did. People who sever ties with their families of origin, or who live with their parents until they're forty. Straying from the mainstream—whatever that mainstream might be—is what sociologists call deviance.

People tend to think of the term "deviance" as referring to illegal and/or immoral actions, and that's certainly part of the picture. But there are also deviant acts that violate *norms* rather than laws or morals, like sitting down right next to someone on the bus when there are empty seats available elsewhere. You won't get arrested—you may not even get a dirty look—but you'll almost certainly make the other person uncomfortable. And there's another type of deviance even milder than norm-breaking: people who just do things a little differently. In 2022, in much of the world, not having a cell phone makes you deviant; so does having twelve children. Ditto skydiving, or having a tarantula for a pet.

Your society will have all these forms of deviance. There will be people who commit crimes (actions that a government deems undesirable for one reason or another), there will be people who do immoral things (often actions that a religious authority deems undesirable), and there will be people who do weird things and think outside the box. The motivations for these actions could be anything you can imagine. What if there were a Dothraki in George R. R. Martin's series *A Song of Ice and Fire* who was allergic to horses? What if there were a Hogwarts house elf who had a vision from the gods and started preaching that the house elves needed to go join Voldemort's cause, or that they needed to use their magic to destroy the humans?

The people in your world will be born into a culture, and that culture will shape their thoughts and beliefs and actions. But no thinking person can conform completely to every aspect of their culture, no matter how constrictive that culture is. You'll always have variability.

This might all sound like a lot of work, and I'm certainly not suggesting you come up with a hundred incarnations of every culture that could potentially appear in your story. But for the main cultures, I'd suggest it's worth thinking about these things. Because the more nuance you can put in your cultures, the realer they'll feel to your readers—and, who knows, you may even find opportunities for new stories! The messianic house elf seems like it has potential to me . . .

LANGUAGES IN FICTION

ᥫᩣ

BY CHRISTINA DALCHER

I once saw a graph depicting a fact I've long suspected: The probability that a book is good varies inversely with the number of words the author invented. My advice? Believe it. When I read science fiction, I read Heinlein. It's good stuff, I don't need a glossary, and my eyes don't roll at unintelligible strings of punctuation marks in dialogue.

Of course, exceptions exist. Burgess's *A Clockwork Orange* comes to mind. With a Nadsat vocabulary drawn from Cockney rhyming slang, Slavic roots, and Burgess's neologisms, it worked. It worked because Burgess knew his linguistics (he was a phonetics lecturer in early life). He knew it so well that he got away without including the Nadsat glossary in the first edition.

Not everyone who writes, whether it's sci-fi, fantasy, or a Lee Child–esque thriller, can have an expert-level background in everything. Most of us know our limitations. When it comes to linguistics, the problem is this: Unlike chemistry or engineering or genetics, knowledge of language is an inherent part of the human condition. By the time we're three years old, barring pathologies, each of us speaks our native language perfectly. It's precisely this fact that can lead writers down the garden path and permit the delusion that everyone is an expert when it comes to something as universal as language.

Don't take this as an attack on you. It's not meant to be. If anyone deserves the blame for lousy linguistics in writing and film, it's probably the language scientists themselves. We've done a substandard job of self-marketing over the past half century.

With that preamble, let's move on to specifics.

Common Linguistic Mistakes

Four things I've seen in novels and movies that make me want to run:

1. The armchair know-it-all

    This [piece of evidence] was obviously written by a woman. You can tell from the syntax.

    Really? Having studied syntax for more years than I'd like to remember, I'm hard-pressed to find a difference between male grammar and female grammar. Want to talk lexicon? Discuss dancing around before getting to the point? Address the fundamental frequency of a speaker's voice? I might buy the gender assumption from sociolinguistic or acoustic clues. But, as far as I know, the syntax of a language doesn't vary much between women and men. Whatever anatomical features we have, we still need subjects and verbs and objects, and we need them in a certain order. The take-home message here is simple: If you're going to make a statement about language, you need to do more than toss out a term of art.

2. The strong version of a flawed theory

    There's no word for [concept] in [language]. That tells you something about the culture, doesn't it?

Ah, the good old Sapir-Whorf Hypothesis (SWH, henceforth). Combine the strong version of this chestnut with hearsay, and you're guaranteed to be the life of the party. Unless, of course, a linguist is standing nearby. Or worse, a native speaker of whatever language you've just made a sweeping generalization about. There's an easy way to avoid getting yourself stuck in such a situation: Don't do it.

Whorf went there and earned himself a trophy in the Linguistic Hall of Shame (unfortunate, because he did make other very sound contributions to language study). While linguists may accept the weaker version of the SWH—the claim that language shapes our thoughts and behavior to some extent—very few agree to the most robust form of linguistics relativism: that our thoughts and actions are constrained by the language we speak.

3. The tiresome chestnut

The [cultural-linguistic group] have [made-up number] of words for [word].

Here we have the corollary to the previous problem. You've heard it before, usually with words like "Eskimo," "one hundred," and "snow" to fill in the blanks. Please don't fall for it. The Eskimo Snow Word Swindle sprouted from—you guessed it—a combination of lazy research and misquoting. Use something like this in your writing, and readers will gasp in awe, quote you at their next cocktail party, and perpetuate the myth by telling their kids. Linguists, on the other hand, will be shaking their heads, wondering why they failed at educating Joe Public. Like I said—lousy marketing. And think about it for a minute: Don't we English speakers have a passel of snow-related words? When we don't, we can create snow-related phrases along the lines of "nice packable snow suitable for snowman-building." The only real difference between that phrase and an Inuit "word" meaning the same thing is that one of them includes some spaces. Not a very interesting distinction, in my mind.

4. The faulty comparison
Language X is more primitive than Language Y.
Sigh. Here's a fact: All languages are complex. And every single one of them can handle any concept. If a language doesn't have a word for "quark" or "cornflower blue" or (heaven forbid) "snow," guess what? If it needs one of those words, it'll add it into the lexicon.

Tips for Talking About Language in Your Writing

1. Accents versus dialects versus languages—know the difference
There's an old saying: "A language is a dialect with an army and a navy." This does a great job of encapsulating the fuzzy difference in meaning between dialect and language, but I'll try to sort things out in a bit more detail.

Linguists generally use the term "accent" when referring to speech patterns carried over from a speaker's first language to a second language. Example: Giuseppe, from Naples, speaks English with a marked Italian accent.

We use dialect when we're talking about mutually intelligible variants of the same language. Example: Mary's Brooklyn dialect is notable for dropping final *r* sounds, but anyone who speaks English understands her perfectly.

Languages get tricky. I could say that one speaker of Language X will always understand another speaker of Language X, and I'd be right—most of the time. But what do we do about Chinese? Or Italian? Both of these languages comprise multiple variants that might be considered dialects. But they're not. In Italian, we've got everything from Sicilian to Neapolitan to Venetian to Genovese, primarily due to the relatively recent unification of small city-states in Italy. Put a Neapolitan and a Venetian at the dinner table, and you might as well put a Neptunian and a Venusian in their places. Those so-called dialects are different enough to be mutually unintelligible. There's a sense in which they're languages on their own, minus the armies and navies.

In sum, if you want to use terms like "accent," "dialect," and "language" in your work, think about the difference in meaning among them. Linguaphiles will thank you for it!

2. Universal grammar—understand it exists

I'm going to borrow heavily from *An Introduction to Language* by Victoria Fromkin, Robert Rodman, and Nina Hyams (2003), because they've said it so well.

All human languages (now numbering around six thousand), whether spoken or signed, share common elements. On the phonetic side of things, every language employs a limited number of sounds or signs. Grammatically speaking, every language has syntactic categories—go ahead, find me a language with no verbs, I dare you! All languages have rules governing the formation of words and sentences, negation, question-making, imperatives, and verb tenses.

In the realm of semantics (meaning), certain universal concepts are found in all the languages of the world: things like "living" versus "nonliving," "male" versus "female," "animate" versus "inanimate." When it comes to spoken languages, each and every one on our big blue planet uses a subset of possible speech sounds; in that subset, you'll find both vowels and consonants.

The take-home message here? Human languages are a lot more similar than they are different.

3. Alien language—it's alien, not human

Here it is—the part you've all been waiting for! Unfortunately, I'm not going to be able to invent an alien language for you.

What I can do instead is give you a short assignment. Go into your (book or film) library and pick out a few of your favorite sci-fi works that incorporate some weird alien language. Read or listen to them. When you're done, ask yourself one question: Do those extraterrestrial languages differ significantly from human languages?

In many cases, I think you'll find what I've discovered: Alien speech in fiction almost always follows the same rules and constraints that human languages do.

Since what I write is grounded in the here and now, I may not be the best person to come to if you need advice on how to make E.T. sound. But I can tell you this: Think outside the box. Ask yourself what features you could bestow on your nonhuman character that would enable him to do something genuinely different. If you're creative enough to write sci-fi or fantasy, you're creative enough to do that.

4. Classical ancestors of English—there's one more than you think

Thanks to the fantasy writers for being patient while I dug into outer space. Let's come back to Earth now.

We all spent part of our school years studying those Latin and Greek roots in English words, and for good reason—there are tons of them. But English, along with Latin, Greek, and a ton of other related languages, falls squarely into the Indo-European family. Yes, Indo, as in India. The next time you dig into linguistic history, have a look at Sanskrit. You might be surprised to find that "saabun" means "soap," and we got "cummerbund" from the word for "loin band."

A Few Authors Who Nailed the Language Thing

Mary Shelley, Robert Heinlein, Marian Zimmer Bradley, Anthony Burgess (mentioned earlier), George Orwell, Neal Stephenson.

Why? Because they kept it simple and didn't try to go too far. There's that old saying "Write what you know," right? It's good advice.

Getting Languages Right in Fiction

You all want me to say "research," don't you? Okay. I'll say it. "Research."

Unfortunately, when it comes to linguistics and its numerous subfields—phonetics, phonology, morphology, syntax, semantics, pragmatics, sociolinguistics, and historical linguistics—delving deep into the abyss of language literature might not be feasible. Not if you need to spend your time banging out the rest of a 100,000-word novel and also need to brush up on chemistry, engineering, and genetics. There's not enough time in the day.

My suggestion, then, is to find yourself a real, live linguist. Most universities will have one or two. Also, consider using the Ask a Linguist feature on the LinguistList: askaling.linguistlist.org/questions.

What Happens If You Get It Wrong?

In short, a linguist will find you and post snarky comments on his blog. Geoff Pullum has done this more than once, but my favorite bit of Pullum snark is a *Language Log* piece entitled "Learn some phonetics, Reacher." In it, he rips apart Jack Reacher's (really Lee Child's) casual toss-out of speech science jargon without having done even a minute of research. As Pullum points out, "in five minutes over a beer with any linguist," Child could have seen the error of his ways.

You don't want to be Pullum's next victim. Trust me. Do your research or ask a linguist (there are tons of us, including yours truly). If you don't have the time to do either of these, kill your linguistic darlings.

LEGENDS AND FOLKTALES IN FANTASY

࿎

BY COLLEEN HALVERSON

Because so much of my research in Irish literature involves faeries, ghosts, vampires, and other spirits, people often ask me if I believe in these things. My answer usually involves me giving my best Kanye shrug while flashing a *Mona Lisa* smile. While I would love to be a lady Ghostbuster someday when I grow up, my interest in the supernatural as a literature scholar is in what a ghost or vampire *means* within a particular text, especially within a modernist or contemporary context.

Folklore and legends function in much more slippery ways than their cousins—myth and religion. Myths and religious rituals are sanctioned stories, with a generally unwavering discourse and structure. Folktales and legends are living texts. Dynamic and ever-changing, they are inherently inconsistent, unstable stories, open to a variety of interpretations and retellings. As Linda Dégh says in *Legend and Belief: Dialectics of a Folklore Genre*, "The legend, more than any other folklore genre, can make sense only within the crossfire of controversies."

In other words, every powerful legend must have its doubters and haters.

The use of folklore and legends in fantasy world-building is essential to creating a believable, complex fictional universe. What follows is not a complete analysis of legend and folklore but a product of my own journey in trying to understand the presence of the supernatural within Irish literature. As a creative writer, I have used this understanding of folklore and legends for characterization, world-building, exposition, plot development, and foreshadowing in my own fiction.

Legends

For the sake of this chapter, I shall borrow Dégh's brief description of contemporary legends to include stories about "spirits, witches, demons, monsters, lunatics, criminals, extraterrestrials, and abilities of certain humans who are empowered with precognitions and magic that can identify these evil forces and protect us from their destructive power." But such designations of "legendary" are culturally relative. As Barbara Walker explains in *Out of the Ordinary: Folklore and the Supernatural*, "Among Asian populations, it is not unusual to believe that honoring dead ancestors is mandatory for avoiding disharmony in one's earthly life, or among Mormons to believe that spiritual interaction between people in this world and souls in heaven is an almost daily occurrence through ritual enactments in Mormon temples. Basically, when regarding the supernatural, what is agreeable within one group may seem superstitious, primitive, uneducated, or ignorant to another." The difference between religion and folktale is that religious beliefs are sanctioned by institutions. However, a far-fetched story that someone overheard from someone else? This is a folktale or "legend" precisely because it is an oral story passed around through various back channels. We should not be quick to privilege one over the other, but should understand how they function differently within culture.

Beliefs in the supernatural can vary even under a single roof. For instance, when I was finishing up my dissertation, I managed my stress by binge-watching episodes of *Ghost Hunters* on SyFy. My practical, skeptical husband (the Scully to my Mulder) would roll his eyes and make disgusted clicking noises as he walked through the living room. But every time football season rolls around, he develops incredible rituals involving the Green Bay Packers. "Belief" or "nonbelief" in the supernatural says a great deal about what an individual values and what they reject. By setting up legends of the supernatural within an SFF novel, we can gain insight into how characters define themselves on both a micro and macro level.

Questions for World-Building: What is the "sanctioned" mode of belief in your SFF world? What are expressions of vernacular culture and how do these beliefs shape cultural practices? How might legends conflict with the sanctioned modes of belief within this society? What does your characters' belief or nonbelief in terms of the supernatural say about them on a personal level? How might their beliefs in certain legends but not others reflect their various cultural backgrounds?

The Faerie Folktale and the Ghost Story

In Ireland, the faerie folktale is a type of grammar for explaining personal and/or cultural trauma, for expressing marginal histories, and for designating and spatializing the "Other." According to Angela Bourke in "Reading a Woman's Death: Colonial Text and Oral Tradition in Nineteenth-Century Ireland," although the faerie story is part of an oral tradition, it possesses highly codified rules of discourse and often involves "the actions of real people in real places and real time." All through the wild green hills of Ireland, one might stumble upon forts, also known as "forths" or "raths," but even still within these rural societies "they are sites of avoidance, overgrown and undisturbed, metaphors for areas of silence and circumvention in the social life of the communities which tell stories about them. They are places out of place; their time is out of time."

Oftentimes, stories about these raths emerged to keep invaders away from these precious archaeological sites. During years of imperial rule, when the English did everything they could to strip away Ireland's language and history, these raths stood, and still stand today, as reminders of the past. Stories abound of greedy English landowners who dismantled faerie forts to till the land beneath only to fall ill to some terrible, supernatural calamity.

Other popular stories include the forts existing as sites where people disappear as prisoners of the fae. Most important to Bourke's argument, the majority of these stories of faerie abduction involve women and children. While the changeling story can often absolve parental guilt from neglect, failure to thrive, or even infanticide, the faerie story in particular often speaks to the "unspeakable" lives of women. As Bourke explains, "Adult women taken by the fairies were usually said to be brides, pregnant, or lactating, and . . . it is not difficult to imagine the variety of physical and mental illnesses, from anorexia to tuberculosis to postnatal and other depression, for which the discourse of fairy abduction might be found appropriate." In other words, the fairy stories become the mode in which to talk about certain experiences that are without "language" in the larger discourse. Even now, I still struggle to find words to discuss my postpartum depression coupled with the experience of having a severely colicky baby. A changeling story certainly would have fit the bill.

The ghost story functions in similar ways as an expression of maligned history, the "return of the repressed," or the resurrection of the abject or disavowed. In American culture, ghost stories often involve women, children, runaway slaves, Native Americans, and so forth. These ghost stories are a way of preserving histories we might not otherwise be able to access: the history of domestic violence, of child labor, of the Underground Railroad, of massacres. Similar to the faerie forts, ghost stories also preserve historical sites, in particular sites of modernization such as the asylum, the prison, the school, the factory.

The site of the haunting often occurs in marginalized spaces such as the attic, the basement, and, yes, the toilet. In the West, we have Bloody Mary (a specter associated with female anxieties about menstrual blood, for sure), and in Japan there is Hanako (the toilet ghost who haunts elementary-aged children). According to Jeannie Banks Thomas in *Haunting Experiences: Ghosts in Contemporary Folklore*, "Hanako wears red clothes, and kids can contact her by knocking a specified number of times on her stall. She murders children, and her hands reach up from the toilet to grab her vulnerable victims." When I was potty-training my kids, all we ever talked about was poop, but, of course, as soon as they began using the toilet on their own, they're told by grown-ups that such conversations are "inappropriate." It would make sense that such childhood ghost stories emerge from these anxieties in terms of what is and is not appropriate to discuss within "polite" society. Again, the ghost story becomes a vehicle for speaking the "unspeakable."

Questions for World-Building: In what way do the legends within your SFF world allow for you to explore oppressed histories or cultural traumas? How do haunted spaces reflect both literal and figurative borders of acceptability? How do your legends reveal the "unspeakable" within your world?

Supernatural tales, even within SFF worlds where certain elements of the supernatural are "normalized," are great vehicles for characterization and world-building. By exploring what cultures accept and what they reject, we can bring layers of complexity within these systems. Every person, every society, is haunted by some specter, and in spite of what my husband thinks, who doesn't love a good ghost story?

REFERENCES
Angela Bourke, "Reading a Woman's Death: Colonial Text and
Oral Tradition in Nineteenth-Century Ireland," *Feminist Studies*
21, no. 3 (1995): 553–86.

Lina Dégh, *Legend and Belief: Dialectics of a Folklore Genre*
(Bloomington: Indiana University Press, 2001).

Jeannie Banks Thomas, "The Usefulness of Ghost Stories," in
Haunting Experiences: Ghosts in Contemporary Folklore (Logan: Utah
State University Press, 2007), 25–59.

Barbara Walker, "Introduction," in *Out of the Ordinary: Folklore and
the Supernatural* (Logan: Utah State University Press, 1995), 1–7.

WOODWORKING MYTHS IN FICTION

‿⁀◡‿

BY DUSTIN FIFE

I'm a statistics professor. I get paid for my brain, not my back. But sometimes I just want to smell the walnut sawdust, spend a day in good-to-the-bone labor that brings a backache and a truckload of satisfaction at the end of the day. I love the release of woodworking—love letting the manual labor pull my mind from the stresses of biased estimates, violations of homoscedasticity, and alpha inflation.

Several years ago, I began woodworking. And I tell you—there's nothing like walking by that piece of furniture you built and knowing that your own hands shaped that wood, planed it, and smoothed it. It's not unlike that feeling you get when you finish your most recent draft of a novel and read through it as a reader, not an editor.

Mighty fine feeling, folks. Mighty, mighty fine.

With that introduction, let me offer a few of my pet peeves when it comes to woodworking in fiction. By correcting these, not only will you spare frustration among my woodworking peers, but you might add some depth to the world you're building that you'd otherwise miss.

1. Everything Smells Like Sawdust

Yeah . . . um . . . what *kind* of sawdust? Is it nutty like walnut? Does it smell like popcorn like alder does? Does it smell like McDonald's BBQ sauce after spending a few hours in the sun? (Red oak.) Is it acrid like pine?

You see, saying that the room smells like sawdust is like saying a kitchen smells like food.

Give us more! Does it smell like pizza? Basil? Broccoli? Tuna? Is it cedar? Is it maple? Is it applewood?

Next time you want to describe the scent of a woodshop or sawmill, spice up your rhetoric a little. I might even recommend going to your local Woodcraft or lumberyard and sniffing out the wood. Seriously! I guarantee you will not be the first to do it! (Woodworkers, too, love the scent of different types of wood, so you'll fit right in.)

2. Mahogany Is Expensive

I see this *all the time* in fiction, so much so that it's become cliché. (Remember Effie Trinket in the first *Hunger Games*—"That's mahogany!")

The truth is, mahogany isn't really that expensive. Sure, it has to be imported, but where it grows, it grows abundantly! In fact, in places like Cuba and Honduras, many of the homes' *siding* is made of mahogany.

Just to give you an idea, I called my local hardwood dealer and they quoted me $7 a board foot for mahogany. Walnut, a homegrown wood, sells for the same price. A bit pricey, perhaps, but not all that exotic. Teak, on the other hand, sells for $20 a board foot!

If you really want to show a character's home as exotic and expensive, why not say it's made of ebony (a whopping $100 a board foot!)? Or how about bubinga ($15)? Maybe some zebrawood ($25) or cocobolo ($35)?

Just make sure you study some pictures online so you know how to describe it. Which brings me to . . .

3. Improperly Describing Wood

Let me begin by saying that I think it's awesome when writers of fiction are specific. Rather than saying the man slept in a log cabin, say he slept in a southern yellow pine cabin! Or instead of saying he rested his hands on the wood table, say he rested them on the white oak table! These sorts of details add dimension to your world.

Just be careful.

Before I talk about this particular pet peeve, let me talk about how wood is milled. There are two categories of woods: softwoods and hardwoods. Softwoods tend to come from conifers. They tend to have a *ton* of branches all throughout the tree and grow really fast. They're great for construction but not so good for fine furniture building. Hardwoods, on the other hand, have massive trunks with few branches until you get to the top. They grow a whole lot slower, but the wood is much harder, and much better for building fine furniture.

Something like pine is a softwood and tends to have a lot of knots in it (because of the branches). Oak, being a hardwood, very rarely has knots in it (because loggers harvest from the *trunk* below the branches).

So, imagine my dismay when I'm reading someone's novel and she says, "She gazed at the knotty oak chair."

Um, excuse me? Oak ain't knotty, pal! If it is, someone probably harvested it improperly. (Or they harvested an "urban" oak, which is a tree that grew in a neighborhood rather than a woodlot.)

Or perhaps someone is describing the "grainy texture of the maple desk."

Not really. Oak has a very coarse grain, the type that will put hair on your chest. Maple has a much more subtle grain.

Or maybe, "The dark maple chest."

I suppose maple *could* be dark, if you stained it. But why open up that can o' worms? Why not just call it walnut?

Nobody expects you, fair reader, to memorize every possible grain structure and characteristic of wood. But if you reference a piece of wood, at least look at a picture first.

Chances are, no agent or editor will refuse your book if you describe "knotty oak" or "the smell of sawdust" or build a table out of mahogany. None but the Dustin Fifes, Norm Abrams, and Nick Offermans of the world will laugh at you. *But* if you do it right, you'll add some depth to your world that you might otherwise miss.

Now go sniff some wood.

WITCHCRAFT IN MEDIEVAL AND RENAISSANCE EUROPE

✧

BY E. B. WHEELER

When people think of witches, they often picture something like the scene from *Monty Python and the Holy Grail* where peasants crowd around an old woman with a long, warty nose and call for her to be burned at the stake. They also might imagine Hallowe'en witches with pointed black hats and green skin, or modern Wiccans worshipping a mother goddess. None of these images are true to historical European witchcraft, though witches were sometimes depicted flying on broomsticks even then. Witchcraft is so buried in stereotypes that its historical facts take a little digging to uncover, but understanding the medieval and Renaissance beliefs about witchcraft can help in creating magic systems—and systems of power and prejudice—in fantasy worlds.

The Roots of the European Witch

The idea of magic—the ability of certain people to control the natural world through supernatural powers—is probably as old as humanity.

Witchcraft and religion are often closely intertwined, since both call on supernatural powers to confront the difficulties and dangers of life. It could be said that the difference is that religion asks for supernatural intervention, while witchcraft attempts to command it.

Most medieval Europeans believed that some people had the ability to talk to spirits, locate lost or stolen objects, create love charms, see the future, control the weather, interfere with livestock, or harm others through supernatural means. Such beliefs had roots in Greek, Roman, Celtic, and other ancient European cultures. These cultures had priests who served as conduits between the human and the divine, and where the cultures had writing, people sought divine or ghostly aid directly by etching curses or spells on thin sheets of lead and tossing them into caves or bodies of water to reach the underworld (perhaps the origins of tossing pennies into wishing wells). Nonliterate societies, no doubt, had their own methods of summoning supernatural aid.

By the Middle Ages, magic often blended these earlier pagan beliefs with Christian ones. For instance, practitioners might invoke Christian saints to rain pagan curses down on their enemies. This was frowned upon by most authorities but rarely prosecuted, often seen as merely ignorant superstition. Such magical activities continued into the Renaissance—the age of witch hunts—when practicing magic was viewed as something more dangerous.

Witchcraft in the Renaissance

Systematic belief in and fear of witchcraft in Europe peaked in the 1500s and 1600s. The Black Death had shaken traditional beliefs and institutions, and Europe was torn apart by religious change and conflict between Catholicism and Protestantism. People were afraid and looked for someone to blame—often someone different or outside the established social order.

Earlier magic invoked either benevolent or malevolent spirits, but in the Renaissance imagination, witchcraft stemmed from pacts that magic practitioners made with the devil to gain supernatural powers. The people who practiced folk magic may not have considered themselves in league with Satan, but church and political leaders now did. Even those authorities who believed that witches did not have any real power (and they were often in the minority) now viewed attempts to practice magic as heresy: a serious crime worthy of death.

This focus on the devil changed notions of what was involved in magic, sometimes becoming quite colorful. Having sex with the devil or with demons was considered a common rite of passage in witchcraft. Witches were thought to harm people and livestock by touching or looking at them, by concocting magical brews, or by sending evil spirits to harass them.

One of the signs of a witch was a mark like a mole, but without sensation—an "extra nipple," which witches were supposed to use to give sustenance to their animal familiars. There were also things witches were said not to be able to do, such as recite the Lord's Prayer, because they had chosen the devil as their master.

Trials and Confessions

Witch trials sometimes showed a sharp disconnect between the views of common people and the beliefs of political and religious authorities. Many people executed for witchcraft insisted that they were innocent or only confessed after being "cleansed" by torture.

A minority of people accused of witchcraft confessed freely to making pacts with the devil in hopes of gaining power. Another group of the accused were those practicing older forms of folk magic, who did not view their activities in the same malevolent light as their accusers. In Italy and other parts of southern Europe, some confessed witches claimed that their consciousness left their bodies while sleeping to battle evil witches and protect the harvests, perhaps hearkening back to traditional fertility rites. Their accusers struggled to make these confessions fit into their view of witchcraft.

Targets of Witch Hunts

Fear of witches wasn't reserved for political or religious leaders; the common people also distrusted those who might disrupt the order and safety of their communities. Towns sometimes hired witchfinders to ferret out witches, and when this happened, the number of witch trials in an area rose dramatically. Outsiders were often the targets of witch hunts—those who were on the margins of society, especially single or widowed women, the mentally ill, thieves, and the poor. Women were suspected of witchcraft more often than men, but men were also accused and executed.

The old stereotype that midwives were viewed as witches is probably false. Midwives filled an important role in society—even holding the power to baptize children if they looked likely to die at birth—and though the growing, male-dominated medical profession began to chip away at midwives' authority, they were still important enough in their communities that they were not often persecuted.

The Salem Witch Trials

The Salem witch trials provide a case study in witchcraft, showing the dynamics of power, class, gender, and race in witch hysteria. In 1692 and 1693, a group of teenage Anglo girls belonging to the upper class in and around Salem Village, Massachusetts, claimed to be persecuted by witches. The town had already been bubbling with tension over religious and legal disputes centered on unpopular Puritan minister Samuel Parris. These tensions exploded when the girls in the Parris household confessed to experimenting with the folk magic of the enslaved woman Tituba, a Black or Native woman Samuel Parris had brought from Barbados. Perhaps trying to deflect blame, the girls also accused a poor beggar woman and a rich widow—who had defied convention and married her servant—of practicing witchcraft and torturing them in spirit form. More accusations soon followed.

Many of those accused fell outside the social norms or were opponents of Samuel Parris, who used the witch hunts to solidify his social power. If anyone questioned the girls' accounts or their "spectral evidence," those people would find themselves accused, too—including at least one of the girls' friends. The girls eventually named around two hundred witches, about three-quarters of whom were women.

Twenty of the accused were executed for witchcraft. Nineteen of the victims died by hanging, and one was pressed under stones in an attempt to force a confession. Another four died in prison; a baby born to an accused mother in prison also died (prisons were breeding grounds for disease). A few women escaped hanging by "pleading their belly"—pregnant women were not executed because of the desire to spare the unborn child from being punished for the crimes of its parent. Still, thirteen of the twenty execution victims were women. Those accused ranged in age from four years old to their eighties, though the majority were on the older end of the spectrum.

One victim, George Burroughs, was a Harvard-educated minister who recited the Lord's Prayer just before his execution, causing a stir among the crowd and increasing doubts about the accusations. The trials finally stopped when religious authorities outside the community became concerned about the court's reliance on unverifiable spectral evidence, and when the accusations reached all the way to the governor's family.

Lessons for Writers

If you're writing about historical witchcraft, it's best to research the exact time period and location you're writing about to see which trials and punishments were used, because they varied greatly across time and place. Some witches were executed by burning at the stake, but many more were hanged, especially in Britain and its colonies. People accused of witchcraft in Britain and America sometimes chose the slow, agonizing death of being pressed under stones to avoid entering a plea of guilty or not guilty and going to trial, which saved their family's property from a government anxious to seize it from convicted criminals.

Witchcraft trials give us insight into a mindset that is mostly lost to the modern world. They came about in part because of an active belief that God and Satan, saints and demons, were not abstract concepts or distant religious figures but actively involved in everyday life. Especially during times of political and religious upheaval, people felt themselves involved in a war between forces of good and evil—not just in a metaphorical sense but as a literal, day-to-day, physical reality.

The lines between the spiritual and physical worlds were blurred. Spectral evidence, such as the dreams and visions of alleged victims, was as important to detecting witchcraft as witnesses and confessions. Understanding this can help us come a little closer to understanding the past and creating settings and characters that will transport readers to another world.

REFERENCES AND FURTHER READING

Carlo Ginzburg, *The Night Battles* (New York: Routledge, 2011).

Richard Kieckhefer, *Magic in the Middle Ages* (Cambridge: Cambridge University Press, 2010).

Daniel Ogden, *Magic, Witchcraft, and Ghosts in the Greek and Roman Worlds* (New York: Oxford University Press, 2009).

Marion L. Starkey, *The Devil in Massachusetts* (New York: Anchor Books, 1989).

Keith Thomas, *Religion and the Decline of Magic* (London: Penguin Books, 1971).

TRADITIONAL EUROPEAN SUPERSTITIONS

༄

BY E. B. WHEELER

Humans are adept at finding meaning in chaos and making themselves feel safe in an uncertain world. Superstition is one way to do that, and the superstitions we embrace grow out of traditions and the way we see the world. If we put ourselves into the mindset of a premodern European (up through 1700 or so), we can see how the physical and mental world of a people help form their superstitions.

Medieval and Renaissance Europe was a dangerous place. Society was violent, and germs had not yet been discovered, so death was common, often sudden, and almost always painful. The world was full of unseen threats like demons, faerie, and witches, as well as helpful forces in the form of God, angels, saints, and perhaps other friendly spirits. Social order was extremely important, so rightful kings had special abilities, too, both to keep nature in harmony and to heal with their touch. People needed protections to navigate this perilous landscape.

Bad Timing

The inhabitants of premodern Europe saw time as a yearly cycle, especially in Catholic regions. Each day was governed by at least one saint or religious observance. Some days were bad luck for traveling, bloodletting, marrying, or other major events because of the religious festivals or saints they were associated with. For instance, Fridays were bad luck because Jesus was crucified on a Friday. It was bad luck to marry during the fasting period of Lent because sex was taboo for that time of the year. In Wales and perhaps other parts of Great Britain, Tuesdays and Thursdays were common times to encounter the faerie. On Hallowe'en, spirits wandered the earth.

Yearly rituals also brought good luck, like eating hot cross buns on Good Friday or a goose on Michaelmas, or giving gifts at the New Year. One always had to be aware of where they stood in the annual pilgrimage through time.

Counting on Good Luck

Numbers were also important for determining luck—especially numbers associated with Christianity. The numbers thirteen and 666 (the number of the beast in the Bible) were bad luck, while three (members of the Godhead), seven (the biblical number of perfection), and nine were lucky. Thirteen people should never sit down to a meal together, since there were thirteen at the Last Supper just before Jesus was betrayed. The belief that people are renewed every seven years dates back at least to the Renaissance, so each seven-year milestone of a person's life was regarded as a time to be cautious, with sixty-three (seven times the mystical number nine) being the most precarious age—if you were lucky enough to live that long.

Searching for Omens

Because life was so uncertain, people were very concerned about know-ing the future. There were many ways to predict future events, like drawing in fireplace ash or putting objects under your pillow to predict your future lover, but astrology was probably the most popular. The belief that the stars guided daily life and events was widespread, not just among the masses but among the educated elite and nobility. The one thing no one should predict? The death of a monarch. It wasn't just bad luck—it was treason.

People spent a lot of time outdoors, so they searched for omens in the weather and in animals. Some of these make sense—like watching birds or clouds to predict a coming storm—but others have no obvious explanation. It was bad luck to disturb a sparrow's nest or have a rabbit cross your path, though carrying a rabbit's foot was considered good luck, as it is today. Crows and ravens were often associated with death, but, depending on the time and place, they could be helpful, and they often helped foretell the future.

Natural Sciences

Medieval and Renaissance society hinged on a belief that God made humans and everything else for a reason and to occupy a certain, fixed position in the Great Chain of Being, with God at the top and miner-als at the bottom. Everything in the natural world had a purpose and mystical properties. Medicine often employed strange (to us) combina-tions of plants, animal parts, and even pearls or gems to treat illnesses and restore the balance of the humors (fluids) in the body. On the other hand, fingernail clippings, hair, or other bodily leavings could be used against people in spells. Alchemy was the science that attempted to change the nature of materials—especially to turn common metals into gold.

Respecting the Dead

Europe before the Reformation had a sense of community that is mostly foreign to the modern Western mind. Community extended not only among living family, friends, and neighbors but also to those who had gone before and those who would come after. The dead trapped in purgatory needed the prayers of the living in their efforts to reach heaven, while the dead who had passed on could help or hinder the living.

Charitable giving, both while alive and in one's will, was good luck, because the subjects of the charity might prove helpful in the next life. For instance, some believed that if you gave a pair of shoes to someone in this life, in the next you would have shoes to wear on your journey to heaven. Yet making a will too early could invite one's death.

Ghosts were known to return to help their friends and to harass their enemies. It could be difficult to distinguish between true ghosts and demons, though. Evil spirits were all around. In some regions, leaving an open window or rocking an empty rocking chair might invite them in. Even sweeping could be an invitation to the forces of evil, and though the traditions vary, it was best not to sweep at night or to use a new broom in a new house.

The Fair Folk

The faerie were also a major source of concern for premodern Europeans. They kidnapped infants and even adults, as well as leading them astray or killing them for entertainment. They punished those who were sloppy or unchaste, and shot cattle with elfshot to make them sick, though they might also reward those who were good.

When there was a baby in the house—especially one who had not been christened—an iron knife or scissors opened to look like a cross placed in or near the cradle protected them. Carrying an iron knife was a good idea while traveling through unpopulated areas, as was turning clothing inside out to confuse the faerie. To keep the fair folk happy, and perhaps even solicit their help, people might leave food and drink out for them while people slept.

Warding Off Evil

An apotropaic is an object, symbol, or gesture meant to ward off evil. Crosses made of straw or rowan branches might protect a home from evil. Other home protections could involve carrying fire or salt across the threshold, often as part of annual rituals.

If the apotropaic failed, a house might be haunted. In Catholic regions, a priest could perform an exorcism. In Protestant areas, the afflicted were left with only fasting and prayer to drive out the evil spirits, unless they turned to a cunning local man or woman who would employ traditional Catholic symbols mixed with popular magic to clear out the ghosts.

Grotesque figures such as gargoyles, which could be either frightening or humorous, were used to scare away or distract evil spirits. Eyes carved or painted on drinking vessels or on ships protected the users from evil. Some animals offered protection against evil spirits, including man's best friend; a spayed dog was especially effective against ghosts.

It wasn't only the spirits of the dead that people were wary of. Corpses often had stakes driven through their hearts to make certain they rested in peace. This was especially important if they died by suicide or were unrepentant sinners. People might also make crosses over them or tie their feet together, depending on if they preferred spiritual or practical solutions to the restless dead.

Some plants had power against evil, too, including roses, rowan, and elderberries. Hawthorn could be protective but was also regarded with caution because of its association with the fair folk—no one was supposed to harm a hawthorn tree, or they might face the wrath of the faerie.

Apotropaic protections could also be carried while traveling. Garlic, silver, and mirrors were supposed to ward off a number of evil creatures. Iron, and especially horseshoes, have long been known to keep evil away. If worse came to worst, the traveler could cross moving water, which stopped most evil beings.

Religious Protection

Objects with religious associations were considered especially good protection. With the advent of Christianity, the Bible, blessed wax, crosses—including making the sign of the cross—and holy water or holy oil were effective apotropaics. Baptism protected infants from being kidnapped by the faerie, and being born on a Sabbath allowed a person to see through faerie glamours.

Bells—especially church bells or those used in funeral ceremonies—also frightened away demons and malevolent faerie. While we may not think of salt as religious today, in the past it was considered so. Spilling it was bad luck, which could be countered by tossing some over your left shoulder, into the face of the devil, who was always lurking there.

Superstitions in Writing

There were so many day-to-day superstitions in premodern Europe that it's impossible to list them all. If you're interested in a particular time and place, it's best to research it to discover the details of what people there did to counter the harmful influences in the world.

It's easy to look down on people of the past because of their superstitions, but they were not stupid; they simply lived in a different world than we do—one more richly populated with things unseen and unexplained. Their superstitions grew out of their beliefs and helped them face uncertainties. Likewise, characters in a fantasy world would probably develop superstitions to try to control their luck or avoid dangers they perceived as part of their world and belief system.

REFERENCES AND FURTHER READING

Katharine Briggs, *The Faeries in Tradition and Literature* (Chicago: University of Chicago Press, 1967).

Ronald Hutton, *The Rise and Fall of Merry England* (Oxford: Oxford University Press, 1994).

Richard Kieckhefer, *Magic in the Middle Ages* (Cambridge: Cambridge University Press, 2010).

Keith Thomas, *Religion and the Decline of Magic* (London: Penguin Books, 1971).

PART 3

HOW TO
MAKE IT UP:
WORLD-BUILDING

HEALTH AND WELLNESS IMPLICATIONS OF WORLD-BUILDING

❧

BY OLASENI AJIBADE

Healthcare is a complex subject. It touches every facet of society, so it can be a challenge to fully grasp. But I can guarantee that because of this complexity, you're already wondering what health and wellness might mean for world-building and crafting a story. I hope the following questions and my thoughts on how to approach them can help you on your creative journey.

How Dead Is Dead?

On the surface it seems like a stupid question, but it's easily the most necessary in any world-building effort. Thinking about death forces you to consider things that will help you flesh out important aspects of your story. These can include the rituals surrounding burial, the characters' cultural understandings of the balance of life, even the level of technological advancement. Many preindustrial cultures might define death by the lack of a visible response to pain or a pulse. Conversely, a more modern society would define it by the lack of brain activity or by complete metabolic collapse.

In the same vein, it is helpful to consider if death is permanent or if there is a supplemental "life repository" that must also be destroyed. This can be a great way to raise the stakes. *Harry Potter*, for instance, uses this to great effect in its treatment of Voldemort's horcruxes. As the story progresses, Voldemort becomes an ever-present danger because he can use his many horcruxes to resurrect himself.

If you are going to use death impermanence as a plot device, it is worth considering the ways that it can bog down your story. J. K. Rowling was smart to hold off on revealing Voldemort's horcruxes until later in the series. This allowed her ample time to flesh out the world and its characters. By the time the reveal came, it highlighted both Voldemort's skill as a wizard and how daunting the task of truly vanquishing him is. At this point, we've learned that the heroes have already disposed of several of them, allowing a more manageable story going forward. If readers knew about the horcruxes from the outset, it could easily have turned the series into a convoluted MacGuffin hunt that readers would have eventually stopped caring about.

What Role Does Technology Play?

The technology of any society or culture will dictate the most immediate advantages and limitations in your characters' lives. The ability to procure and store food safely is one of the easiest ways to show the impact of technology on the broader society. Some of the first civilizations developed in the Fertile Crescent following the advent of irrigation. This would create a more stable food supply that could then spur on a population boom. A healthy population can then branch out to develop more tools and instruments that push society forward.

For writing purposes, the first task is picking a time period. What technologies would be imperative to daily life? What instruments or techniques might be considered bleeding edge for the time? Your characters' feelings about them can help you flesh out their lived experiences. An excellent primer on how technology can shape societies is *Guns, Germs, and Steel* by Jared Diamond.

However, it can also be worthwhile to consider the downsides of technological advancement. The more technologically advanced a society is, the easier it is to spread disease. One of the reasons why the 1918 flu pandemic was so devastating was because of how quickly people could travel. One sick person traveling by train could potentially seed an infection in several cities before succumbing to the virus. Nowadays, air travel has only amplified that potential. The ensuing chaos would fuel a palpable sense of paranoia that could inflame existing tensions and upturn society. The current COVID-19 pandemic exemplifies that pandemonium.

History is full of examples of how these situations can play out, but you do not need specific expertise in epidemiology to write these stories effectively. *Castlevania* on Netflix is essentially a plague story that uses monsters and hell beasts in lieu of pestilence. Consider how the inhabitants of the various cities and towns ravaged by the monsters would feel. Some might have their faith shaken when even priests succumbed to the monsters, seemingly abandoned by the gods they served. Others might be paralyzed, not knowing what to do or whom to trust. The intelligentsia, possessed of all the knowledge in the world, would be struck by their own powerlessness—truly realizing for the first time how little they actually understood. If your story uses societal upheaval as its main thrust, this can be a great tactic to employ.

Who Treats You When You're Sick?

The places we turn to for help in times of sickness can say a lot about us, not only as persons, but also about our experiences, cultural backgrounds, and so much more. The same will be true for your characters.

Premodern societies tend to focus on religious/spiritual dimensions of health and wellness, whereas more developed societies might rely on more established medical practices. The presence of an apothecary suggests a developed but preindustrial society with DIY medicine. In this context, there is no guarantee of quantity or quality control. Conversely, pharmacies suggest not only an industrial society but also a high level of formal education. Location will invariably matter in all these considerations. A pharmacy in a remote or poor enough location might barely approach the standards of a medicine cabinet, or even an apothecary. These dynamics can create opportunities for plot and background elements that could make your story incredible.

The obvious application of this is the "MacGuffin-as-ingredient" trope where the protagonist must go on a quest for the ingredient that will save someone. However, there are other ways to use these ideas. For instance, trying to convince people to try a new medication or medical procedure can be cause for tension. When Albert Alexander was first treated with penicillin, his doctors had no other recourse. Imagine being his doctor, having to convince him and his family to try the treatment even when you're not sure it would work. The hours between waiting and seeing the results would have been harrowing, but maybe his doctor quietly resigned himself to the fact that he had done everything he could. The drug's discovery itself was fortuitous, but the recovery that Mr. Alexander made in just twenty-four hours is now the stuff of legend.

Where Does the Poop Go?

Everyone does it and yet it is so rarely discussed in stories. But I propose that to seriously consider feces is to consider everything about your world. This includes the obvious things, like what the main animal species are, the food sources, and even the climate. In *Life of Pi*, Yann

Martel describes an ordeal where Pi, now out to sea for several weeks, struggles to have a bowel movement. It isn't a very long segment, but it gives the reader a good sense of just how malnourished and dehydrated Pi has become.

Probing the presence of poop and how it is managed will help guide other aspects of the story. One way this can present is in architecture. Preindustrial societies relied on animal labor, so it would not be out of place for there to be smells of animals and their droppings, as well as the consequences of poor sanitation and sewage. These sights and sounds are somewhat less prominent today, and might have gone overlooked back then, unless you were in London during the Great Stink.

There are infinite ways in which you can build out a story simply by asking:

- Whose poop is this?
- How did it get here?
- What can we do about it?

I'm not asking for a multipage exposition on the excrement of your characters (even my gastroenterology colleagues don't want that), but to seriously consider how it exists and is managed can help you fully realize even the most minute details of your world, its people, and their daily lives, and ultimately put your reader wholly in the action.

Final Thoughts

Understand that these questions and the examples I have given are suggestive and not prescriptive. You won't have to use all of these framing questions that we have discussed (and perhaps you shouldn't), but any one of them can easily help you flesh out your story and give your work an immersive quality that will make it unforgettable. If you have the time, I recommend going back through your favorite stories and trying to analyze them in this way. You certainly won't have answers to every question, but you will see how they could be answered in a way that makes sense to that world and hopefully yours.

DESIGNING REALISTIC MAGIC ACADEMIES

ᕧᕤ

BY HANNAH EMERY

When I reread J. K. Rowling's Harry Potter books these days, I have different questions than I did the first time around. Questions like: Who are the great legendary heroes of British wizarding society that every kid learns about? What options does a talented student like Hermione Granger have for postsecondary education? Who taught Ron Weasley how to read?

Anyone who's read or watched the Harry Potter saga knows quite a bit about Hogwarts. But even after reading all seven books, I'm still pretty confused about the education of twentieth-century British wizards. And if you're planning to create a school of magic for your fantasy world, there are some things you should think about to keep your readers from having this same confusion. Most important, you need to figure out the function of your school within its society. Another way of thinking about this is to ask yourself this question: Who is your school's target audience?

At first glance, schools of magic would seem to be pretty common in fantasy fiction. Besides Rowling's Hogwarts, there's the Scholomance in Naomi Novik's series of the same name, the University in Patrick Rothfuss's Kingkiller Chronicles, and loads of others. However, most institutions of magical learning seem to operate on the *trade school* model: Students are a slice of the general population, of various ages and backgrounds, who've come in search of highly specialized knowledge or training. Hogwarts, on the other hand, is presented as a *general education program*: All British witches and wizards between the ages of eleven and seventeen are expected to pass through its doors. Like general schools in most parts of the world, it divides its students primarily by age, and students have relatively little choice in which courses they take for most of their academic careers. Hogwarts students aren't there to get a cosmetology certificate or a law degree: They're just trying to graduate from high school.

If you're thinking of creating a school on the Hogwarts model, the first thing you need to consider is the prevalence of formal education in your larger society. Although human societies have always had to train their children in how to be productive adults, and formal instruction for some elite portion of the population (on topics including literacy, mathematics, philosophy, theology, and science) has existed in almost every society throughout history, widespread education of "the masses" is a relatively new concept. Laws requiring formal schooling for all children regardless of their background first appeared in parts of Protestant Europe in the seventeenth and eighteenth centuries; compulsory schooling didn't become the general law in the United States until 1918 (though many states mandated it decades earlier).

But let's set aside the question of prevalence; let's say your story is set in a version of our modern real world, like Rowling's is. That means that some sort of formal education for children is almost certainly mandatory in your society, at least through the mid-teenage years. So you know you've got a school system designed to serve the general population. Your next task is to think a bit about the people who designed the system, and figure out their most important goals. Because a quick look at the history of the modern Western educational system shows that the people putting together public schools have had different goals at different times, and these goals have affected our complicated modern system.

Scholars of education pretty much agree that in the twenty-first century, the general Western education system has had a few main purposes:

- Instilling practical life skills. Although there are a lot of debates these days about what schools ought to be teaching students—how human sexuality should be discussed in school (or if it should be discussed at all), whether programming courses should be mandatory, whether teachers should make sure every high school graduate can manage their finances and change the oil in their car—there are a few skills the modern world takes for granted. If you're an adult living in an industrialized country, it's expected that you can read, write, and do basic math. That's one reason standardized tests focus on these skills: Someone who's illiterate or innumerate will have a really hard time in the modern world.

- Developing loyal citizens. The first public schools in Protestant Europe came about because religious leader Martin Luther thought it was important for all citizens to be able to read the Bible. In the United States, widespread public schooling became popular during the massive immigration of the nineteenth century, and one of its main goals was to teach immigrant children how to be Americans. The Pledge of Allegiance was developed with this goal in mind; ditto the story many American children still learn about President George Washington chopping down a cherry tree as a boy. Although many modern schools in the US and elsewhere try to take a more multicultural approach to their curricula, it's still expected that schools will teach children about their country: geography, civics, and, perhaps most important, history. What's included in that history is a matter for constant debate in countries all over the world. Public schools put together a country's entire next generation in a room to learn about the world. It's unavoidable that part of that learning will involve establishing some basic norms about what it means to be American/Australian/Japanese/a British wizard.

- Establishing cultural literacy. If you grew up in the United States, there are certain books you probably read in high school: *The Grapes of Wrath*, *The Catcher in the Rye*, *To Kill a Mockingbird*. If you grew up in the English-speaking world, you probably have at least a passing acquaintance with *Romeo and Juliet* and *Hamlet*. The markers of what constitutes "an educated person" are different from one place to another, but education almost always includes more than facts and figures. And depending on which rank of society you're planning to move in once you've finished your education, the type of "culture" you're expected to be familiar with could go beyond literature. You might be expected to speak a foreign language fluently, or to recognize classical music or fine art, or to know which fork to use at a fancy dinner party. Which brings me to the final role of formal education . . .

- Gatekeeping and credentialism. As I mentioned earlier, in much of the world throughout much of history, formal education was the domain of an elite few. As education expanded to the masses, that wealthy few began creating additional prestige markers to set themselves apart. For a while, it was only the elite who attended high school; then it was only the elite who pursued bachelor's degrees; now—well, you get the idea. This phenomenon, called "credentialism," is one thing sociologists point to as a cause of "degree inflation" (where bachelor's degrees are increasingly not considered sufficient education for a professional job). The harder it is to get credentials for a job—credentials that imply specialized cultural knowledge as much as practical knowledge—the longer that job will stay in the hands of the elite.

With these goals in front of us, we can see that Hogwarts has an odd curriculum for a modern comprehensive school. As far as we can tell from the books, it focuses very heavily on the acquisition of practical skills; like Novik's Scholomance and Rothfuss's University, it feels much more like a trade school than a place for general education. I'm not suggesting that Rowling should've given us long accounts of Harry and his chums doing algebra and reading Dickens (or, you know, nineteenth-century wizarding-world novels with titles like *The Goblin Lord of London*). But she could have given us a little more cultural backdrop than the one almost universally disliked History of Magic course that appears briefly in *Order of the Phoenix*.

If your school of magic is a specialized place where people go to learn the wizarding arts, then you can feel free to make the classes as content-focused as you want. But if you're designing a place for general education, you'll want to include at least a little of the other stuff. What cultural touchstones are young people in your magical society expected to be familiar with by graduation? What does "an educated person" look like? Who teaches students the basic intellectual survival skills? (These could be reading and fundamental math; they could also be something completely different.) And how do the elites in your society (because every society has people who'd rather not mingle with "the masses") set themselves apart? Are there private magic academies that teach spells in ancient languages known only to the wealthy? Does your school have the equivalent of AP courses, or a PTA pushing the school to offer Mandarin to give their kindergarteners a jump-start on the road to Harvard?

You don't have to put it all in; you probably shouldn't. Like all world-building, a little in the text goes a long way. But thinking about these aspects of education will help you build a better magic school, and with it, a better world.

PROPHETS, PREACHERS, AND PRIESTS IN FANTASY

⌇

BY JAY S. WILLIS

"Always look on the bright side of life. . . . "

Hearing that phrase followed by whistling conjures for me poor Brian during the crucifixion scene from *Monty Python's Life of Brian*. Brian's wordless look of bewilderment and impotent anger sums up his entire story. The poor guy gets dragged around the entire movie and unwittingly becomes the prophet and savior figure instead of Jesus of Nazareth. Blasphemous to many, I'm sure, but the absurdity of *Life of Brian* is a strong lesson not only about the unbridled power of religion and faith but, more specifically, from a writer's perspective, the importance of the choices you make for characters' actions.

Fiction, especially science fiction and fantasy, is filled with various belief systems, and the priests, penitents, and petitioners following said religions form strong foundations for good world-building and typically drive the story. Imagine Star Wars without the Force and the Jedi, Dune without the Bene Gesserit, The Wheel of Time without the Children of the Light or the Aes Sedai. All of those religious institutions are important, but what is truly vital in driving them and the stories about them are the characters' actions and reactions to them.

In the real world, the same holds true, and examining events and the people who instigated or impacted these events can be instructive. There's no doubt that the Reformation and growth of the Protestant movement was historically significant. However, let's not lose sight of the fact that people shaped and drove that story. Would the Reformation have happened without Martin Luther? Probably. But did Luther's actions and reactions impact the final outcome? Most definitely.

The Catholic Church was the center of life during the Middle Ages. Control over the religious and political aspects of society were vested in the Church. However, crises such as the Babylonian Captivity (1309–77) and the Great Schism (1378–1417) had strained the loyalty of the faithful and devastated the unity of the Church for more than a century. A number of problems, such as the search for new sources of income and forms of corruption, plagued the Renaissance papacy. These factors came into play as root causes of the Protestant Reformation.

Luther's theology, which went against the very foundations of the Catholic Church, and his ideas on institutional changes needed within the Church greatly impacted the religious and political sectors of society. In no way did Luther purposefully try to bring about the Reformation or try to break away from the Church. He wanted to change the Church from within, doing away with the corruption that was taking place and stopping the teaching of false doctrine, returning to the true doctrine of the New Testament. Luther was the most important figure in starting the Reformation. However, there could have and most likely would have been a Reformation without him.

The ideology developed by Luther came from his own personal quest for assurance of salvation and his questioning of his righteousness in the eyes of God. The two basic doctrines developed by Luther were justification by faith and the priesthood of all believers. Luther's first doctrine was based on Saint Paul's Epistle to the Romans (1:17). He concluded that one could be saved by the grace of God alone through faith in Christ.

Justification by faith taught that good works and indulgences had nothing to do with one's salvation. This new ideology destroyed the basis of the Church's system of grace given by the Church and questioned the foundation of Christian belief at the time.

Luther's second doctrine was the idea that everyone is a part of a priesthood of believers. In his address to the Christian Nobility of the German Nation (1520), Luther stated: "It follows then, that between layman and priests, princes and bishops, or as they call it, between spiritual and temporal persons, the only real differences are one of offices and function and not of estate. . . . "

This doctrine touted that priests and Church officials, including the pope, had no special powers and weren't totally infallible.

Luther's teachings and actions had various social and political implications as well. Socially, he advocated the allowance of clergy to marry, which was against the Church's teachings. Politically, Luther realized his need for support from the German nobles and upper class. He clearly sympathized with the Peasants' Revolt (1520), but he had to support the nobles due to his need for protection.

Luther felt strongly about stopping the corruption in the Church, especially the sale of indulgences. Luther spoke out about his beliefs that the Church should abandon false doctrine and realize that scripture, not Church officials, should be the source of authority for Christians. He challenged the Church over the indulgences issue with his Ninety-Five Theses, which were presented as a theological debate, but the Church's response and public uproar resulted in the beginnings of the Protestant Reformation. What transformed Luther from a quiet educator seeking reform into a towering figure of world history was the dramatic image of Luther nailing his Ninety-Five Theses on the doors of a church; that iconic historical moment has power and remains memorable.

Luther was the immediate cause of the Protestant Reformation in that he filled the leadership role required for it to take place. However, the Reformation could have happened without Luther. A number of other theologians and humanists, such as Ulrich Zwingli and John Calvin, were contemporary forces for religious change as well. Luther's ideology and actions, which gave the Reformation its personality, came along at a time when conditions were prime for a change in the Church and all religious aspects of society. If Luther had not been around, someone else with a different theology would have come along, instituting changes, and modern religion would probably look much different today.

In developing fictional religious systems, good writers avoid allowing their characters to be swept along like Monty Python's Brian with good reason. Our protagonists, our antagonists, and every character in between shape our stories with their actions or inactions, especially in terms of religion. The truly memorable characters are the ones who struggle and effect changes to their own lives, the world around them, and even the gods.

Locke Lamora was trained as a con artist by Father Chains, pretending to be a blind priest in *The Lies of Locke Lamora*. The Wheel of Time's Rand al'Thor fights against multiple prophecies and expectations from various factions to define himself as the true Dragon Reborn. We love and read all these stories because of the struggles these characters face, whether they fail or succeed. Likewise, you can write the most intricate, complex, and original religious system, but nobody will care or read about it if your characters don't have great reactions and interactions within those systems.

MONEY MAKES THE WORLD GO 'ROUND

BY A. R. LUCAS

My goal when I set out to write this chapter was to make it as difficult as possible to categorize. This is untrue, but the concept of value, on both a micro and macro level, is so fundamental to us that we often overlook it when we build our science fiction and fantasy worlds. I have read countless fantasy novels where there are whole chapters devoted to complex mythologies and magic systems, or science fiction novels where there are pages upon pages about wildly imagined technologies, but both use a similar variation of a monetary system we would recognize today. It may be a form of precious metal currency in fantasy or some greater abstraction of our current credit system in science fiction, but often, money and economic systems aren't given a lot of thought by writers.

The Purchase of Manhattan: How We Value What We Value and How Different Value Systems Collide

There is an urban legend that the island of Manhattan was purchased for beads by an officer of the Dutch West India Company in 1626.

Research supports that this isn't true, but let's look at this supposed transaction more closely.

Why the Dutch?

Feel free to insert "English" or "Portuguese" here as well. It is not a coincidence that many great naval powers are smaller countries with comparatively few natural resources. Wealth (i.e., control of resources) is a fundamental component of power. If there's a war in your story, it's about control of resources at some level, and the better you understand this, the more believable your conflict will be.

In your fantasy or science fiction novel, what resources do your various groups have access to? How can they improve their resource portfolio? What social mechanisms enforce or detract from their claims to resources (war, legal systems, social and political alliances, etc.)? How are religious or cultural differences used to justify the acquisition of resources from another group? How do resources contribute to the balance of power in your society?

What's in a Deed?

The idea of landownership is one that most of us take as a given. However, systems of landownership and allocation vary widely throughout history. For many years, the common theory was that the Native Americans didn't believe in landownership; however, there is evidence to the contrary. They did have concepts of landownership and responsibility, but they differed from the European systems. Thus, the tribe who apocryphally sold Manhattan may have had a fundamentally different view of what they were giving up than the Dutch did. Also, the deed was said to have been signed by the Canarsee, a Lenape tribe, who didn't control a portion of the territory they signed away.

In your book, how does the social system support resource claims? Do you have groups with very different legal or social structures regarding resource ownership, and how might they clash? How are the rules of economic transactions governed by laws and social mores, and how well does each party understand the views of the other? For instance, throughout much of history, usury, or the lending of money at interest, was considered a sin, most notably in the Christian and Islamic worlds. Views on moneylending after the fall of the Roman Empire did much to shape the course of European history.

Utility

When the Dutch supposedly purchased Staten Island less than five years later, the deed records that the rights to the land were traded for a variety of equipment, including kettles, axes, hoes, Jew's harps, and, most important, drilling awls, which were used to make wampum, the local shell bead currency. For the local tribe, European metallurgy was a superior resource, and thus held a great deal of value to them, regardless of the actual cost of production from a European perspective. Plus, the tribe also had a different view of landownership, as described earlier.

On paper, from a Western point of view, the transaction looks wildly imbalanced, but it occurred because of the vast difference in the way each party viewed the same transaction. Of course, the Europeans' metallurgical advantage also provided them with superior weaponry, which may have also influenced the transaction.

How do concepts of utility, law, and social mores and differing perceptions of value at a societal level shape the interactions between groups in your novel? What happens when groups have similar views? What happens when they have different views?

Macroeconomics

Macroeconomics deals with the structure and interaction of larger-scale economies at the national, regional, or global level. Trade, currency systems, the interaction of currencies (exchange rates), technological advances, unemployment, and policy are all macroeconomic concepts.

Monetary policy is how your society controls money.

How centralized are your cultures' banking systems? What do your cultures use for money? How abstract is the currency? By this I mean, is it gold or is it paper? Is it paper backed by gold? Is it seventh-generation bitcoin on steroids?

In *The Philosophy of Money*, Georg Simmel discusses the psychological effects of living in a society where life is increasingly measured in money, and where money itself has become ever more abstract. He posits that money psychologically divorced man from life, making us hyperrational and less human. The recent Netflix film *Worth*—about the 9/11 victim compensation fund—explores this concept. How does value in the monetary sense shape value in the philosophical sense? What do your characters believe constitutes a good life, and how do they value life? What social, religious, and philosophical concepts influence this?

Fiscal policy is how the government influences the economy through instruments like taxes, expenditures, and debt. When governments break down, such as after the fall of the Roman Empire, fiscal and monetary systems break down as well, and the more unique to your culture or abstract your currency, the bigger the effect this will have on society. If your book has an empire that is collapsing, and its currency is gold and all its neighbors' currencies are also gold, then the fall of the empire will have less effect than if the modern US government were to fall, and with it, the US fiscal and monetary systems (think banks, credit, and markets). But as a rule of thumb, if your government is weak or collapsing, expect this to show up in day-to-day transactions somehow, at minimum as a wariness of the local currency and likely as an increase in barter transactions. A currency with no intrinsic utility (like paper money) is completely dependent on a functioning society to provide its value.

Mesoeconomics

The term "mesoeconomics" is not as well known as its macro- and micro- counterparts, but is sometimes used to describe those economic concepts that are between macro- and microeconomics. Two areas that are commonly thought of as existing in the realm of mesoeconomics are game theory and information theory. For our purposes, I would like to use it to describe societal interactions within a nation or culture.

In your work, how does society organize itself with respect to values? Is there a division of labor? If so, how does the society ensure that general needs are met? What are the social constructs that either lift your society up or tear it apart? How do people negotiate with others to get through daily life? How do transactions form bonds within your culture (e.g., a gift economy)?

For example, Robert Wright, in his book *Nonzero: The Logic of Human Destiny*, makes the argument that social progress is the effect of societal non-zero-sum games (a zero-sum game is a game where if one party wins an amount, the other party loses that same amount). Non-zero-sum games are not strictly competitive, and thus have elements of cooperation that can benefit both parties in certain situations and "make the pie bigger." Wright describes technological change as a key non-zero-sum event.

If technology makes the pie bigger, how is the pie shared? And what effects does this have on your society and between societies?

Microeconomics

Microeconomics is the study of how we as individuals allocate our scarce resources (time, energy, money, etc.) to create value. To understand our characters' microeconomic situations, we need to know what they value and what resources they have at their disposal to obtain what they value. Disconnects of resources and values can make for rich internal and external conflicts.

Enter my friend Maslow's pyramid.

Maslow's hierarchy of needs states that humans will strive to meet these needs starting at the bottom and moving up, and will allocate their resources accordingly (e.g., if you are dying of thirst or starving, you will not be allocating your resources toward gaining respect from others).

Where are your characters on Maslow's pyramid? Are they searching for self-actualization, striving to be the best they can be? Or are they struggling to survive? What happens when life forces a character who was once concerned with self-actualization to beg for food? Or steal? How would a character who is searching for belonging react differently to the same situation from a character who is searching for esteem? How can a mismatch in resources and values cause difficulty for your characters?

Values and value systems at a personal and societal level are fundamental to the human experience. A little thought about resources and resource allocation can add depth to your characters and nuance to your world-building.

POLITICAL PHILOSOPHIES FOR FICTIONAL WORLDS

~

BY KATE HEARTFIELD

The decisions we make as writers of speculative fiction depend a great deal on how we see our own world.

If we create a fantasy world, an alien planet, or a future Earth, do we want to use the modern concept of states as articulated by the philosopher Max Weber (a monopoly of the legitimate use of force within a given territory)? Or do we want some other model for how people govern themselves?

If we're writing about a period of anarchy, or the rise of tyranny, what can we predict about how people would react? What assumptions have we built into our utopias and dystopias? Why do villains succeed or fail? Does history happen in cycles? What long-term effects does colonization have?

Here's an introduction to some of the political philosophers I use as touchstones in my own work: Thomas Hobbes and John Locke, John Rawls and Robert Nozick, Steve Biko and Frantz Fanon, and Hannah Arendt.

A few caveats: I don't necessarily agree with all the work I'll discuss below. I just find these particular writers to be useful starting points or representatives of a particular worldview. And it's certainly not intended to represent the whole field of political philosophy. For one thing, my own education was heavily skewed toward (patriarchal, white) Western philosophy. But I hope it's a useful demonstration of how these ideas can inform speculative fiction. At the end, I'll briefly list a few more names that might be useful to writers working on particular topics.

Thomas Hobbes and John Locke

I had to start with Hobbes because, let's face it: He wrote a book with the very fantastical title of *Leviathan* and with a very fantastical illustration for the frontispiece. Hobbes was an Englishman who lived from 1588 to 1679, so the backdrop to his work is the English Civil War.

He is best known for his theory about the condition of humanity in a "state of nature." In the absence of government, he wrote, a human life is "solitary, poor, nasty, brutish, and short."

To avoid that, according to Hobbes, human beings surrender their rights to the sovereign in a "social contract." The sovereign's power derives from the people, but the sovereign's will is incontestable. Civil society is a massive beast united under one will: the Leviathan.

John Locke also wrote about social contracts, but he had a much rosier idea of how humans would act without an authority to tell them what to do. He wrote that the state exists to protect inherent rights, not take them. His observation that "princes" exist in a state of nature is a precursor of the notion that international relations are fundamentally "anarchic"; that is, states do whatever they can get away with—but often they act well toward their neighbors, because it's in their interest to do so.

So if you set down to write, say, a *Game of Thrones*–style fantasy, you've got to decide (even if subconsciously) how you understand the social contract—and perhaps more important, how the rulers in your world understand it.

John Rawls and Robert Nozick

I'm going to depart from dueling white men in a moment, but before I do, here's another fundamental disagreement about the nature of society that I find really useful as a writer. This one comes from two American philosophers of the twentieth century.

What is the best society?

John Rawls began his answer with a thought experiment: the "original position." Imagine you are behind a "veil of ignorance" that prevents you from knowing what your gender is, or your aptitudes or abilities, or your cultural background, your sexuality, your religion . . . In this situation, Rawls says, it would be irrational for anyone to propose, for example, race-based slavery, because no one would know whether they would end up enslaved. It's in every individual's interest to ensure freedom. Rawls argued that it would also be in every individual's interest to ensure a certain level of equality, since one can't know whether one would be born into a poor family or a rich one.

Robert Nozick argued against the idea that justice requires the redress of inequality. He began with the axiom that individuals have rights, including a right to use their property as they see fit. One of his famous thought experiments goes roughly like this: If hundreds of thousands of free people want to pay small amounts of their money to see an athlete play, and the athlete becomes wealthy as a result, it is not just to take the money away from the athlete and give it back to the people who paid it with full consent in the first place.

Another of Nozick's thought experiments will be familiar to any reader of science fiction: the "experience machine." If you could choose to plug into a fail-proof machine that would perfectly replicate all of your dreams—a happy romance, say, or a million-dollar book deal, or the birth of a child—would you do that rather than live your life? Nozick thought people would not choose the machine, because being and doing are central to the human experience, beyond mere comfort and pleasure.

Speculative fiction writers are, after all, engaged in creating thought experiments of their own. What happens when someone wants to leave the perfect society? Are "freedom" and "equality" two words for the same thing, or are they fundamentally opposed? What is a just government?

Steve Biko and Frantz Fanon

Steve Biko is best known as an activist murdered by the South African government in 1977. He was a brilliant writer and political thinker; his essays and articles are collected in the book *I Write What I Like*.

His observation that "the most powerful tool in the hands of the oppressor is the mind of the oppressed" should inform every book that portrays oppressive societies (including our own). As a proponent of the Black Consciousness movement, he argued against the sort of blithe assurance of post-racialism that many white liberals espoused, the superficial integration in which white power structures remain intact. "I am against the intellectual arrogance of white people that makes them believe that white leadership is a sine qua non in this country and that whites are the divinely appointed pace-setters in progress. I am against the notion that a settler minority should impose an entire system of values on an indigenous people."

Biko wrote those words in an article titled "Black Souls in White Skins?" It's an echo of the title of the Frantz Fanon book *Black Skins, White Masks*. Fanon was born in Martinique and went to France to fight with the Free French Forces in 1943. He eventually moved to

POLITICAL PHILOSOPHIES FOR FICTIONAL WORLDS

Algeria and supported the independence movement there (and wrote
in defense of violence in liberation movements). He wrote about the
psychological oppression and the obliteration of culture that are part
and parcel of colonization, and ended his book *The Wretched of the Earth*
with this call: "Let us reconsider the question of mankind. Let us reconsider the question of cerebral reality and of the cerebral mass of all
humanity, whose connexions must be increased, whose channels must
be diversified and whose messages must be re-humanized."

Any speculative fiction writer who is tackling themes of oppression, subjugation, genocide, and colonization needs to consider the
psychological and cultural effects, both in a set of characters and in
the author's mind.

Hannah Arendt

We writers spend a lot of time dreaming up our larger-than-life,
mustache-twirling villains. I love writing those characters. They're
fun. Often, the misunderstood and crotchety are not as evil as they
seem: Think of Elphaba in Gregory Maguire's novel *Wicked*, for example, or Maleficent in the film of the same name.

But when Hannah Arendt found herself facing a real-life villain,
she saw something both more evil and more ordinary than any invented
antagonist: "Justice insists on the importance of Adolf Eichmann, the
man in the glass booth built for his protection: medium-sized, slender,
middle-aged, with receding hair, ill-fitting teeth, and nearsighted eyes,
who throughout the trial keeps craning his scraggy neck toward the
bench (not once does he turn to face the audience), and who desper-
ately tries to maintain his self-control—and mostly succeeds, despite a
nervous tic, to which his mouth must have become subject long before
this trial started." Her report for the *New Yorker* on the trial of Adolf
Eichmann, one of the main architects of the Holocaust, became the
book *Eichmann in Jerusalem: A Report on the Banality of Evil.*

That evil is banal does not make it any less terrifying; quite the opposite. It's comforting to think that evil must be committed only by comic-book masterminds. "For all this," wrote Arendt of the task facing those in the courtroom, "it was essential that one take him seriously, and this was very hard to do, unless one sought the easiest way out of the dilemma between the unspeakable horror of the deeds and the undeniable ludicrousness of the man who perpetrated them, and declared him a clever, calculating liar—which he obviously was not."

Many novels tackle the nature of evil, and many novels fail. It's difficult for any writer to capture how evil can sit in the most pitifully human breast without making the grave error of seeming to sympathize with it. I turn to Umberto Eco's essay "Ur-Fascism" over and over again, in which he wrote, "I can even admit that Eichmann sincerely believed in his mission, but I cannot say, 'OK, come back and do it again.'" For writers, I think the job isn't to humanize our villains but to portray how villainy can so easily infect humanity.

I could go on and on. But I'll just mention a few more of my personal touchstones and reference points: Mary Wollstonecraft and Virginia Woolf on the rights of women. Edward Said on orientalism. Francis Fukuyama on history and progress. Machiavelli and Sun Tzu on strategy and leadership. Michel Foucault on power and social control. Jeffrey Sachs and William Easterly on poverty and development. Alexis de Tocqueville on tyranny and democracy.

Happy reading!

LEGAL SYSTEMS IN FANTASY WORLDS

‿᷍⁀

BY J. R. H. LAWLESS

When you're busy slinging spells, pillaging dragon lairs, or fulfilling destinies, there isn't always time to stop and think about the legalities of the affair—and even less time to stop the action and write about them when crafting fantasy stories.

And yet, from the seats of lords and kings to the court of faerie, it seems that, even when laws are not a central element of the plot, they are baked deep into fantasy narratives. The need to design and incorporate convincing and compelling legal systems for fantasy worlds is even more important for creators and world-builders to take full advantage of the opportunities they present to create conflict and character development in service of a compelling story.

I've had the opportunity to speak on the subject at various conventions while promoting my novels, *Always Greener* and *The Rude Eye of Rebellion*. This chapter will sum up some of the key points from those presentations, to help readers and writers alike understand the importance of legal systems in fantasy, as well as how to create believable laws for your own worlds.

Just Because You Do Not Take an Interest in Law Doesn't Mean Law Won't Take an Interest in You

One of the first things they teach you in law school—at least, the ones I went to—is that law is everywhere. In one example that really stuck with me, even the relatively simple act of buying a loaf of bread from a shop is forming a contract between you and the vendor. As a consequence, no transaction in a character's world, even one as simple as buying bread, can take place without having a legal framework in place. And just as with everything else in world-building, the iceberg theory applies, serving as fantastically concise shorthand for a submerged mountain of exposition: We see a character buying bread, but how that transaction happens says a huge amount about the legal system behind the world, including property and business law, plus the fact that there is a power that defines those laws, as well as a power that enforces them and that could be called upon to execute the contract if either side does not live up to its obligations.

While this is true of any world-building, especially in speculative fiction, there are also major considerations that are more specific to fantasy. Faerie courts, for instance, often follow their own rigid legal system, and discovering the rules of that system, alongside the human characters, is often a large part of the joy of such stories (the Dresden Files come to mind). Magical pacts, be it through geasa or through the obligations that are a counterpart of the magic system itself, are also a rich source of fantasy-specific legalities. When you add demonic laws and pact terms, divine justice systems, or even mundane feudal hierarchies, from emperors and kings all the way down to local lordlings, it soon becomes apparent that legal systems are at the heart of any fantasy story that isn't limited to a *Robinson Crusoe*–style isolation.

And since these legal systems provide the necessary framework for all the characters' trials and tribulations throughout the story, then we as creators had best make sure we don't leave them up to assumption or chance by designing the best legal systems we can come up with to serve the narrative.

One Does Not Simply Walk into a Fantasy Legal System

There are two interlinked key notions that provide a solid first approach to conscious legal system world-building design.

First off, and perhaps surprisingly, it is distance, both physical and in terms of communications, that is one of the most defining elements in the structure of any legal system. Naturally, this will vary with every setting, but within the framework of classic fantasy technological levels, and barring magic systems that might include generalized teleportation or at least magical telecommunications, any attempt at designing a coherent legal system will usually lead to a decentralized organization, based on the limitations of the world's travel possibilities. These same constraints led to the formation of counties in medieval Europe, and other forms of decentralization in societies all around the world. For practical reasons, the court—both in the sense of the seat of law-making and law enforcement through judicial power—can't be more than a certain reasonable travel distance away, be it on foot or by animal mount.

One of the main reasons for that is, in fact, the second major point to keep in mind when designing your legal systems: effectivity. Laws mean nothing if they cannot be enforced. Once again, there are many fantasy-specific elements that can complicate having an effective legal system: in portal fantasy, for instance, one can easily end up with stories spanning multiple universes or planes. It can be incredibly difficult within such complicated world-building to maintain an effective legal system—but then again, the complications can also be a boon to powerful storytelling. The breakdown of effectivity, which is the source of many possible and compelling story plots, from Robin Hood to fantasy Westerns, is a tool that can be very useful for the fantasy storyteller, so long as it is a design choice and makes sense within the world-building.

For all these reasons, it is important to make conscious world-building choices up front, and design legal systems that are adapted to the geographical, technological, and magical constraints of your world. The last thing you want is to be stuck having to rework the entire foundation of law and how society works in your world after you've written an entire draft to make the story work the way it needs to, just because you neglected to take these factors into account early on. And perhaps most important, legal systems are one the best opportunities that we, as creators, have to avoid easy assumptions, break with the status quo, and create something different, compelling, and meaningful for our readers.

BUILDING CREDIBLE AND INTERESTING POLITICAL SYSTEMS

๑๛

BY CARRIE CALLAGHAN

When I was a kid, I hated when my parents talked about politics. Names floated above my head at the dinner table: meaningless people doing silly things. The conversation was abstract, and I wanted to talk about the real world.

What I couldn't see then was that politics, the search for power, is the web underlying our interactions in the real world. The human struggle for survival embroils us in interpersonal power dynamics in our search for resources. People live in groups; therefore interpersonal power aggregates, like streams flowing into rivers, until the power forms the political systems that guide our societies.

Every fantasy realm will have a political system, and every story takes place amid politics, regardless of whether those politics are distant or the driver of the plot. Relationships carry power dynamics, and even the most intimate of relationships expresses some sort of politics and represents some sort of placement in a political system.

My political science professor taught us that power was the ability to make others do as you please, but I think a better definition is the ability for *you* to do as you please. There is power in agency.

But unless your characters are all isolated monks (and even then), the political systems of your world will involve some coercion. You'll need to determine what allows your characters to coerce others or do as they please.

Where Does Power in Your World Come From?

Resources confer power, whether we're talking about rare diamonds that a crony elite can trade for rifles or the fervor of religious devotion that fuels a god's strength. In Ann Leckie's *The Raven Tower*, a massive god embodied in a huge rock gains strength from being rotated. The humans who do this rotation become his attendants; he is dependent upon them for magical strength, and so he cares for them by secretly adding additional nutrients to their poor food. It's a transaction that benefits both parties.

Whom Does Your Ruler Depend on to Stay in Power?

This brings us to a crucial political point. Every—yes, every—political leader has what political scientists call "key supporters." In democracies, those key supporters are the voters who make the winning difference, the (often small) voting coalitions without which a candidate cannot win. In autocracies, the key supporters might be certain members of the business elite, generals in the army, or priests who control the masses.

How do you know who is essential? Look where the leader dedicates resources. Think about who, if they withdrew their support, would cause the leader's government to collapse (or the leader to lose the next election). Leckie's stone god needs his attendants to protect him and generate his power; without them, he is vulnerable. Some supporters are more essential then others; the most essential will get the most resources. The less "essential" the supporters are, the less valuable the rewards need to be—to the point where perhaps the demagogue's supporters in the street (among whom no individual is essential) receive only emotional validation and promises of future wealth.

Leaders want to give us the impression that they alone rule, but, in truth, they rely on the collaboration of underlings. In royal courts, this means the king or queen is less powerful than appearances suggest. In Samantha Shannon's *The Priory of the Orange Tree*, Ead learns that Queen Sabran, revered leader of Inys, is subject to the machinations of her many dukes and duchesses. Sabran has legitimacy but little control of the levers of power. In Inys, the dukes and duchesses are Sabran's key supporters (some more essential than others), and her control over them is weak. Her grip slips even further when her one potential source of power, her ability to deliver a dragon-defeating heir, vanishes. Sabran has lost access to powerful resources, and thus loses some key supporters until she can figure out how to reestablish control.

What Binds the Key Supporters to the Ruler? How Does the System Reward That Support?

Power systems are almost always fractured, with power flowing from the key supporters up to the ruler (the general grants the king ability to direct the troops) and down from the ruler to key supporters (the ruler pays the general her salary from the royal coffers). In Robert Jackson Bennett's *City of Stairs*, Shara discovers a powerful secret: the magical Divinities are guided by their believers' wishes just as much as those believers are guided by the Divinities' injunctions. In your fantasy world, think about which supporters benefit from the political system and what benefits they want. If you have a broad base of supporters, like in a democracy, the benefits will probably also be broad. This is, by the way, why democracies tend to get better things from their governments, or at least services that benefit a broad set of people (public schools, national park systems), as compared to systems of government that benefit more narrow constituencies.

This is where we start to encounter what might look like ideology to some eyes. An ideology of, say, "feeding the poor" won't get an aspiring leader very far unless those poor people have the power to install that leader and keep them there—a tough challenge, since impoverished individuals, by definition, tend to lack power.

Instead, think of ideology as the way in which your characters find their most important supporters (do they look to a few rich merchants, or hundreds of armed peasants?), and benevolence as a tool in the character's political arsenal or a trait that a leader needs to counterbalance (because those free loaves of bread to the poor don't pay for themselves).

Or, as Silas Octakiseron in *Gideon the Ninth* says, "Since when was power goodness?"

If you want to write about a benevolent monarch who scoffs at the nobles and cares only for the downtrodden, consider how that regent will maintain power. What confers power in your world? Chances are, the aristocracy already have a lot of that power, whether in the form of money, weapons, or magic. What will prevent the elite from banding together to oust the monarch? Tradition probably won't be sufficient to protect the monarch, because it's not *actually* power. Tradition and lineage are stories about power, but not actual control. In the end, that monarch will probably have to devote some resources to placate the nobles—or spend some resources, military or otherwise, to quash them.

On the other hand, a leader—even a criminal boss like Tomas Piety in Peter McLean's *Priest of Bones*—can make good moral choices (like opposing violence against children and sexual assault), because those values, in the long run, help build a more stable coalition. People grant him their loyalty in response to his good governance, and he can trade on that loyalty for power.

Who Is the Opposition?

Politics make for a great spectator sport, because the dynamics are always in flux. One adviser moves up, another falls. The people who are not key supporters clamor to have their needs acknowledged. Inside the ranks of any political system, some people have power, while others want it. This creates opposition.

Who in your fantasy world represents the opposition? It could even be senior advisers, like Prime Minister Crupo and Chatelain Pira in *The Grace of Kings* by Ken Liu. They conspire to eliminate Emperor Mapidéré and change his heir because they fear their interests are at risk. The more power the individuals in the opposition have, the fewer of them are necessary to create political change and defend it.

How Do Privileged Groups Defend Their Power Against Nonprivileged Groups?

The powerful will protect their interests. Part of that protection will involve identifying groups who pose a potential threat. In N. K. Jemisin's Broken Earth series, society marginalizes the earth magic–wielding orogenes, better allowing Guardians and the Fulcrum to corral and control them. Orogene power threatens the establishment, so they are demonized. In other worlds, these lines can be drawn around gender, sexual orientation, race, class, or nearly any other categorization. Knowing whom the elite class marginalizes in your fantasy world will add a layer of complexity that will allow you to bridge the gap between your fiction and contemporary society.

Every fantasy world has sources of power, and no matter how informal those may be, they manifest in political structures. Thinking about the continual contest for controlling power will enrich your worldbuilding, making your unique realm echo with a truth that readers will recognize.

In summary, questions to consider include:

- Where does power in your world come from? What are its limits?
- Whom does your ruler depend on to stay in power? Who are the key supporters, and what binds them to the ruler?
- Who is the opposition?
- How do privileged groups defend their power against nonprivileged groups? What are the costs to the privileged groups of limiting access to power?

WORLD-BUILDING WITH FOOD AND DRINK

৵৹

BY CRYSTAL KING

We all have to eat, and there's a good chance that the characters you are writing about need to eat, too. It's such a fundamental part of who we are that it's easy to overlook the power that food can bring to your story. Your characters sitting down to a meal is one thing, but there are many other ways that the world of food can influence your characters and your plot.

Let's walk through how our own world is impacted by food. Consider this "food for thought" as you imagine the worlds you are building. How can these same things affect your characters and plots?

Food and Drink in Religion

Food is a central element to nearly every religion on this earth. Thousands of years ago, people sacrificed food to the gods, whether it was food made on the hearth or by animal sacrifice. Wine has been used as a libation for centuries. People also buried food with the dead so that the person could be fed in the afterlife. The ancient Romans even left their scraps on the floor so that the ghosts of the family's ancestors, or the household gods, would be nourished. Mosaics, frescoes, and paintings across the ages depict the gods having feasts, and we humans have always imagined what those feasts might be like. The ancient Greeks believed that the gods had a magical fruit, ambrosia, that gave them their power and strength.

Religions around the world have developed their own sacred rituals and rules involving food, by requiring or restricting food at certain times (no meat on Fridays if you are Catholic), by developing specific food taboos (no pork in the Jewish and Muslim cultures), or by specifying the ways in which you can eat some foods (e.g., the food must be blessed before eating).

Food becomes symbolic in many rituals as well. Consider transubstantiation in the Christian faith, the idea that the body and blood of Christ is transformed at consecration, with the physical bread and wine left as representation. That is what practitioners are taking in when they have Communion—they are, essentially, consuming Christ and taking him into them directly.

Religious food also turns into tradition in societies, for example: honey cake at Passover, hot cross buns at Easter, baklava having thirty-three layers to correspond with the years Christ was alive, ghee as the sacred food of the Devas, dates to break the fast at Ramadan, dumplings eaten at midnight to welcome in the Chinese New Year.

In what ways does food impact religion in your stories? Are there specific foods used in the rituals of your people? Are there foods that symbolize certain religious actions? Are there foods that have traditional meanings for your characters, that give them comfort or represent something deeply religious to them? Are there taboos or rules regarding food?

Food and Drink in Politics

Wikipedia defines "food politics" as "the political aspects of the production, control, regulation, inspection, distribution, and consumption of food." That's a mouthful, definitely, and it carries with it a deeply complex number of issues regarding how food entwines throughout our political systems.

You might be familiar with the term "bread and circuses." Roman emperors and politicians rose to power by appealing to the poorest citizens by introducing a grain ration. This ration, plus giving the people the gladiatorial games, helped those politicians receive the valuable votes needed for laws in the Senate.

As we progress through history, we see farmers paying taxes with chickens and pigs, serfs toiling on the land to earn their keep. Trade routes helped many countries grow rich from their valuable imports. Being able to obtain costly foodstuffs has been a priority of the nobility from the earliest times. And of course, once those trade routes are established, eventually the food may become a commodity.

Our food politics today are complicated. Many countries have programs that help feed the homeless and the poor, and many also run services to make sure the housebound elderly are fed as well. Most countries have strict regulations that govern the sale of alcohol, especially across state lines and into other countries. During wars, countries often ration food, and soldiers receive specific rations designed for convenience and travel. In the US, we have the FDA to regulate food safety, and our government provides subsidies to our farmers to keep them economically viable. And this is just the tip of the iceberg.

The Impact of Access to Food

Consider how food affects the governments and systems you are creating in your novels. You don't have to dive as deep as Suzanne Collins did in her Hunger Games novels, but giving your reader a sense of how the characters are affected by governmental systems can bring tension and, perhaps, empathy or affinity to your readers. Can all your characters afford the same types of food? What do the nobility eat? How do the poor get their food? What types of trade routes are in place? How does the government regulate and control food? Does this regulation come from a desire to manipulate the people, or to help them?

Food in Societal Relationships

How many times have you met up with a friend for coffee, a cocktail, or dinner? Nine times out of ten, our social connections with others involve food. We have business lunches, drinks with our girlfriends, summer picnics with our kids, and potluck dinners and cake to celebrate special occasions with our families.

There are also patterns and propriety that go along with these social food meetings. If a man asks his single female coworker out for a drink, that probably carries a different meaning than if he suggests a group of fellow employees meet at the corner bar after work. A gathering that has an invitation carries a different gravity than a meeting that is organized via text message. The type of food or style of restaurant might dictate certain behaviors such as what one might wear. These are subtle things, but understood within a culture.

Additionally, how the wealthy dine is quite different than how the poor dine. Everything hinges on what one can afford, ranging from the silverware and plates to the type of food that sits upon them, and even the manner in which one eats the food.

Using food and drink, you can build tension between your characters and devise simple ways to show the reader more about them and the world in which they live. How does food factor into the way that characters relate to one another? What memories of family and friends does food trigger for them? Are there specific relationship rituals such as dating, marriage, or death that involve food?

Conclusion

Food and drink play a central role in so much of our lives, and they should in your characters' lives, too. Food is love, politics, religion, history, memory, consolation, and conviviality. Food identifies who we are. We cannot exist without it, and our lives revolve around it, even when we don't think it does. Finding deeper ways to weave the impact of food into the stories you are telling will make them more realistic, credible, and, importantly, relatable.

PLANTS IN WORLD-BUILDING

◈

BY AMBER ROYER

I learned early that botany can be an important part of world-building. One of my favorite books as a kid was *The Green Book* by Jill Paton Walsh. In it, colonists land on an alien planet and plant crops they brought from home—only the alien soil infuses silicates into the Earth crops, rendering "glass grass" and the like. If the people can't overcome this botanical problem, the colony fails and they all die. Which makes for huge stakes, especially when you're reading it as a ten-year-old.

But plants have a huge impact on more sophisticated works as well. They can be used to cement a setting and make a statement about the story world, as with Jurassic Park, where the park designers' use of poisonous plants because they look cool is brought out in both the book (Michael Crichton) and the film, in order to highlight the carelessness with which the whole project had been put together.

Plants can be used as characters. In Sue Burke's *Semiosis*, her colonists land on a world where the plants turn out to be sentient, and finding a way to communicate with them becomes vital.

Plants also can be used to foreshadow and explain. When you read the first Pern books (by Anne McCaffrey), you'll notice this beverage made from the bark of a local tree that everyone treats like coffee, so after a while you wonder, "Why didn't the author just use coffee?" But when you realize in later books in the series that these people came from Earth and remember real coffee, the revelation doesn't come out of left field.

Deep World-Building in Fantasy

Deep world-building (as opposed to wide world-building) focuses in on one thing, and looks at different implications it has for your characters' world and lives. For example, the Force in Star Wars was used in different contexts and different ways: to move things, communicate telepathically, even fly through space.

This repetition of a concept allows a reader to feel like they are in on how the world works, and to applaud the characters for using that one thing in unique ways to solve problems (as opposed to giving them a different whiz-bang technology, weapon, or concept to get out of each situation). You could create an entire world-building system based on plants. Or even centered on one plant.

If you are building a fantasy or science fiction world, you can riff on some of the oddities of Earth's plants to create your world's more fantastical versions.

Case Study: Cacao

Let's break down the usual questions you ask when world-building and center them on real-world cacao to show how you could design a fantasy or sci-fi setting around a fantastical or alien plant.

Theobroma cacao is a tropical evergreen in the family Malvaceae. It also happens to be the tree that chocolate comes from. Other members of the family include okra, cotton, and durian. There are several other trees in the *Theobroma* genus that produce edible fruit/seeds, but none have gained the world's attention like cacao.

Plants and Geography

What does this story's setting look like?

If cacao is growing in your setting, your characters are inside Earth's "chocolate" belt, roughly twenty degrees north and south of the equator. They are in an area with relatively comfortable temperatures (cacao trees don't like to get colder than fifty degrees or warmer than ninety degrees Fahrenheit) and plentiful water: high humidity and frequent rainfall. The best elevation is under a thousand feet above sea level, which means you're not on the side of a mountain.

I am experimenting with growing cacao indoors, as office plants, and the office turned the heat off during a cold Texas long weekend. Months later, the youngest plants still have crinkled, brown leaves.

Plants in the Ecosystem

What flora and fauna flourish here? Are any dangerous?

While there are cultivated cacao plantations, which require careful shading of young trees, wild cacao trees are under-canopy plants, surrounded by taller rain forest trees and by other understory/forest floor plants, including ground plants such as ferns, orchids and bromeliads, and climbing vines. Characters in a story about cacao might be local farmers—but could also be chocolate sourcers from anywhere in the world.

Cacao trees will attract animals who want to eat the sweet pulp from the cacao pods. One animal especially connected to cacao? Bats. Fruit-eating bats help disperse the seeds, while insect-eating bats help protect the trees from pests. One study found that excluding bats from an area of cacao trees made the production yield fall by 22 percent. Some insects, though, are required for cacao's survival. Without several species of tiny flies known colloquially as chocolate midges, the cacao trees' flowers couldn't be pollinated.

Also expect: monkeys, birds, and squirrels. And anything that eats bats, monkeys, birds, and squirrels—and possibly unwary characters.

World Economics

What is the economic system like? Do people invest? Barter?

In pre-Columbian times, the Aztecs and Mayas used cacao beans as money. Charts listing the exchange rates were documented by the conquistadors. A 1545 list of commodity prices in Tlaxcala (exhibited online by the Columbia University Library) gives an idea of the purchasing value of cacao:

1 good turkey hen = 100 cacao beans

1 turkey egg = 3 cacao beans

1 fully ripe avocado = 1 cacao bean

1 large tomato = 1 cacao bean

Under Aztec rule, the need to turn over large amounts of cacao as tribute, and the pervasiveness of cacao as barter currency, led to the rise of counterfeiting, which became widespread enough that archaeologists have found examples of faked clay cacao beans still in existence. Beans were also counterfeited by carving avocado pits into bean shapes and waxing them to give the appropriate sheen.

Today, chocolate is seen as a reasonably priced luxury that serves as an interesting economic indicator. In the UK, Cadbury makes Freddos, small frog-shaped chocolate bars. The Freddo Index charts the percentage the price of a Freddo (and presumably other luxury items) has increased versus overall inflation rates. It has been consistently higher than expected (in 2016 it was 25p when inflation suggested it should be at 15p)—until 2018, when the price actually dropped.

At the other end of the production chain, farmers may easily lose 30 percent of their trees' yield per year to pests and diseases, while the global prices for cacao fluctuate daily, affecting how much they will earn for the remaining beans. As a result, many farmers join co-ops to leverage selling power, and some chocolate makers and chocolate sourcers visit farms to make deals directly. Some of these professionals are educating farmers in ways to create more desirable beans (focusing on how the beans are fermented and dried, including details as small as the type of wood that fermentation boxes are made from) to maximize their profits.

Trade and Conflict

What resources are plentiful here? What shortages might cause conflict?

Chocolate is grown in rural, tropical areas. Areas where solid eating chocolate can be processed efficiently are usually more temperate or have access to plentiful refrigeration and air-conditioning. This is why chocolate processed in industrial Monterrey, Mexico, is often grown in Chiapas and transported north. (One Monterrey-based chocolate maker I visited is partnering with Chiapas University to educate farmers within the country.) Many cacao farmers never taste the finished chocolate made from what they have grown, though locally the beans are often stone-ground to make beverages.

While some small makers import beans from all over the world, it is more likely for someone in the United States to import beans from South America than from Africa (though most of the world's chocolate is produced in Africa) because of shipping costs and logistics.

There is some worry that the world might run out of chocolate as demand outstrips production, or if predicted global warming significantly changes the growing region. But you can design something more cataclysmic for your fantasy plants. Just imagine the conflict created if Earth's axis changed and a massive ice storm rolled through the tropics, so that suddenly the bars of chocolate already in stores were the only ones left.

Personal and World History

What has happened in this place? How has history shaped your protagonist's life?

Chocolate houses in Europe were all the rage in the 1600s—and they may well have shaped history for several reasons.

They were places where people met for pointed social discussion. In 1675, Charles II tried to ban chocolate houses for, among other excesses, political plotting. (These were rowdy places. If you decide to write about one, look up White's, where the regulars once stopped people from assisting a man who had collapsed because that might affect the outcome of a bet they'd made as to whether he was dead.)

Chocolate houses fed into the notion of chocolate as a highly desirable luxury item. People went to the chocolate houses to be seen with other upwardly mobile social or political types. And that in turn fed into a growing craving for chocolate that took over Europe. (An Irishman brought chocolate to the United States in 1765, after learning his craft as a chocolatier in England. But the company was run by physician Dr. James Baker, which is where we get Baker's Chocolate.)

The history of early chocolate making is fascinating. For instance, Baker's Chocolate had nothing to do with baking. Rather, American physician Dr. James Baker became sole owner of one of the most successful early chocolate companies after his business partner disappeared during a sourcing trip to the West Indies in 1799. Then, as major companies emerged, epic rivalries ensued. (Look at a couple of books on the history of chocolate production to see how personalities, business tactics, and even belief systems clashed—and then think how something as seemingly frivolous as chocolate could drive major conflict in your story. World-building can be interesting, but it really comes to life when it starts affecting your characters' lives directly.)

Chocolate has also been present for important events throughout history. It was included in World War II rations for soldiers, and later even taken into space (where M&M's have been used in educational demonstrations of low gravity). In 2020, an intact tin of chocolate that Queen Victoria had commissioned to improve morale during the Boer War was found among the possessions of a woman who was a daughter of one of the soldiers—when she died at age one hundred. And you can find chocolate tins commemorating Prince Charles and Princess Diana's wedding on eBay. You can also find antique chocolate pot sets made by Nippon and Limoge.

Any of these artifacts could easily draw characters into a story about history. What kind of artifacts might surround your invented plant? How could your character discover them?

Roughly 70 percent of the world's chocolate is grown in Africa, but cacao isn't native to that continent. You know how some of the world's best coffee is grown in Costa Rica, Colombia, and Brazil? Nope. Not native. Chocolate, not coffee, is native to Central and South America. Many sources consider Mexico to be the birthplace of chocolate. So how did some of the most sought-after cacao beans in the world come to be produced in Madagascar? The American Revolutionary War in 1776, followed by the War of 1812, made the Atlantic Ocean a dangerous place for trading ships to cross. Christian missionaries showed up with cacao beans in West Africa, planning to take advantage of a hot, rainy climate similar to that in Central America—while skirting around the wars and social instability. There are records of chocolate in Africa as early as 1819. This led to a complicated, ugly period in chocolate's history, with the demand for cheaper products at odds with fair treatment of workers.

Honestly, there were a lot of ugly periods relating to chocolate (as you'll also see in Aztec culture described later in this chapter). Think how crop desirability conflicts could affect your speculative characters' interactions in unique ways.

Food and Food Preparation

What do people in your story eat? How is it prepared?

If you crack open a cacao pod, the sweet flesh tastes like pineapple or guava. But the seeds inside? Don't bite into them. They're nasty. And yet . . . that's the part that becomes chocolate. Cacao beans go through several steps to become palatable. First, the pods are cracked open, and the beans are allowed to ferment in the pulp. (I've done this in micro-batches on the counter, and the beans go through stages where they don't smell like anything you'd want to eat.)

Then they have to be roasted to bring out the flavors. There's a whole science behind flavor notes achieved at certain time and temperature combinations, but simply put: Lighter roasting preserves fruity and floral notes.

Chocolate makers are like winemakers—they want to put their own signature on the finished product, so what two makers do with the same beans can be dramatically different. Chocolate making is a very sensory experience. The fragrance of the beans changes as they roast. When you're roasting chocolate, you're waiting for the sound of the "first crack," which sounds more like firewood popping than popcorn. And then, afterward, you have to get the outer skin off the beans, which can be messy. (Chocolate makers who are just starting out—or people like me, making chocolate at home—often do this step with a hair dryer while tossing the beans in a bowl.) Then, if you want solid eating chocolate, it has to be ground down into something that comes close to a liquid, with particles under thirty microns, so that your tongue won't taste the grit of individual particles. That can take several days in a melangeur. Stone-ground chocolate has much larger particles, and you can grind it by hand with a metate.

Chocolate is classified by the amount of cacao solids in the finished product (dark chocolate has at least 65 percent, milk chocolate at least 10 percent plus 25 percent cacao butter, and white chocolate contains just cacao butter).

It takes about four hundred beans to make a pound of chocolate, which leaves a lot of waste. Traditionally, cacao pulp has been made into booze. It is also pressed into juice, which is now available in boxed form in the US. The exterior part of the pod is technically edible, but your character would have to be really hungry to want to go through all the work of processing it for the thin layer of squash-like flesh that's palatable. (I tried it—it's slippery and I nearly cut myself.)

Has the way that food's been prepared and eaten changed over time?

Chocolate was originally served as a spicy drink, which may have occasionally been sweetened with honey but was usually just bitter. As foodstuffs started making their way around the world and chocolate met new supplies of cane sugar in Europe, sugar was added to the beverage (along with milk, which was an innovation at the time), and then, much later, techniques were developed to make solid eating chocolate in the mid-1800s. This led to the invention of decadent chocolate cakes and desserts in the years surrounding 1900, including Italy's Torta Novecento, which was created by Canavese master pastry chef Ottavio Bertinotti to celebrate the turn of the twentieth century. The need for chefs to outdo each other and to develop recipes worthy of being named for famous people of the day led to the creation of classics that are still popular, such as torta tenerina, which was designed to honor Elena of Italy, the queen of Montenegro and the wife of the Italian king Victor Emmanuel III.

Customers demanded a consistent product, so beans were brought in from different sources around the globe to create something that would taste the same, batch after batch, year after year, and provide consistency for baking (this is still considered an asset in making desserts).

But, more recently, customer attitudes have changed, and chocolate is seen as more akin to wine, with regional flavor differences considered an asset, so that chocolate bars—and even baking recipes—are being designed around beans grown in a particular region, sometimes even a single farm or collective. The farmer's story has become part of the customer's story, and small-scale craft chocolate makers are gaining customers who are looking for a personal touch and a way to know how the product was produced and paid for. There are now awards for craft chocolate bars, in a number of categories from several different recognized organizations, as well as festivals where people can meet the makers, chocolatiers, and chefs. With so many things going digital, in 2020, I attended two virtual chocolate festivals, where makers sent samples in a box so you could taste at home while virtually touring their factories and interacting with growers on-screen. There are so many possibilities here for a speculative situation—from the inherent conflict in two ways of doing things (each of which makes valid economic sense), to the need of people to view or participate in processes (and potentially cause them to go wrong).

Technological Innovation

How can innovation be used creatively in the story?

The chocolate chip cookie was invented by accident. The baker in question thought the chopped chocolate in her cookie batter would melt uniformly into it. Nestlé bought the recipe from her—in exchange for a lifetime supply of chocolate. At the time, it probably seemed like a great deal, because who could have imagined how ubiquitous the chocolate chip cookie would become? (A setup like that would be great in a story, as the character slowly starts to realize she didn't make such an amazing deal after all.)

In 1828, Dutch chemist Coenraad Johannes van Houten created a hydraulic cocoa press, allowing enough cocoa butter to be removed from chocolate liquor (the ground chocolate mass) to create cocoa powder. In 1847, Quaker chocolate manufacturing company J. S. Fry & Sons recombined the cacao butter with cocoa powder and sugar, making the first solid "eating chocolate."

When your characters look at their fantastic plants, what similar potential do they see?

Spiritual Life

What do people value here?

Cacao pods are shaped somewhat like the human heart, and the Aztecs drew parallels between the heart and chocolate. Chocolate beverages were featured in rituals and were therefore set aside for priests, soldiers, and royalty. If you were a commoner or a prisoner of war and were served a fancy chocolate beverage, chances were that you were about to be sacrificed. (Think of the ominous foreshadowing you could set up with one character who knows the meaning of your fantastic world's special plant—and another character who has no idea what they've been given.)

Violence and Danger

What in this environment could be used as a weapon?

The exterior pods of cacao fruits are often used for mulch. But the mulch will still contain theobromine, which is the component in chocolate that dogs cannot handle and has resulted in poisoning. Symptoms of theobromine poisoning include tremors, seizures, and irregular heartbeat. The onset is usually marked by severe hyperactivity.

Technically, a human can suffer theobromine poisoning. But your bad guy would have to get your character to consume around twenty pounds of chocolate, unless said character's allergic to chocolate . . . or the theobromine was somehow extracted and concentrated. I've read several mystery stories involving poisoned chocolates, because the strong flavors mask other tastes. Rumor has it that chocolate hid the poison that killed Pope Clement XIV in 1774.

Weapons could more easily be hidden in the chocolate, either to help a character bust out of a situation or to threaten someone. The Nazis tried to assassinate Winston Churchill with an exploding bar of chocolate. The weapon was made of thin metal, coated in real chocolate, and if you broke off a piece, it would pull out a piece of canvas—and the bar would start ticking ominously.

Build on Your World's Foundations

Inspired yet? Now that you have some idea of how to use botany in world-building, think about how you can make your fantastic plant special. Cacao leaves can move up to ninety degrees to shade younger leaves or catch better sun. What don't Earth plants do that you think would be cool? Change color to hide? Uproot themselves to migrate with the seasons?

REFERENCES

Deborah Blum, "The Poisonous Chemistry of Chocolate," *Wired*, February 14, 2013, wired.com/2013/02/the-poisonous-nature -of-chocolate.

K. E. Carr, "Chocolate and Africa," Quatr.us Study Guides, June 21, 2017, quatr.us/african-history/chocolate-and africa-2.htm.

"Cacao Production Guide," Business Diary PH, June 9, 2020, businessdiary.com.ph/2191/cacao-production-guide.

"Fun Facts About Chocolate," National Confectioners Association, accessed January 11, 2022, candyusa.com/story-of-chocolate /fun-facts-about-chocolate.

Dan Lewis, "100 Delicious Facts About Chocolate," The Fact Site, last updated April 16, 2021, thefactsite.com/100-chocolate-facts.

Eoin McSweeney, "Royal Box of Chocolates from 1900 Discovered in War Helmet," last updated April 1, 2021, CNN Style, cnn.com /style/article/chocolate-boer-war-scli-intl/index.html.

Jess Righthand, "A Brief History of the Chocolate Pot," *Smithsonian Magazine*, February 13, 2015, smithsonianmag.com/smithsonian -institution/brief-history-chocolate-pot-180954241.

Peter F. Stevens, "It Happened in Dorchester: Dr. Baker and the Chocolate Factory," Dorchester History, accessed January 11, 2022, web.archive.org/web/20120406172003/http://www.dotnews.com /bakerchoc.html.

"10 Most Popular European Chocolate Cakes," last updated January 13, 2021, tasteatlas.com/most-popular-chocolate-cakes-in-europe.

Ker Than, "The Rich and Flavorful History of Chocolate in Space," *Smithsonian Magazine*, February 10, 2015, smithsonianmag.com /science-nature/rich-and-flavorful-history-chocolate-space-18095 4160.

Merlin Tuttle, "Bats and Chocolate Production," Merlin Tuttle's Bat Conservation, June 13, 2018, merlintuttle.org/2018/06/13 /bats-and-chocolate-production.

"When Money Grew on Trees," *Chocolate: Food of the Gods*, Cornell University Library Online Exhibitions, accessed January 11, 2022, exhibits.library.cornell.edu/chocolate-food-of-the-gods/feature /when-money-grew-on-trees.

ORGANIC WORLD-BUILDING THROUGH ECOLOGY

BY SARAH J. SOVER

Let's talk about porgs.

You know, those divisive winged creatures plaguing Luke Sky-walker's island refuge in *The Last Jedi*. Their features are familiar, if somewhat exaggerated—big eyes, rounded bodies, stubby wings—the features of a puffin. There's a reason for that. Puffins were so plentiful on Skellig Michael, the island setting that doubles as a wildlife pre-serve, that getting a shot without them dotting the horizon and rocky outcroppings was nearly impossible. So one of the concept designers came up with the brilliant solution of disguising the puffins as a species more suitable for the Star Wars universe—porgs. And it works! Be-cause the various settings of Star Wars are built upon realistic frame-works containing individualized ecosystems, an indigenous birdlike species that's as adapted to the rock island as an Ewok to the forests of Endor or a Jawa to the sands of Tatooine simply makes sense. Main-taining the reader's suspension of disbelief is integral to the success of a story, whether it be on the screen or on the page. Had that same designer imagined a creature that made no sense in the habitat, it would have stretched believability and exposed a crack in the world-building. One little crack can spread and shatter the illusion completely.

For writers, keeping the reader immersed is integral to our world-building. To do that, we need to consider every aspect of the worlds we create. Every species on earth is adapted to its environment, so it's important to consider those adaptations, even when writing about other worlds and universes. George R. R. Martin's direwolves, for instance, wouldn't last long roaming sunny Dorne, and placing them there may give the reader pause. But their thick fur, pack mentality, and sizable body mass are well suited to the cold northern climate where the reader would expect to encounter such creatures.

Another way to pull a reader away from a well-written story is to remove the plot and characters from their environment entirely, treating them as if they exist in a vacuum. Unless you're writing a story taking place in a laboratory where all variables are controlled or manufactured, the world is a messy place filled with nuisances and needs, smells and sounds, cockroaches and puffins. A plot that is untouched by its surroundings is too convenient and, frankly, boring to read. Ecosystems are complex and interconnected, but in order to provide an immersive reading experience, you need those messy ecological elements to be a part of your world-building. A long-running joke among fantasy writers is that everyone must be constipated, because nobody ever stops to answer the call of nature in high-fantasy novels. Basic body functions such as eating and breathing are sometimes overlooked in the name of plot progression, but if the reader isn't immersed in the world, the plot falls flat. That also applies to the ecosystems we inhabit. A journey through a forest is far more believable if there are mosquitoes biting necks, owls calling in the distance, and squirrels scurrying along branches—or at least creatures that fill those roles.

But ecology isn't limited to animal species. It also includes the natural resources that provide the foundations for life, and human societies are formed primarily around meeting those needs. Just like humanity doesn't exist in an environmental vacuum, societies don't simply exist as independent entities. They don't run on currency, but rather the resources that currency represents. Fictional societies must take into account the foundational needs of the inhabitants in order to provide for the masses. You may not want to diagram the agricultural and irrigation systems of your world, just like you probably don't want to note every time a character pees in the woods or chugs some blue milk, but neglecting to acknowledge fundamental needs or show how they shape society makes for abysmal world-building.

By viewing your characters as members of a society existing within an ecosystem, you'll begin to see how much their surroundings influence their actions, and your plot will feel more organic. Building a cohesive world requires a basic understanding of the characters' place in it. An apex predator behaves differently than a decomposer, and that doesn't change just because they're caught up in a major plot point. Ecology influences animal behavior like air influences breathing—you can't separate the surroundings from the actions without losing a driving factor.

So, how do we create believable worlds that come alive on the page? First answer a few questions:

1. What natural resources do your societies utilize, and how do they procure them?

2. What creatures belong in the ecosystems your societies inhabit, how are they adapted for their specific habitats, and how do they, in turn, utilize and procure natural resources?

3. How do your societies interact with the environment and creatures around them?

4. How is your plot affected by the environment and eco-systems?

5. What does your world look like without your characters in it?

The answers to these questions can help add depth and realism to your story in ways you may not expect. For examples, look to the master of world-building himself, J. R. R. Tolkien. From the eating habits of hobbits to the physical adaptations and social constructs of his many fantasy civilizations, Tolkien's Middle-earth is alive with or without rings, mirrors, or swords. I argue that ecology is more powerful than the One Ring.

With the ring, you can dominate, but with ecology, you can create. Besides, when your book scores that bank movie contract, it never hurts to have some adorable, big-eyed creatures lined up to pitch to merchandisers. As for me, Grogu and I have a date with a delicious roasted porg.

REFERENCES

For more on the hatching of the adorable nuisance creatures known as porgs, see the interview "Designing *Star Wars: The Last Jedi*, Part 1: How Porgs Were Hatched," Star Wars (website), December 15, 2017, starwars.com/news/designing-star-wars-the-last-jedi -part-1-how-porgs-were-hatched.

PART 4

∾

WEAPONS AND WARFARE: WHEN IN DOUBT, ADD THESE

REALISTIC KNIFE FIGHTING

༒

BY ERIC PRIMM

It did not last long. It is only in the movies that knife
fighters stab and miss and slash and miss and tussle
over several city blocks.
—James Jones, *From Here to Eternity*

Bladed combat is a commonplace of fantasy fiction, with most stories
focusing on swords, axes, and spears. However, knife fighting is rare in
stories, but in reality, knife attacks are a common form of violence.
They are used in robberies, muggings, gang fights, drunken brawls,
and self-defense.

Around the world, many martial arts claim to study knife fighting.
However, a quick look through any catalog of instructional videos
results in finding a lot of bad, bad advice. For example, without super-
powers, no one will ever kick a knife out of an attacker's hand; it just
won't happen. In modern America, no one will lunge and thrust like

they have to punch a dagger through plate armor. Real world knife attacks are short, brutal, and terrifying. Here are six realities of a knife attack.

First, there is no guaranteed knife defense. In knife attacks, the outcome always favors the blade. Skill and knowledge only increase a person's odds of surviving. A saying attributed to Filipino martial artist Edgar Sulite describes it best: "If I have more skill than my opponent, he dies. If my opponent is more skilled, I die. If we're of equal skill, we both die." Note the severity of the language. In knife fighting, win and lose are meaningless terms. The only outcomes that matter are survival or death.

Second, if running away isn't an immediate option, the fighters will get cut. With body positioning and movement, skilled fighters try to limit where the cut happens, but defending one part of the body exposes another. The higher the skill level of the people in the fight, the higher the chances of being cut.

When it comes to knife defense, without fail one person will claim, "All you need is a gun." This is one of self-defense's Dunning-Kruger equivalencies. The third reality is that, due to the body's built-in reaction times, there exists a range of distances where knife beats gun every time. Most people know of the flight-or-fight response, but no one considers the time between observation and reaction necessary to initiate fight or flight. Neither response is instantaneous. A smart fighter takes advantage of that gap.

Police and military training, by design, aim to minimize the gap between observation and action, but it will never disappear. Or, more simply, guns are not the get-out-of-a-knife-fight-free cards that people believe. Search YouTube for Tueller Drills as confirmation. These drills are commonly and incorrectly known as the twenty-one-foot rule because the gun fighter requires twenty-one feet of separation to draw and fire a gun without getting stabbed. Due to the biased nature of the test—participants know to be ready—it's debated that twenty-one feet is too short. However, all distances within twenty-one feet resulted in a stabbing of the gun fighter.

The fourth reality is that how the knife is gripped says nothing about the fighter's skills. Whether the blade protrudes above the thumb or below the pinky finger, there are advantages and disadvantages to both grips. Typically, when you close your fist around the handle, if the blade is above the thumb, it is called a hammer grip. If the blade is reversed so that it protrudes below the pinky, it is called an ice-pick grip.

The hammer grip is comparable to a fencing style of fighting. The blade moves like a swashbuckler's sword, fast and attacking from many angles, with the attacker needing to be close enough to strike but not so close as to lose maneuverability.

The icepick grip requires fighters to move in close like two wres-tlers clinching. Think of the icepick grip as a grappling hook that is used to dig into the body. When the blade has a single edge, the direc-tion of the edge matters in the icepick grip because an attacker can pull with the edge.

How a person grips the knife tells the victim nothing about that person's abilities, but it can indicate which tactics to use against the person, provided there's enough time and light to glimpse the grip. For self-defense purposes, a person must learn both grips to know a com-plete system of defense. Neither grip is superior to the other; in fact, the different attributes of a chosen grip can be negated by an opponent skilled in the other grip. As with all other fighting, the only attributes that matter are training, knowledge, fitness, and the mental capacity to do violence. How a knife is held often depends on how it is drawn or picked up.

In movies, the attackers wave their blades back and forth in front of their targets. This is a poor tactic when the goal is to assault some-one. If the victim can see the knife, it is meant to scare the target into compliance, i.e., a threat more than a promise. (To be clear, complying and not testing to see if the attacker will back up the threat with action is the best course of action.)

Fifth, knives are small and easy to hide, which is what makes them dangerous. Anyone could be carrying one or more blades at any time. If someone decides to use their blade, they will hide it until the actual attack. Why let the target see the knife and defend against it? Allowing the victim to see the knife also allows the victim time to draw their own weapon. As any tactician throughout history says, the surprise attack improves the odds of success. Thus, the knife should remain hidden until the very last moment.

Because of their compact nature, knives are close-range weapons. An attacker needs to be close to the target to do damage. Distance management becomes key to achieving an objective. The closer the attacker gets, the higher the chance of damage. With more space between opponents, the target has better chances to escape. While the attacker could throw the blade, once the weapon leaves the person's hand, it loses maneuverability and is easier to avoid.

Proximity is why hiding the blade becomes important; an attacker can approach a target without hinting at intentions. If distance is key, then it follows that jogging is the best thing a person can do for their own self-defense. For the victim, safety means putting as much space between themselves and their attacker as possible. Or, in simpler terms, being safe means running away. Jim Butcher in the Dresden Files makes a point about how much Harry runs and why, which is self-defense preparation done right.

Since knives are small, they are more agile than swords, axes, and blunt weapons. Knives slice and stab at high rates from many angles of attack. In all fighting, the defender must be successful 100 percent of the time, whereas the attacker needs to succeed only once. Because the knife moves faster, the increased rate of attack makes a breach of a person's defenses inevitable.

Any time the defender fails to stop the attack, they will be cut, which, with loss of blood, increased lubrication from the blood, and increased panic at being cut, means their ability to defend will degrade quickly. Knife attacks are often short and fierce because the knife moves so fast. In many attacks, the victim is stabbed before they even know they're in a fight. To see how brutal knife fighting can be, watch *The Hunted* with Tommy Lee Jones and Benicio del Toro. (For the sake of the story, the fight is drawn out to heighten the drama, but it remains an excellent display of the horrors of knife fighting.)

Finally, being stabbed is more critical than being slashed. Slash wounds from knives look horrific and result in ugly scars, but stab wounds cause more damage. Slashes, while bloody and large, tend to be superficial. Stab wounds, however, go deep into the body and might injure an internal organ. In terms of visual horror, stab wounds don't look like much, but in terms of survivability they are far scarier.

Due to the nature of a blade, slashing versus stabbing depends more on the movement than the fighting style, and often one can be reversed right into the other. Any slash can become a stab, and any stab can become a slash. With the speed and versatility of the blade, both will be present during knife attacks.

Knife fighting can be a technical art, and this chapter left out the detailed mechanics, but the points covered can help a writer think differently about knives. In urban settings, regardless of time period, knives and daggers represent hidden dangers that seed everyday environments with the potential for violence.

The clarifications made here are meant to open possibilities for the author, not be a definitive argument for realistic knife fighting. Instead, they present ways for the author to add danger into a scene. By their very nature of being a useful tool, knives have persisted through human history and will continue to persist well into the future. Whether in sword and sorcery, urban fantasy, or space opera, the knife exists. How it is used in the story is limited only by the author's imagination.

MEDIEVAL VERSUS MODERN ARCHERY

∾

BY DAN KOBOLDT

The bow and arrow is one of the oldest projectile weapons in history, dating back as far as 30,000 years BCE. It's been around forever—particularly for hunting—but the bow's use in warfare rose to prominence during the Middle Ages. I'm talking about the English longbow, also called the Welsh longbow. Its first recorded use in Britain was around 633 CE, when an arrow shot by a Welsh longbow killed Edwin, the son of the king of Northumberland.

Advantages of the Longbow

The crossbow was the main rival for the longbow in the Middle Ages, and popular because it required minimal training. Yet it could only deliver one to two bolts per minute and had an effective range of twenty to forty yards, whereas a longbow could deliver six arrows per minute at a range of three hundred to four hundred yards. Longbows were also relatively easy to make; modern bowyers can build a longbow in about ten to twenty hours.

Bows in Battle

In the Middle Ages, the longbow saw use in various civil wars for which the period was rather famous. It also played a key role in several battles of the Hundred Years' War. One of these was the Battle of Crécy, which took place in northern France on August 26, 1346. On one side were the exhausted French forces, whose crossbowmen had just endured a long march in the rain that damaged many of their weapons. On the other side were the English, who'd chosen the field of battle, rested, and kept their bowstrings dry. The French tried a crossbow volley, which had no effect.

How did the English respond? Froissart, the renowned French chronicler, tells it this way:

"Les archers anglois découvrent leurs arcs, qu'ils avoient tenus dans leur étui pendant la pluie."

Translation: "The English archers uncovered their bows, which they had kept in their cases during the rain." (Hey, I knew that French degree would come in handy someday.) And you don't need Froissart to know what happened next. Wet crossbows were no match for the Welsh longbow, which could shoot four hundred yards and deliver five to six arrows per minute. The French forces were soon routed and took thousands of casualties.

Longbows Versus Chain Mail and Plate Armor

An interesting question that comes up, both in scholarly history and in fantasy novels, is whether longbows could put an arrow through armor or chain mail. A bodkin arrow, whose tip has a stronger, narrower point (essentially a squared, spear-like shape), was probably developed for this purpose. Compared to the broadhead, which had a wider cutting radius, bodkins were more likely to punch through armored enemies.

Though it's a matter of debate among historians, many believe a bodkin would have difficulty penetrating solid armor, especially high-quality plate armor covered with a gambeson (a sort of cloth worn on the outside to protect against projectiles). Against nonmagical chain mail, however, a longbow with bodkin arrows was likely very deadly. Especially at close range (less than fifty yards), where archers could aim with some precision.

Very few longbows from antiquity survive. Unlike swords, armor, shields, and other weapons, bows wore out and were replaced instead of handed down from one generation to the next. Much of what we know about English longbows comes from the *Mary Rose*, a warship from the navy of King Henry VIII that sank in 1545.

When rediscovered in the 1970s, the wreck was like a Tudor-era time capsule. Among the countless historical artifacts were about 175 longbows and four thousand arrows, the analysis of which rewrote our understanding of English longbows in the Middle Ages. It's what I use for the comparison below.

Modern Archery

Firearms eventually replaced the bow and arrow in warfare, but archery remains popular today for sport and recreation. I know more about the bowhunting side, where bows, arrows, and related equipment are modern marvels. According to the US Fish and Wildlife Service, there are roughly three million bowhunters in the United States, and they spend $935 million each year on bows, arrows, and other archery equipment. Most hunters prefer the compound bow, for reasons I'll explain. How does their modern equipment compare to that of King Henry VIII's archers? Let's find out.

Longbow Versus Compound Bow

Here I'll compare some of the important features of longbows from the *Mary Rose* to a typical modern compound bow used for hunting.

FEATURE	ENGLISH LONGBOW	COMPOUND BOW
Length	72 inches	32 inches
Limb Material	Yew, ash, or elm wood	Metal alloys or carbon fiber
String Material	Hemp, flax, or silk	Polyester
Draw Weight	150 pounds	50–70 pounds
Range	350-400 yards	20–500 yards*

* The maximum range for hunting is generally fifty yards. Most deer are taken from forty yards or less.

One thing you'll notice is that the longbow was considerably larger (six feet) and had a much higher draw weight. The draw weight is essentially how much force is required to pull back the string. My own bow has a draw weight of sixty-two pounds, so each time I pull it back it's like lifting a sixty-two-pound weight with three fingers. At times, I've had trouble drawing it (especially in the cold). Drawing a 150-pound bow repeatedly, especially in battle, is hard for me to imagine. In fairness, bowhunters in most areas of North America don't really need more than a sixty-pound draw for any game they might encounter. An arrow is a cutting weapon, so accurate shot placement matters far more than arrow speed. Most deer are taken from twenty to forty yards, the optimal distance to make an aimed shot without being detected by the animal.

Flatbows and Recurve Bows

Other kinds of noncompound bows have evolved throughout history. The cross section of an English longbow would be a *D* shape: flat on the side that faced the archer, and rounded on the other side. A flatbow is a different design, with flat, relatively wide limbs that have a rectangular cross section. It's superior to the longbow because the flat surface spreads the stress more evenly. It generally takes longer to construct a flatbow than a longbow, but a wider variety of timbers—such as elm, maple, and hickory—can be used.

The recurve bow is yet another design, but one in which the tips of the bow curve away from the archer when strung. This also means that the string rests against the limb of the bow at the top and bottom. A recurve stores more energy and delivers it more efficiently than straight bows, which means that they can be shorter in size, but with the same punch. Horse bows, which had to be shorter so that they could be shot while on horseback, were often recurves for this reason.

Bow and Arrow Myths in Fiction

Because we're debunking common myths and mistakes in this book, I thought I'd touch on a few things I see—especially in the fantasy genre—that are not really accurate.

1. Myth: Learning to Shoot a Bow Is Easy

Longbows in particular were difficult to master. King Henry III made the following declaration in 1363 to encourage all Englishmen to practice with the bow.

"Whereas the people of our realm, rich and poor alike, were accustomed formerly in their games to practise archery—whence by God's help, it is well known that high honour and profit came to our realm, and no small advantage to ourselves in our warlike enterprises . . . that every man in the same country, if he be able-bodied, shall, upon holidays, make use, in his games, of bows and arrows . . . and so learn and practise archery."

2. Myth: Bows Shoot Arrows Flat

An arrow shot from a bow falls with gravity, and the less powerful the bow, the greater the effect. With a modern compound (sixty-pound draw), I'd estimate the arrow drops six to ten inches every ten yards.

With historical bows, this also meant that archers "aimed up" to account for the rainbow-shaped flight path. If you don't believe me, go watch a longbow or recurve shooter at an archery range sometime. It's scary.

3. Myth: Skinny Boys and Girls Can Shoot Longbows

Sorry, Katniss, but shooting a longbow that could kill a man at distance, or punch through armor, required considerable upper body strength. We're talking eighty to 120 pounds of force. I myself probably couldn't draw one. I certainly couldn't shoot it repeatedly. The skeletons of English longbowmen showed visible adaptations (enlarged left arms and bone spurs on the right fingers) from prolonged longbow use.

Smaller bows with lighter draw weights (especially recurves) are more realistic. Many compound bow manufacturers now make lighter models specifically for use in the growing female bowhunter demographic.

4. Myth: Ten Arrows a Minute Is Reasonable

Surviving documents and historical accounts of English longbowmen suggest they shot, at most, around six arrows per minute. It would be wasteful to do otherwise, and most archers were supplied with sixty to seventy arrows before a battle. Unless your character is an elf named Legolas, it's wise to put a cap on the rate and number of arrows they can shoot.

Compound Bow Advantages

The reason that compound bows are so popular is the draw curve: the strength required to pull back and hold an arrow. With a longbow, that draw curve is essentially linear: It takes more strength to hold a bow the farther you draw it back. That's why some of those Katniss-like moments are a little unrealistic. Longbows are hardest to hold when they're fully drawn, so there's not a lot of time for aiming and releasing. A strong man would have trouble holding a longbow at full draw for more than a second.

The compound bow's design offers a different draw curve: It's hard at first, but as the pulleys (the gear-shaped things at each tip) turn over, a compound requires less strength to draw. Holding an arrow at full draw is much easier. I'll routinely hold at full draw for five to ten seconds to take steady aim at the target.

Modern bows also have something called a peep sight: a small donut-shaped plastic ring located in the string (near where you nock the arrow). At full draw, you look through the hole at sighting pins on the bow itself. You set the pins at different heights for different ranges (twenty, thirty, and forty yards). Thus, the peep sight helps with both centering and distance.

Modern bows have other luxuries, too: stabilizers to make them easier to hold, shock absorbers to preserve the limbs, fancy arrow rests, and rubber "string silencers" to reduce the sound made at release. Most hunters now use carbon arrows, which are narrow and strong but provide the flex required to counter the archer's paradox. In other words, the arrow needs to bend out of the way of the bow to continue traveling the way it's pointed. Modern hunters can employ a variety of arrow tips, including field points, fixed-blade broadheads, mechanical broadheads, and even blunted arrowheads for small game.

Despite all the technological advances, the fundamentals of the bow and arrow haven't changed in thousands of years. Draw, aim, shoot. It's challenging to hunt with a bow instead of a rifle, but millions of us do anyway. I like the challenge. And when I carry my bow into the woods, it's like taking thousands of years of history with me.

WRITING REALISTIC SOLDIERS FOR FUN AND PROFIT

❧

BY MICHAEL MAMMAY

I write about soldiers. Sure, I write about other things, too . . . mystery and science fiction and scheming . . . but soldiers are at the center of it. I spent twenty-seven years in the army before I ever had a book published, so soldiers are pretty important to me. Here are some of the things you might want to think about if you're putting soldiers in your books. I'm going to stick to universal characteristics that will apply whether you're writing fantasy, sci-fi, or any other genre.

1. Soldiers Aren't Uniform Just Because They Wear Uniforms

I don't care how regimented your force is or how oppressive the leadership, unless you've got clone troops or robots, soldiers still have individual personalities. In a really rigid force (say, where minor infractions are punished by imprisonment or death), soldiers might suppress their personalities, but they still have them. They find different things funny, they like different things, and they have different dreams. Some are happy to be there. Some are just serving because they don't have a better option. Some actively despise the military.

Every soldier is different, just like every teacher is different, every doctor is different, and every truck driver is different. It's a job, not a personality. Try to give every soldier their own personality.

2. Soldiers Come from Somewhere

A military doesn't just spring up from nothing—that's an obvious enough concept. But it's important to know how your force came into being. Is it conscripted or volunteer? Where do the soldiers come from? If it's a big military, chances are that soldiers are coming from across a wide region. Is that entire area culturally homogenous?

Probably not. Even in a rigid culture, there will be differences between people from the city and rural areas, different levels of education, different economic statuses, and different views of the world. How do they see each other? How do their differences interact?

3. Soldiers Aren't All on Time, and They Don't All Love Working Out

They don't *all* do anything. This is similar to number one, but I've seen this so many times on TV and in books, I had to mention it specifically, too. I don't like getting up early. Hate it. During my twenty-seven years in the army, I got up early. But only because I had to. When I was on vacation, I slept in. I'm not the only one. There isn't some miraculous distribution of early birds in the army. Yes, soldiers are trained to get up early. Some of them will grow accustomed to it and keep doing it. Some won't.

The same thing goes for being on time and exercising. While they're in the service, soldiers will do both of those things. It doesn't mean they like it, and it doesn't mean they'll do it when they don't have to. There were people in the army with me who loved to run. There were people who loved to lift weights. There were some ridiculous people who liked to do both. But there were a lot of people who didn't.

4. Soldiers Can Think

Getting this fact wrong is probably the one thing that will make me quit on a story fastest. I quit on *Supergirl* because of it. I remember the episode. There was a four-star general, and he was so rigid in his thinking that he couldn't allow for any variables. I'm sorry . . . that's impossible.

To get to that high a position, the man led countless organizations, consisting of thousands of people, through all kinds of changing situations, and he was successful. If not, he wouldn't be there at the highest possible rank. So, in all that time, he didn't develop at least some level of flexible thinking? Again . . . impossible. And while there is a certain amount of "just following orders," even then, a soldier still has *thoughts* about those orders.

Granted, you can build a military for a totalitarian society where there's less free will, and some of that will bleed into your force. That's the thing . . . soldiers are a product of the society from which they come. The military will try, to some extent, to change some of that. But they'll be only partially successful. Especially in a free society, soldiers will think for themselves, for good or ill.

Obviously, there are different levels of intelligence in any group of individuals. Soldiers are individuals. Some of them barely passed the entrance test. Some have genius-level IQs. Most are somewhere in between. Just like everybody else in the world you build.

5. Soldiers Break the Rules

This one doesn't bother me when I see it, but it does make me laugh. I think somehow people have this idea of soldiers as rule followers. But think that through. A military force is primarily comprised of young people. Think about yourself at nineteen, and how well you did what you were told. Now add explosives and guns. But wait, you say . . . if they get caught breaking the rules, they'll get in trouble! So . . . you never sped while you were driving as a teenager? Never drank when you were underage? Never did something that would have gotten you thrown out of school if you got caught?

Young people don't plan on getting caught . . . they think they're invincible. If anything, that idea is stronger in soldiers. After all, they're trained to think they're not going to die. I remember one deployment where someone higher up than me enacted the ill-fated order that soldiers were not to have sex while deployed. So I'm sure none of the thousands of eighteen-to-twenty-one-year-olds ever did, because that would be breaking the rules.

But of course they did. A couple was caught literally having sex in a dumpster. Soldiers are nothing if not expedient. Or, if you're an optimist, love will find a way.

6. Soldiers Break Everything

I worked for a general once who was fond of saying that if you leave ten soldiers in a room with an anvil and come back in fifteen minutes, it will either be missing or broken. It's not a malicious thing. It's a combination of youth, boredom, and curiosity. What will happen if we put the auto-injector up against a piece of cardboard? What will happen if we shoot one of our own guys in the chest with a forty-millimeter sponge round?

Nonlethal weapon? That sounds like a challenge! I bet you don't dare to get tased.

Just in case any military officials are reading this, please remember that I'm a fiction writer. These are merely hypothetical situations that sprung from my own imagination. As far as you can prove.

A vendor once brought a computer to me that he was diligently trying to sell to the military. I was a young officer at the time, so I had no say in the matter, but for whatever reason, he wanted to convince me. As part of his pitch, he said it was soldier-proof. It was a nice enough computer for the nineties . . . I'll give him that. But when he said "soldier-proof," I dug in.

"Can you pour a Coke on it?" I asked.

He looked at me like I was joking.

"Can you hit it with a big hammer?"

Blank stare.

"What if you tossed it across the room and someone didn't quite catch it?"

All I'm saying is that if you're going to advertise something as soldier-proof, you better bring your A game.

7. Soldiers Do a Lot of Different Jobs

Not everyone carries a rifle every day. There are cooks, pay specialists, truck drivers, mechanics, supply techs, fuel handlers, explosives experts, chaplain's assistants, military police, and a thousand other jobs. They have varying skills. Not every soldier has every skill. A computer tech might be nearly useless with a rifle. Sure, they've had training, and they probably carry one around with them. But make no mistake, nobody wants them to use it. (Note: This is a generalization. Some computer techs can also shoot. But really, nobody cares, as long as they can make hot computer magic.)

Sometimes these differences come with different attitudes, or even completely different subcultures. Soldiers in different areas of expertise might have their own language, norms, and habits. They may look down on other groups. They may look up to them. In most cases, they probably do both, to some extent.

8. In the End, Despite Everything I've Said, the Main Purpose of Soldiers Is to Kill People and Break Things

They are often trained in this way and behave accordingly. Sometimes, when you see them all shined up in a parade, you might forget that. But that's a front. They get in fights . . . with outsiders, with people from other units, with each other. They swear a lot. Not all of them. Again . . . individuals. But more than average. I'd have some serious questions about a G-rated war story.

Soldiers are amazing. They do things you never thought people could do in both good ways and bad. They are absurd. I once found a group of my soldiers playing video games after eight hours out on patrol in Iraq. They were playing *Call of Duty*. You can't make that up.

REALISTIC FIGHTING
FOR AUTHORS

୬

BY ERIC PRIMM

A trained fighter beats an untrained one. Skill, of course, trumps no skill. But what really constitutes fighting skills? Different martial philosophies define skills in different ways. The martial arts are a generic term, equivalent in specificity to a word such as "vehicle." Just as there are many types of vehicles with different purposes, there are many martial arts with varied goals, training methods, and fight objectives. Some are for self-defense, others are for sport, and still others maintain cultural traditions. But certain basic skills, such as cardiovascular conditioning, distance control, and development of muscle memory, are common across disciplines. Each art may emphasize or explore these skills differently, but without them, the martial artist is in trouble.

Characters with a martial background would understand the need for these skills. An author needs to know that a character who fights also practices those skills. Without training, it would take luck, surprise, or, most likely, both for an unskilled character to beat a trained one. Like writing skills, martial abilities require maintenance. If a skilled fighter is important to a story, then that fighter has put in hours upon hours learning and maintaining three basic aspects of fighting: endurance, range, and muscle memory.

Fighting is exhausting. It is mentally, physically, and emotionally draining in a way that no other experience can be. It is a three-dimensional, dynamic puzzle with a side of pain and the risk of injury. Fighting is also a transformative process that induces a Zen state of mind. It is scary, exhilarating, fun, and frustrating. It can be short bursts of strength and speed that drag out over several minutes. It can also be a grueling grind that wears everyone down.

Depending on the situation, fighting can be the best experience of someone's life, the worst, and/or the stupidest. Each time, the struggle is new and different. Each of the factors of a fight—physical, emotional, and psychological—exhaust the fighter. In fact, when skills are equal, the fighter who fatigues faster will lose without luck or third-party intervention. Sport fighters dedicate equal time to staying in peak condition—including exercise, diet, and mental conditioning—as they do to skill training.

Fatigue is such an important factor in a fight that strategies are built around making an opponent exhausted first. In striking sports, punches and kicks to the body, leaning on your opponent, and pushing and pulling are all strategies to wear down an opponent. In wrestling or grappling, the fighter makes their opponent carry their weight. Covering the airways and constricting the diaphragm are excellent strategies as well. A fighter understands that the only way to beat an opponent with more skill is to wear that person down until they make a mistake. Or the fighter has to cheat, which means weapons or allies.

Characters who are accomplished fighters must be in shape and understand energy management during a fight. The longer the encounter, the more energy required. In *Words of Radiance*, Brandon Sanderson has Adolin Kholin duel for shards (magical swords or armor), and

Adolin's strategy is to drain his enemy of stormlight, a brilliant modi-
fication of a fatiguing strategy.

Distance is another trait that fighters learn. Martial artists refer to
fighting distance as range, and the easiest way to understand this is in
terms of weapons. In the single-stick fighting portion of Filipino martial arts (FMA), there are four ranges: long (largo), medium (medio),
short (corto), and stick-grappling. These ranges affect targeting, footwork, use of the empty hand, blocking, trapping, kicking, joint ma-
nipulation, and which portion of the stick is used.

This even applies to fighting without weapons. A long-range punch,
such as the jab, can strike an opponent from farther away than a hook
punch to the body. A kick hits farther away than an elbow strike. A
character with a martial background instinctively understands that distance dictates the options available during the fight. Changing range
can expand or contract the options available to a fighter. The movie *John
Wick* demonstrates this well. Even though the protagonist has a gun, he
utilizes judo throws when close to his enemy. Wick understands that,
even in a gunfight, grappling options are available in the right range.

Fighters gain this sense of distance from sparring. They learn techniques in all ranges, but everyone develops a preference for a particular
range. Certain fighters like to grapple, others like to kick, and still
others like to punch. Fighters build strategies around getting into or
maintaining their preferred range. In mixed martial arts (MMA)
competitions, fighters who like to strike need defensive grappling to
maintain striking range. Grapplers must move through punches and
kicks to grab their opponents.

Fighter preferences are dictated by what each person enjoys and
believes to be their strong suit. A character who has fast feet, is tall,
and has good flexibility might enjoy keeping his opponent away with
long kicks, straight punches, and footwork. A shorter character might
prefer to wrestle or use knees and elbows. Physical traits don't always
dictate the characters' preferences, though. Mindset, personality, and

temperament do. In fact, some fighters rely on their favorite techniques instead of their best ones.

When building characters, the author should build the fighter around their personality. What does the fighter enjoy, what does the fighter think are their strengths, and what is their goal during the fight? Does the fighter enjoy the knockout more than, say, a submission? Does domination mean more to the character than simply finishing the fight? Is the warrior uncomfortable with killing up close and prefers using the long sword as opposed to the dagger? Will your character stab someone in the back or need a so-called fair fight to ease their conscience?

Martial training instills technique into muscle memory. For this chapter, "muscle memory" is defined as "without conscious effort," meaning that an action is performed without having to think through every step. When a child is learning to tie their shoes, they think of every step until they've practiced enough that the task is automatic.

Martial arts skills are the same. The action in a fight occurs so fast that if a character has to think about blocking, they've already been hit. Muscle memory, however, goes beyond reaction times. As a child is learning to tie their shoes, an adult can see what the child is doing and anticipate the next step. The same happens in fighting. An experienced martial artist can counter an opponent with less practice.

In the early Ultimate Fighting Championship, Royce Gracie beat a number of skilled opponents because he possessed ability in a range they did not. After all of Gracie's training, when his opponent moved, his muscle memory anticipated what was happening, allowing him to stay one step ahead. In FMA single-stick fighting, a master recognizes a strike from the angle that it enters on and can counter an opponent at the beginning of an attack.

Among fighters of equal skill, muscle memory can be used in chess-like strategies to set a trap. For example, one fighter may figure out that each time they swing their stick horizontally, their opponent tries a vertical block that is braced with the empty hand. The next time, the fighter fakes a strike, anticipating the block, and switches to punch their opponent in the face with their other hand.

The author's job is to build a character who has muscle memory in certain skills. Every martial artist is human; thus, every martial artist has flaws, which the correct opponent can exploit. These flaws are built from the fighter's preferences. A character needs weaknesses that are exploitable based on their lack of knowledge. The overconfident boxer can be wrestled to the ground, and the overconfident wrestler can be boxed into unconsciousness. Characters need skills that are automatic and second nature. But to be human, the character cannot be perfect in all skills.

By having better conditioning, being able to be in the right spot to apply the right technique, and executing said technique without thought, the fighter's skill is evident. These are the universal skills that fighters need, and any character that is built as a fighter needs to understand these. Any character who isn't a trained fighter will fail in at least one of these areas. Drama is built from the failure, and suspense is built by application of the principles. By having these skills evolve from the character's tendencies and traits, the author earns believability. These skills also add depth to the character.

A sickly character who raises their sword to fight a strong man speaks of bravery. The woman who slips a punch into a double leg takedown as a defense is an agile thinker under pressure. The thief who stabs a mark in the back for a few gold pieces is a practical murderer. The soldier who shoots an unarmed villager kills too easily and probably has mental problems. Each of these examples is spoken in the language of physical conditioning, range, and muscle memory, and each speaks of character. By showing the reader how their character fights, the author engages in the most hallowed of writing advice. They are showing, not telling.

BUILDING A FANTASY ARMY

ᕙᕗ

BY MICHAEL MAMMAY

Before we look at where individual members of an army come from, let's look at the army as a whole. War is expensive. One of the first things you have to do is figure out how you pay for it, and one of the biggest cost considerations is whether your soldiers are professional or whether they show up only when it's time for war. A lot of fantasy books have preindustrial societies, and that affects your ability to field a standing army. In *The Wealth of Nations*, Adam Smith discusses how in preindustrial societies war tended to be supported by the actual participants. If you wanted an army, you, as an individual, paid for it. The ability to bear that expense is a key factor that an author must consider when it comes to the size and composition of the army. We'll look at three possibilities: standing armies, wartime call-ups, and mercenaries.

Standing Armies

Standing armies are expensive. You have to pay them even when you're not using them, and you have to equip them. Most preindustrial

economies were founded on manual labor, and maintaining nonpro-
ductive people creates strain, especially over time. A professional soldier isn't participating in the economy unless that economy is based on
war. You can create a nation that can support a standing army by giving
it natural resources or industrial capability (whether by science or
magic) or by centering the economy on war. A nation that uses war to
take resources from its neighbors can shift the economic burden to
defeated foes, for a time. Consider the example of sixteenth-century
Spain: They were the most powerful nation in Europe because they
funded their armies (and, more specifically, navy) using the gold and
silver that they stole from the New World.

Even in the most advanced societies, the size of a standing army is
limited by cost. If you consider the Roman Empire, most estimates
suggest the standing army reached a peak of between 300,000 and
400,000. The peak population was somewhere around seventy million,
which means the army was roughly half of one percent of the population. In an economy driven by industry (mundane or magical), the cost
of your army will be divided between the technology and the number
of people required to maintain and operate it.

Wartime Call-Ups

A more common means of building an army historically in the time
periods associated with a lot of fantasy novels involved calling on troops
only when needed. This was especially true in agrarian societies where
farms required large amounts of labor in the spring for planting and the
fall for harvest, leaving the summer free for a nice skirmish with the
neighbors. This pattern is visible even today, as fighting often slowed in
Afghanistan during poppy harvest season. As farmers or other manual
laborers convert to soldiers, some factors to consider in world-building
include their skill level, types of weaponry to which they have access/
training, who supplies their arms, and how important it is to get them

home. For example, it would be pointless to win a war while your harvest rotted in the fields, starving everyone during the winter.

Of course, if your country/home/family is threatened, some of those considerations go by the wayside, but only for so long. If your homeland has no choice but to defend, it might have to keep an army it can't afford, putting pressure on the economy and potentially leading to widespread hardship even for those not directly involved in the fighting.

Mercenaries

History is filled with mercenary companies. The White Company (multinational, but fighting mostly in Italy), the Catalan Grand Company (Spanish), and the Varangian Guard (Norse) are three famous examples. If your nation can't afford a standing army but needs a better-trained force than you can get by rounding up the peasants, mercenaries could provide a reasonably priced alternative. There's always a war somewhere, so a company of mercenaries need never be out of work, and they could bring a level of skill and training to an employer for the right price.

Not all mercenaries followed the same ethical code, and a contract is only a contract if both sides continue to abide by it. For a writer, the use of mercenaries can add some nice twists to your plot, as they could threaten to change sides at a pivotal moment, or perhaps just delay their attack by a few minutes to reduce their losses. When war is a business, expect the leaders to make business decisions, and those decisions might not align with the interests of their employer.

Manning and Equipping Your Army

Once you've figured out your economy and how you're going to field a force, you need some soldiers. Where do your fighters come from? As a rule, soldiers reflect their society. What is it that makes your soldiers join the army, and what skills do they bring when they arrive? Are they volunteer or conscripted? Do they see it as a duty—an inherent part of the culture—or is it a means to a different life? Are they respected for joining, hated, or somewhere in between? What class of citizen is likely to choose military service?

These are just some examples of questions you can ask yourself as you gather your fantasy soldiers.

Some other questions to consider:

How do the soldiers learn to fight? Do they join as recruits and then learn? Because that's a significant overhead cost, as you're now paying for soldiers who aren't ready to fight, as well as for the people to train them. And that takes time.

Or do soldiers show up already trained?

Perhaps they're from a warrior culture (like the Vikings, Cossacks, or Spartans) where fighting is baked right into the way of life. If so, consider showing how that affects your culture (such as children playing martial games, for example). A culture that values fighting from an early age will always have a replenishing base from which to draw soldiers for an army. Or you could create a culture/nation where war is inevitable, so everyone prepares to some extent. A great example of this is the rise of the English longbow in the thirteenth and fourteenth centuries. In 1252, the Assize of Arms ordered all Englishmen between fifteen and sixty, by law, to have bow and arrows. Edward III took it further in 1363 with the Archery Law, which basically outlawed all sports except archery and mandated practice for all men on Sundays and holidays. The expertise of the British with the longbow directly led to major victories against the French at Crécy, Poitiers, and Agincourt during the Hundred Years' War.

If you don't have trained warriors, soldiers might come from whatever civilian life they led. If you have a culture of hunters, they might fight with bows. A region with an economy based on logging might produce soldiers who fight with axes. If you don't have a significant standing army, peasants might show up with the tools of their trade—or modifications of those tools—and turn them to war.

One thing to consider when planning to run your war with conscripts is what makes them fight. There is more to an army than training, and especially in a time of edged-weapon combat, the will to close with and destroy the enemy—the fighting spirit of a force—could be as important as skill with a weapon. This is often why leaders stood behind their formations, ready to "encourage" anyone who thought it might be safer to go backward instead of forward.

And of course you can create a noncontiguous force, comprised of a mix-and-match of professionals, volunteers, and conscripts, and give them all different advantages and drawbacks. It can be as complicated or as simple as you like.

And that's where your leaders come in.

Leading Your Army

Someone has to be in charge, and the more complicated the army, the more important your leaders are. So now that you've got your soldiers assembled, who is going to lead them into battle?

Do your monarchs or societal leaders lead their own fighting forces? If so, by what authority do they lead? Are they the strongest fighter? The smartest? Or do they gain their authority from inheritance, or, as in some societies, are they considered to be ordained by their god to lead? Whichever you choose, consider how it's received by their subordinates. Does everyone accept their leadership without question, or are soldiers constantly watching, ready to desert if a leader shows any kind of incompetence?

I've seen a trope in quite a bit of fantasy that has leaders trained in an academy setting, and you can include that in your story, but understand that it was a fairly late invention (eighteenth century) and comes with a high overhead cost. Honestly, I think the prevalence is more because authors like the setting of the military academy and the options it opens up for the story more than it being a realistic way to prepare leaders. Academies are usually more appropriate to a large standing army in an industrial society.

Once you decide who will lead your army, consider the training inherent in that responsibility. Where does the leader get the skills necessary to fight, lead, and employ troops? What might they have to sacrifice in order to gain those skills? After all, there are only so many hours in a day, and a leader who is focused only on military matters might not have as much time for learning other things.

The problem expands when you consider the common fantasy trope of a young ruler. Have they had time to learn strategy and tactics for every kind of force they will need to deploy or counter? Do they have enough fighting skill to protect themselves? Have they earned the respect of their soldiers? What about other leaders, who have perhaps done the job for twenty years? Count on veteran soldiers to ask those questions of a young leader, even if they're too afraid to ask out loud.

Perhaps, lacking training, your novice ruler hires someone to lead the military or turns to a trusted uncle for guidance. Now you've got someone who controls all your forces but isn't the ruler. Enter human nature: You've constructed a situation ripe for a coup. In cases like this, consider what conflict this causes, or what measures your leader might have put in place to protect themselves from their own forces. If you forget, all of a sudden Caesar is crossing the Rubicon, and Rome has a new leader.

Some potential ways for a leader to buffer themselves against their own forces include:

- **Distance**. A ruler could station powerful generals far from the seat of power to deny them direct access to allies within the centralized power base. An army stationed on the frontier poses less risk to the capital city.

- **Family.** Tapping a relative as leader of the army should offer some added level of trust, but it's no guarantee.

- **Keeping generals relatively weak.** This could come by hiring generals who don't inspire a lot of loyalty, playing generals off of one another and keeping them watching their backs, keeping control of their families or loved ones, or really anything that's going to make it hard for a general to thwart the will of the national leader. Just remember, generals are people, too. If you put them in bad situations, they're going to do what they can to extricate themselves and gain their own advantages. But hey, the conflict is the fun part.

- **Culture.** Why has there never been a military coup in the United States? Culture. We're raised to believe in civilian control of the military as right. US Army officers swear an oath not to any person, but to the Constitution. Loyalty to the nation comes before loyalty to the army. This is certainly not unique in history, but it is rare. If you choose to build an army based on that, consider showing the culture in enough detail to support it.

Command and Control: How Do You Lead the Army?

Unless it's a small army, your general needs some help. How much help depends on the size of the force, but, more important, on the tactics and the ability to command and control the army. To lead an army, a leader has to be able to communicate their intent to the force and signal changes to that intent as the battle develops. If everyone is together in one formation, it might be as simple as "Follow me and do as I do." But the more you spread out, the more your leader is going to need a system to help guide their troops to the right actions.

As your army grows in size or spreads out, a good rule of thumb is to have a leader for every formation, and your formations should only be close enough together that they can effectively communicate and receive orders. Orders could be relayed visually (flags, usually on a hill that can be seen from multiple directions), by sound (bugle or drum), or, if your army has it, by magic, which could give you a lot of options.

Logistics: How Do You Feed Your Army?

The size of your army is dictated by your ability to keep it supplied. An army on the move can send out provisioning teams to strip the countryside bare of food, but a stationary army has to bring in food (and water, if you don't have a local source). Your ability to move food and supplies then creates a need for transportation assets—wagons and animals, in a lot of fantasy situations—and those assets require their own food as well. The longer you stay in one spot, the farther future food shipments have to travel as closer supplies run down.

For fantasy army purposes, ask yourself how your soldiers eat. If you can come up with a way to feed your troops, you're probably okay. If not, then perhaps your army is too big to sustain.

In Conclusion

There are, of course, dozens of other factors you can consider when building your fantasy army, and you can make it as complex as you want. But if you keep these basics in mind, you'll get a somewhat realistic solution for your fantasy fighting force.

MARTIAL ARTS MAGIC: BUILDING A FIGHTER FROM THE GROUND UP

ॐ

BY EMBER RANDALL

Fantasy is full of swashbuckling swordfights, brutal fistfights, and general mayhem. Such fight scenes are often fun to write, full of high-energy acrobatics and witty dialogue, but they're not always as fun to read, especially when the protagonist ends up sounding more like a many-tentacled octopus than a human-shaped being. (If your protagonist is indeed an octopus, this chapter may not help you.)

However, assuming you do have a relatively humanoid protagonist, you can make them sound like a kick-ass fighter without needing any real martial arts training of your own—just a bit of research and imagination.

Tae Kwon Do? Aikido? Jiu-Jitsu?

The style that your protagonist trains in is going to shape a lot of how they fight, so start with that.

Most martial arts can be classed as either striking or grappling arts—striking arts rely on punches and kicks, while grappling arts focus on locks, takedowns, and wrestling. If your protagonist is going to be getting into fights in the street, they probably want to specialize in a striking art, since going to the ground is a hazardous proposition when you might get run over or land yourself on a broken bottle. But if they aren't prepared for the real world, a grappling art might be perfect to showcase how training and the ability to survive a fight don't necessarily go hand in hand.

Something to keep in mind is that a practitioner of a striking art tends to be weak in grappling, and vice versa, unless they've spent equal time mastering both. And that's a lot of time! Earning a black belt takes years, and while it's a definite achievement, it's the start of your journey toward mastery, not the end. As an old sensei of mine liked to point out, getting your first-degree black belt means that you know how much you don't know. (And, to be clear, not all arts use a belt system.)

However, this doesn't mean that your protagonist needs to start training as a young child, the way the Shang warriors in Tamora Pierce's Tortall novels do. Anyone can learn an art with enough practice, and while children do have some advantages, starting as an adult has benefits as well. Adults can focus better than most children can, and adults have a better sense of their bodies than rapidly growing kids. So adults often pick up certain parts of an art, like forms (also called kata), more quickly than children.

Of course, adults don't heal as fast and don't have the flexibility that most kids do, unless they spent their teenage years stretching. And starting as a kid does mean your protagonist can put in a number of years of training before hitting adulthood, which is useful if your protagonist is on the younger end—no one, no matter how amazing, can master an art in a month and hope to defeat someone who's been training for far longer.

If you're going to give your protagonist skill in a real-world martial art, I'd suggest picking one that you yourself practice—videos can get you a sense of how fighters move, but they won't teach you everything. And real martial arts have long, complicated histories that deserve respect, not appropriation. It's often easier—and a good excuse for some world-building—to invent an art that exists only in your world.

What style lets my protagonist do all the fancy flip-spin-jump-kicks?

I hate to disappoint you, but the fancy tricks you see in martial arts movies are discouraged in real fights by most schools. Once you're in the air, you can't change direction, which makes you vulnerable to a well-timed punch or kick. Such tricks also tend to be slower than grounded moves, which gives your opponent more time to react. Your protagonist might learn such acrobatics, for use in either forms, competitions, or partner work like the capoeira roda, but, as several trainees learn in Mercedes Lackey's *Exile's Valor*, using them in a real fight often leads to tragedy.

Okay, no flips. What can they do, then?

Once you know roughly what style your fighter uses, it's time to figure out how they make that style their own. Are they quick on their feet, relying on reflexes and fast dodges to keep them out of trouble? Do they go straight for their target, using their power to bowl over weaker opponents? Most styles are flexible enough to allow for a variety of approaches, and some even codify those approaches—Shaolin Kempo, for instance, uses the five Shaolin animals to describe five different ways to apply the basic punches and kicks in a fight. Most protagonists won't be equally comfortable with all variations but will have a preferred way to execute the techniques that their schools teach.

Stereotypes don't tell you everything—for instance, big guys can be as fast or faster than anyone in the room. Similarly, you don't need size to be a feared grappler if you have enough training. But physical limitations do play a role. I'm a pretty small fighter, so I'm never going to have the power of my 6'5" sensei—if I'm fighting him, I either need to be in super close the whole time, or I need to be very fast to get in and out of his range before he can hit me.

Personally, I prefer the latter. But another black belt at my dojo, who's the same height as me, takes a much more direct approach to the fight, pressing and staying in close without ever letting up. Both approaches recognize the mass and power difference, but they're very different ways to deal with it.

How do they learn all this?

Nowadays, most martial arts are taught in schools, some stand-alone and some part of larger networks that span states or countries. The exact structure of the school differs based on the art and the philosophy of the teachers, so you can have everything from small, family-run businesses to major for-profit organizations. There aren't any accreditation programs to guarantee quality, so schools do vary a lot.

In your story, your protagonist may attend a formal school, or they may learn one-on-one from a master in a kind of apprenticeship. Either way, a key thing to consider is the philosophy that the school or master espouses.

This is one of the places where schools differ the most, and it affects everything that they teach. Some are strict and formal, discouraging questions, while others encourage camaraderie and banter during rest breaks and urge their students to interrupt if they're confused. Some take an eclectic approach to teaching, using whatever skills come to hand, even if they're not strictly part of the art, while others enforce rigid discipline. And some, I'm sad to say, are quite toxic.

Cobra Kai, from the movie *The Karate Kid*, is an exaggerated example of the way a dojo can turn nasty, but it's not too far from the truth for some schools. At one point, shortly after I'd earned my tae kwon do black belt, I went to a boxing gym to inquire about classes for the summer. When I told the owner about my prior experience, he looked me up and down, sneered, and said that my nose didn't look like I'd ever learned to fight. Given that kind of attitude, I wasn't surprised to see that the classes were 90 percent male and the sparring heavily prioritized strength over control.

So what does your protagonist's school teach? Does it respect other arts, or scorn them for being weak? Does it encourage students to find nonviolent solutions first, or does it urge students to throw their weight around? The dojo environment will shape how your protagonist fights, as well as how they interact with the world at large.

STABBED IN THE CHEST: MORTAL WOUNDS AND MEDICINE

〜◦〜

BY JEN FINELLI

So, you want to stab a hero.

It lacks the charming ring of "Do you want to build a snowman?" but when *your* heroine takes an icicle through the heart from her magical sister, you may want medical fact on your side to strengthen your tension.

Or you can rely on the power of love to suspend disbelief, but where's the fun in that?

Psh, *love*. Ha!

Let's talk chest-icles. Or claymores, or *Ninja Gaiden* fantasy blades. Whatever your villain's preference, contrary to portrayals on popular TV, the heart is not the only (or even the most likely) fatal blow in the chest. In fact, there is a more lethal chest wound, and there is a heart injury your daring damsel can survive.

Before we touch those delicious teasers, though, we have to clear up the number one injury that makes authors look stupid: the "I'll just walk it off" stab to the right chest.

Unless you're exceptionally lucky, right-sided chest wounds are actually pretty fatal if not treated. That's because you need lungs to breathe, and you happen to have your largest lung on the right side. Anywhere from just above your collarbone to about a handsbreadth and a half below your breast, even a blade just four centimeters long can pierce a lung in a thin person. The villain would just need to stab into the gaps below the bone anywhere from the first to the ninth ribs. (Those gaps below ribs are called "intercostal spaces," by the way.) Keep in mind that your lungs taper up while your ribs taper down, so at the bottom, in that last intercostal space below the ninth rib, the villain must stab toward the hero's back, or literally *in* the back, to hit the lung: The front part of that space contains chest cavity for your lung to expand into, and some chunks of liver.

What does this mean for you, as an author, and for your characters?

Well, with what we know, let's say Jumpin' Jolene takes that elf arrow to the right chest in the heat of battle. Or perhaps in a crowded, candlelit ballroom, her romantic rival dances up beside her, and she almost doesn't feel the prick of the small knife . . .

She will not walk away talking, she will not run, she will not do crazy acrobatics off the top wall.

She *will* start to suffocate. This is because air is now getting into the chest through the wound, and it's crushing the punctured lung. She might even hear a short whooshing or sucking as the air hisses into the hole and the lung shrivels up. Light-headed dizziness will overwhelm her, and her vision may blur; an observant person may notice the injured side of her chest is higher than the other, or not rising and falling all the way with each breath like the other side. In her neck, her trachea will shift away from the side of the injury as her chest fills with air, and she'll have a crushing sensation, like a giant troll sitting on her chest. If the knife didn't go in cleanly, and it nicked the bottom edge of the rib on the way in, it'll cut the blood vessels there, and she'll bleed into her chest with a boiling-hot sensation—burning, even, because the blood feels hot compared to the cold air rushing into the hole.

I hope you're starting to see that medical realism isn't clinical sticklerism but meaningful human experience, with all the sensations that bring intimacy into your description and suck your reader into the world.

So how can your superpowered sweetie survive without critics calling a plot armor foul?

First, if the arrow or blade lodges entirely into the bone and doesn't penetrate the chest cavity at all, she can breathe and do her acrobatics. This will depend on her mental and physical resilience and experience, of course. She'll feel the blunt force *thud*, the sharp penetrating pain, soreness, and maybe a feeling of shock/surprise just because of the body's reaction to the intrusion. She'll bleed some, but she can breathe.

Second, if she's got a lot of body fat, or Schwarzeneggerian musculature, the blade might need more than four centimeters to reach a lung. It's actually possible in some cases for a blade to penetrate a thick chest wall but *not* reach the lung—this will still result in a sucking chest wound, but because the lung's still intact, the person doesn't crash right away. Instead, she'll feel progressively smothered every time she exhales. Why? Well, every time we exhale, our lungs shrink, right? With a wound in the chest wall, when the lung shrinks, air from outside rushes into the chest space it left behind. Then, when the person goes to inhale, there's a bunch of air in the way, and the lung can't expand. So, with each breath, she takes less and less air into the lung as it shrinks—shrinks—shrinks—crushed by the air seeping into the chest with every exhalation. Still, for the purpose of plot, this buys you some time, and whether the blade crosses the chest wall or stops in fat and muscle, thickness is a definite advantage for the initial injury. Thickness is a disadvantage for trying to save a life once the blade penetrates the chest wall, though, whether the lung's punctured or not, and you'll see why in a moment.

The initial emergency treatment for any sucking chest wound, punctured lung or not, is the same, and doable on the battlefield or at the ball. Your heroine or her friends need to create a way for the air trapped in the chest to escape; they also need to stop more air from entering the chest.

First, a three-sided seal on the injury will make it hard for more air to enter the chest. If you vent one side of the seal so it's a flap—hence why I said three- not four-sided seal—air should be able to escape, but not get in. That's often not enough, though: You may need a "back door" for the air to blow through.

Ironically, to save someone who's been stabbed in the chest, you need to stab them in the chest.

The incision is done with a needle or similar sharp object about nine centimeters long, in the second intercostal space, below the middle of the collarbone. Your heroine can find that space by counting ribs—feel the sternum and the ribs connected to it? Your first rib is under your collarbone, your second rib below that, and the space you want is below the second rib. Keep in mind that blood vessels and nerves run immediately under the ribs, so you want to stay near the top of the third rib instead of the bottom of the second. A thin tube—in modern medicine we use a catheter—keeps the tiny hole open for air to escape after the needle punctures the wall. The procedure takes seconds, but requires some force. Someone stabs the needle with the tube around it through the chest, holds it in place for five to ten seconds, and then takes the needle out, leaving the little tube in place. During my military service, I heard about a soldier trying to help a rather portly man whose chest wall fat kept squeezing the catheter closed; the soldier used a hollow pen as the tube instead and saved the man's life.

You can see this makes for extremely dramatic story options. The improvisational action alone: In the modern military, if we don't have actual chest seals on us, we're taught to rip up the plastic bags from our meal kits, so in a fantasy tale, a super-seamstress could tear a tunic and adhere that over the wound; or under some psychic dark elf's command, a sentient biochemical ooze could cover the hole . . . You're the writer, you figure it out. Imagine the dramatic moment when your heroine stabs herself above the breast with a wicked-looking iron spike, or her true love kneels beside her to do it, jaw clenched, needle-like blade clutched in his hand as she gasps for breath.

There's a saying I heard when first learning how to train combat medics: "No one dies without two needles in their chest." A hidden wound does happen, especially in gory battles with blood everywhere, and if puncturing one side doesn't fix the breathing, we puncture the other side. There is, of course, also a lung on the left, and it takes up more space than a heart, so a left-sided lung injury can happen just like we've described for the right—with one important distinction. The largest vessels to and from the heart live in the left chest, and air from a sucking chest wound crushes everything. You can think of it like squeezing a water hose: As the large vessels squeeze shut, that's blood to the heart, to the brain, that can't go anywhere. The crushed heart struggles to pump against the pressure—there's chest pain, a pounding headache, tunneling vision or seeing white starbursts, a sensation of choking as the large veins in the neck can't drain, and terror closes in! This is where Lady Lorraine of Leverland can die of cardiovascular collapse even though the injury's actually respiratory. Of course, the story changes yet again when we consider large lung lacerations—perhaps caused by an axe or a broadsword—instead of simple punctures caused by the tip of an arrow or a knife. (Lung lacerations require significant surgery.)

There are so many other factors involved with stabbings, and we haven't even left the lungs to cover the fatal large vessels that bleed out in under four minutes, or a puncture to the heart sac instead of the heart itself. Bottom line, for traumatic injuries, there's a lot of benefit in just knowing basic real estate, so for further research, you should check out one of the anatomy texts recommended at the end of this chapter. You don't have to memorize them, but it's helpful, when writing an injury, to flip to a picture, see what damage your scimitar could do, and just make sure you're not writing something stupid. To get those really dramatic details, I would highly recommend you download the free Deployment Medicine app, a veritable treasure trove of easy-to-understand medical injuries that teaches even soldiers with very little medical experience how to save lives on the battlefield. Because the app lists symptoms as well as low-resource emergency treatments, you can really get into the mindset of the suffering each injury inflicts, and even get good plot ideas.

Because when your heroine walks it off—you want your reader to believe it.

FURTHER READING

Deployment Medicine App: 2019 TCCC Guidelines

Grant's Atlas of Anatomy

Lippincott's Illustrated Q&A Review of Anatomy & Embryology

Moore's Essential Clinical Anatomy, Third Edition

N. Nishiumi et al., "Diagnosis and Treatment of Deep Pulmonary Laceration with Intrathoracic Hemorrhage from Blunt Trauma," *Annals of Thoracic Surgery* 89, no. 1 (January 2010): 232–38.

PART 5

❧

YOU DON'T KNOW HORSES, BUT WE DO

HOW TO DESCRIBE
HORSES IN FICTION

❧

BY AMY PERKINS-MCKENNA

An author's use of incorrect or archaic terminology is one of the quickest ways to break a book's spell. When it comes to horses, some of the main indicators of an author's level of knowledge are in the description of the horse itself and the tack involved.

Describing Horse Height

Horse height is measured in "hands." The unit originated from the breadth of a human hand, but is now standardized to four inches. So, if you had five horses between 15 and 16 hands, and each was an inch taller than the previous horse, they would be 15 hands, 15.1, 15.2, 15.3, and 16 hands (15.4 = 16 hands). This system of measurement started in ancient Egypt and is most popularly used in English-speaking countries. There are other units that are used in regulated sport, but for the novelist's use, the hand is best.

The height of a horse is measured when the animal is on level ground, from the ground up to the top of the withers. The withers are a bony process that is most equivalent to the scapula of a human. It is the point between the neck and the back. So, a horse that is fifteen hands tall is five feet at the withers. It can carry its head higher or lower depending on its mood and conformation.

In addition to height, there are other classifications of equines, from miniature horses to ponies to horses. A pony is not a baby or young horse. A pony is an equine that measures less than 14.3 hands when fully grown. By contrast, there are no specific height classifications for draft horses; it is breed dependent. Similarly, a miniature horse is a breed in itself, though it happens to be the shortest breed of horse.

Horse Coloring: Fifty Shades of Brown

Horse coat color genetics can be confusing and complicated. For the purposes of the writer, however, the most common colors are listed below, as well as some quick distinguishing notes:

- **Chestnut:** The whole body is a copper to liver brown color with or without white markings and no black points.
- **Bay:** A copper red, red-brown, or chocolate-brown body with black "edging" like a fox would have. The legs, muzzle, tail, mane, and ear tips are black. With or without white markings.
- **Black:** A black horse in the summer is often a deep, dark brown unless otherwise protected from sun exposure.
- **Gray:** A gray horse ranges from steel or rose gray to almost white. Gray is a color that overlaps on other coat colors. A horse who is gray is on an inexorable march toward a loss of coat pigmentation but is not a true white.
- **Pinto/Paint:** A horse with patchy colors of white with black or brown.

- **Appaloosa:** A horse with spots. The spots can range from concentrating just on their rump to being distributed across their entire body like a dalmatian. Spots are black or brown on a white background.
- **Roan:** A black- or red-base horse with a mix of white hairs, giving them a muted blue or even pink look.
- **Dun/Buckskin:** A light tan horse with a darker brown to black dorsal stripe running along their spine toward the tail. Black mane and tail.
- **Palomino:** A golden horse with white to silver mane and tail.

True white horses are very rare but are not impossible to find; however, in a fiction world, that rule can be broken, as always.

Horse eyes are brown or black, with an occasional blue eye. Blue eyes are genetically linked to horses with white markings that cross the face, or certain coat colors like buckskin, paint, or Appaloosa.

The white markings on a horse also have specific terms, depending on their size and body location. Horses may have one marking on the face or legs or a combination. Have fun with this one.

- **Star:** A mark on the forehead that does not extend down the face.
- **Stripe:** A thin strip of white running from forehead to nose.
- **Blaze:** A wide strip of white running from forehead to nose or mouth.
- **Snip:** A mark on the nose between the nostrils that does not extend up the face.
- **White face:** A large expanse of white that covers the eyes and nose.
- **Coronet:** A small strip of white just above the hoof.
- **Pastern:** A white marking that reaches only the pastern.
- **Sock:** A white marking that goes past the fetlock.
- **Stocking:** A white marking that extends past the knee.

HORSE TERMINOLOGY: GAITS AND ANATOMY

❧

BY AMY PERKINS-MCKENNA

For this chapter I've included some pictures of my own horse, an eight-year-old mare named Gwyn. If you read the previous chapter, you'll see that she is an Appaloosa, broadly speaking. Specifically, she is a varnish roan leopard Appaloosa. She is only one-fourth Appaloosa, however! She's also one-quarter Percheron, a draft horse breed commonly used as a driving horse, and half Friesian. The Friesian is a horse breed most commonly idealized as the knight in shining armor's grand black horse with long, flowing mane and tail.

A. The Head

Horses have whiskers like a cat or dog, and in the winter, some grow an additional mustache of hair on the upper lip. Their ears can rotate from facing forward to facing backward and are the single most expressive feature of the animal. Ears are heavily involved in

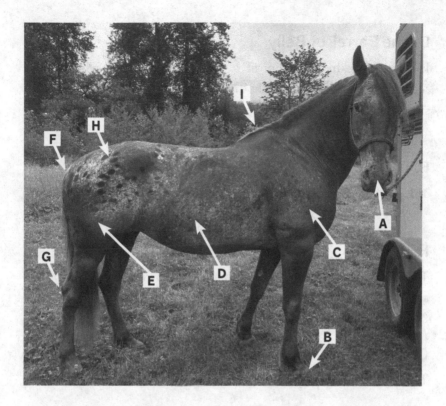

communication both from horse to horse and from horse to human. The forelock is the bit of hair that falls down on the face. The mane is the hair that rests on the neck.

B. The Feet, or Hooves

Singular—hoof. A horse can go with or without horseshoes.

C. The Shoulder

The shoulder of the horse is powerful and is where most of their pulling power originates from.

D. The Barrel, or Belly

If a horse is malnourished or filled with parasites, this is where you'd see their ribs quite prominently. The top of the barrel is where the rider sits astride.

E. The Stifle

This joint bends forward, similar to the human knee.

F. The Tail

There is a bony length of the tail that comes down about a foot or so, and the hair grows down from that.

G. The Hock

This is the joint between the upper and lower bones of the hind legs.

H. The Butt, or Rump

A horse moving with ideal biomechanics is balanced onto the hind end, and the power originates here.

I. The Withers

The withers are the point at which the horse's height is measured.

Parts of a Horse's Leg

The anatomical terms for the parts of the leg run from where the leg meets the body to the hoof.

A. Knee (front leg)

B. Hock (hind leg)

C. Fetlock

D. Pastern

E. Coronet

F. Hoof

G. Feathers on the fetlock
(the hair that hangs down)

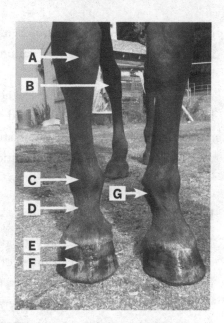

Some breeds have more feathering than others. Clydesdales have the classic, fully feathered legs, while other breeds, such as Arabians and Thoroughbreds, have next to no feathering. For the finer points of anatomy, you can easily find excellent visual resources online. I highly recommend Pony Club or 4-H resources for more in-depth accuracy.

The Hoof and Horseshoe

A horse's hoof is integral to the animal. There is a saying, "No hoof, no horse." Hoof maintenance and integrity is a constant focus of horse owners and caregivers. This is achieved through farrier work—trimming the hoof to an ideal shape or attaching a horseshoe to prevent excess wear to the hoof.

A horseshoe is attached by small nails that are hammered into the outer hoof wall. The hoof wall is like a really thick fingernail and has no nerves. A horseshoe allows the animal to traverse rocky and gravelly ground without wearing their hooves down or causing tenderness or lameness. Horseshoes have also been present throughout history, dating back to 400 BCE. If a civilization can work metal, they can create horseshoes.

Dirt in hooves needs to be cleaned and removed, whether a hoof has a horseshoe or not. Dirt can hide stones, which bruise soft tissue, causing pain. Packed dirt and moisture can also lead to a condition called thrush, a type of fungal infection.

Horse Gaits

With few exceptions, the standard gaits of a horse are the walk, trot, canter, and gallop, listed in order of increasing speed. Some breeds have more than these standard gaits, typically called a pace or rack.

The **walk** is the slowest gait, averaging four miles per hour. It is a four-beat gait, as only one foot leaves the ground at a time. It's the easiest to ride and can be very smooth.

The **trot** is a two-beat gait and is faster at an average eight miles per hour. However, there is a wider variation in the speed of a trot compared to a walk. Some breeds of quarter horses can trot as slow as a walk—this is known as a jog. Other breeds, such as the harness racing Standardbred, can trot as fast as nonracers can gallop. And based on experience riding such a Standardbred, it jostles you quite a bit as a rider! There's a reason they use small racing carts called sulkies to go that fast. The Standardbred also has a variation gait called the **pace**, which is also two-beat, but the legs move parallel (right hind and right front move together) instead of diagonal in the trot (right hind and left front move together).

The **canter** is a three-beat gait, generally faster than the trot, with an average speed of ten to seventeen miles per hour, depending on the fitness and size of the horse. Since the canter is not symmetrical, either front leg can "lead," and that will change how the feet fall within the gait.

The gallop is the fastest gait, with speeds ranging from twenty-five to thirty miles per hour. While this is an impressive speed, for the purposes of using horses as a means of travel, they cannot maintain that speed for more than a mile or two. Not all horses will run until they cannot go farther. They get winded, and some animals are more self-preserving than others.

Horse Pace and Endurance

I compete in endurance in the mountainous Pacific Northwest, and my mare tends toward self-preservation more than most horses. While riding on any hilly terrain, she will stop mid-trail to catch her breath before moving on again. This characteristic became evident at our first endurance ride, which took place on Nordic ski slopes. The trails were rolling hills and wound around a mountain with constant, steady inclines and declines. We'd often build up momentum on the decline and start the incline at a canter. As we cantered up, the path would curve around the mountain, and when we reached the curve only to see more incline, Gwyn would just stop and walk. No amount of urging could keep her moving. She was tired and didn't want to go, while her buddy, a very fit Arabian bred for endurance, was willing to just go and go and go. Once she'd rested, my horse was more than willing to pick up a trot again to catch up, but she needed that rest to catch her breath and let her muscles recover.

I share this to illustrate a few points. The first being that **the personality of a horse can dictate how they handle travel** over long distances or how they respond to the emotions of a rider in stressful situations. I wasn't willing to fight Gwyn over being tired. It was the longest ride we'd ever done, and I wanted to keep her spirits and health up, because horses remember, and first impressions and experiences matter.

Secondly, **the fitness of the horse is also important**. My mare was not used to the long distance I was expecting her to travel. I ride frequently, but I do not ride long distances frequently. My friend on the Arabian had been conditioning her horse for such a distance for a month, and he was barely breaking a sweat on the ride. This means that a horse kept by nobility for casual riding or hunting might not be fit enough to maintain a faster pace over the course of a day in flight, unless otherwise exercised by a groom. In contrast, a horse used by messengers or even a horse used to haul carriages would definitely have the fitness to cover ground with less effort being expended.

Third, **the fitness of the rider is also very important**. I mentioned how my friend was conditioning the Arabian for endurance. In doing so, she was also conditioning herself for hours in the saddle. It takes effort to ride and ride well. Riding a horse is a whole-body workout. You don't just sit; you are an active participant. Although I go on hour-long rides a few times a week, I found the four hours of intense riding at a constant trot and canter to be very tiring. My muscles screamed in pain about an hour in, and my legs pretty much went numb. I thought I was going to fall off because I didn't think that I could hold myself in the saddle. My friend, however, was fine. Her riding fitness was much greater than mine.

These are things that your characters could experience, and they are worth considering as story elements to add some realism. If a character has never ridden before and suddenly undertakes a long journey, especially at a speed faster than a walk, there will be negative physical effects at the start of that journey.

HORSE TERMINOLOGY: TACK AND RIDING

୧୬

BY AMY PERKINS-MCKENNA

Horses are capable of covering a variety of distances. The factors affecting the distance include the fitness of the horse and rider as well as the maintained pace. While a gallop could get you farther in a shorter time frame, the average horse is unlikely to maintain the speed for extended lengths of time. A trot, by contrast, can be very easily maintained by most horses, even animals that are out of shape.

If you look to the endurance world for guidance, horses are capable of traversing a hundred miles in twenty-four hours, and some can safely cover that distance in twelve hours. If the horse is kept moving at a trot for most of the day, it can reasonably cover fifty miles during daylight hours. More is possible if the horse and rider are fit and athletic.

Tack, the equipment used when riding a horse, is diverse. Form often follows function, but the basic terminology remains the same.

The saddle is what you sit in on the horse. The core of every saddle is basically the same. There is a wooden tree that provides the structure and distributes the weight of the rider across the horse's back. Ornamentation and padding are then built around the tree. Historically, a very basic saddle was little more than cloth wrapped around that wood. There were no stirrups (where the feet rest) on early saddles. Contemporary saddles have a wooden or composite tree, and natural wool or synthetic fiber in pockets used to pad the tree to fit the horse, and the whole saddle is covered in leather.

The saddle is attached to the horse by a strap that wraps around the barrel, or belly, of the animal. In English riding, this is called the girth. In Western riding, it is called the cinch.

Additionally, pieces can be added to help keep the saddle in place on the horse. A leather piece that goes around the front of the chest and often clips onto the girth is called a breastplate, breast collar, or martingale. This helps prevent the saddle from slipping back.

Leather that goes around the butt of the horse is called breeching. This keeps the saddle from slipping forward on the neck and can be especially useful if the horse is navigating steep terrain. You can also have a simpler piece, called a crupper, that attaches to the tail.

A halter is a basic leather or rope piece used for general control of the horse from the ground. Halters typically are not used for riding. There's little stopping power unless the animal responds well to seat aids.

Types of Bridles

The leather headpiece used for riding is a bridle (not "bridal"!) or headstall. Bridles can vary from bitless versions, which use nose or head pressure, to bitted versions where a metal bit rests in the horse's mouth in a gap between their front incisor teeth and back grinding teeth. The reins (not "rains" or "reigns") attach to the bit or hackamore on one end and are held by the rider on the other.

Bits vary widely and could take an entire book to describe, but the details shouldn't be vital to a fantasy reader unless somehow integral to the story. What is important to know is that even a simple, mild bit can be very severe in abusive hands.

A bridle is composed of the following parts:

- The **bit** rests in the horse's mouth against the gums, in a space between the incisors and molars.
- The **noseband** wraps around the face, above the nostrils and chin but below the cheeks. The noseband is not required for the bridle to function, nor is it part of every variety of bridle or headstall.
- The **browband** goes up over the forehead, and the throat latch loops under the neck and is tightened only enough to prevent the bridle from being rubbed off the face by the horse.

Pressure on the reins means direct contact with the horse's sensitive mouth. This is why soft hands are important. The mouth should be the last resort for a horse to receive a cue. In some riding styles, there is no direct contact between the rider's hand and the horse's mouth. Communication occurs from the seat of the rider and rein pressure on the neck, a style of steering called neck reining. It is very handy when you need one hand for something other than controlling the horse, such as wielding a sword or lance. If the horse and rider are skilled enough, reins become unnecessary, and the rider can direct the horse by shifting weight in the saddle alone.

Steering off of the seat requires the rider to shift weight and apply leg pressure, shoulder direction, and hip direction. Flexing the core can cue a horse to increase its pace or slow down or stop. The horse is sensitive to many signals from the rider, and learning how to send the right signals in sequence is what makes a skilled rider appear to work in harmony with the horse.

HOW TO WRITE HORSES WRONG

~⁂~

BY RACHEL ANNELISE CHANEY

So, you're writing a book with horses in it and want to write the equines right. Fantastic! Maybe you've already done some research, watched a lot of movies with horses, or read horsey books.

I've got some bad news.

Nine times out of ten, those movies and books are teaching you bad information. The same errors get passed down from movie to movie, book to book, with the creators blissfully unaware of their horse-knowledgeable audience groaning in despair. But you don't have to follow in their mistake-ridden footsteps!

You want to write your horses right, right? Watch out for these eight red flags found in fiction.

1. Rearing

Movie Myth: Rearing is awesome, exciting, and super normal. It's not dangerous, *obviously*, because horses rear with people riding all the time. Make your horse rear!

Reality: I'm trying to think of anything horse-related more terrifying than an unexpected rear. Nope. Nothing comes to mind.

Unlike the controlled movement you see in the movies, rearing is frequently dangerous, sometimes deadly, and always precarious. A rearing horse is balancing on two small hooves. Half a ton of horse and a moving human. On two hooves. If the rider pulls on the reins or loses their balance, the horse can fall backward. If the horse rears on an uneven surface, it can fall backward. If *anything* unexpected happens, the horse can fall backward.

Even if the horse stays upright, the rider can suffer serious injuries if they come out of the saddle. If the horse *does* fall backward, you're looking at a definite spill for the rider, compounded by the risk of a horse landing on them!

If your fictional horse rears, your rider better have them trained for it, be an insanely expert horseperson, or have their life flash before their eyes. In the movies, you usually see horses perform a partial rear, either a pesade or levade, 45- and 35-degree angle rears, respectively. They are highly advanced dressage movements that evolved from cavalry maneuvers. If your character and horse are professionals, a collected rear wouldn't be totally unbelievable.

2. Stallions

Movie Myth: Stallions are the coolest, most exciting horses. Put everyone on a stallion!

Reality: *Don't make stallions your default.* As a whole, stallions are the most unpredictable, dangerous horses to ride. Calm stallions do exist (like 2015 Triple Crown winner American Pharoah), but they're the exception.

Do *not* put your character on a stallion unless they're an experienced rider and there's a reason for it. When in doubt, go with a gelding or mare.

3. Dangling Reins and Ropes

Reins

Movie Myth: Does your character need to hop off their horse and do something? Just flip the reins over the horse's head and leave them dangling while your character gallivants around. No big deal.

Reality: Dangling reins snap legs. Dangling reins injure necks. Dangling reins damage mouths. Dangling reins mean disaster.

Here's the deal: If your character is riding Western and using split reins, they'll be in minimal to zero danger of injuring themselves on those reins. But not all Western riders use split reins.

If your character is like the majority of riders and uses closed reins, flipping reins over a horse's head and leaving them unattended is a recipe for disaster. Why? Closed reins are seven or eight feet long. If the horse is trotting, cantering, or galloping, they can easily step through the dangling loop. The *best*-case scenario would be the horse freezing or snapping the reins without injuring themselves.

Not likely.

If a horse gets their leg tangled in the reins, they can damage their mouth by yanking on the bit, wrench their neck trying to jerk free of the restriction, or even freak out and break their leg trying to run.

Ropes

Movie Myth: If a horse is wearing a halter, you can just drop the rope to "ground tie" him. He'll wait like a faithful dog while the character does their thing!

Reality: With significant training, some horses can ground tie like pros. But horses are prey animals. Even the most well-trained horse will leave your character in a lurch if there's a threat.

If you decide to have your character leave their horse unattended in a halter and lead rope, you better establish (a) they've been trained to do it, and (b) they know and respect their rider.

4. Leaving a Horse in Tack

Movie Myth: When your character reaches their destination, they can hop off their horse and leave them in bit, bridle, saddle, and everything. Just throw the horse some hay.

Reality: Um, no. I won't go through the list of skin, coat, and mouth ailments that can arise from leaving an unattended horse in full tack for extended periods of time, but, at the minimum, a horse can't eat or drink right with a bit in their mouth.

I've seen more than one movie in the past year commit this horse error. Looking at you, *Beauty and the Beast* (2017). Don't copy Hollywood.

5. Turning Horses Loose in Tack

Movie Myth: Your character can turn horses free with tack still on. Running around in the wild with a halter buckled and lead line dragging is A-okay!

Reality: The fastest route to injury? Turn a horse loose with tack on.

Leave a horse in tack in a stall, and you might have some problems. Turn them free with tack on, and you're setting them up for injury and/or death. Out in the wild, or even in a pasture, tack left on can get caught on trees, fences, and rocks and trap the horse. It can cut into the horse's skin. Cause them to trip. Help a predator take them down.

If you want to free your fictional horse, do him a favor and take everything off!

Unfortunately, *The Lord of the Rings: The Two Towers* (2002) committed this horse error in the extended cut. After Aragorn tells Éowyn to set Brego free because he "has seen enough of war," we next see Brego when he finds Aragorn while roaming free. Still with his halter and rope on.

Millions of voices cried out in terror. (Okay, maybe that was just me.)

6. Noise

Movie Myth: Horses neigh, nicker, scream, and whinny all the time! (As I type this, *A Knight's Tale* plays in the background. Though Heath Ledger's performance is delightful, the amount of horse noises in the joust scenes is *off the scale*.)

Reality: As prey animals, horses communicate mostly through body language and ear movement. Most aren't that noisy.

I've noticed that a lot of films and TV shows have the same "horse noises," which leads me to suspect that they're using similar noise tracks. Like laugh tracks for sitcoms. Unfortunately, these noise tracks are misleading.

Unlike humans or dogs, horses don't communicate a lot with noise and prefer to "talk" with body language first and foremost. Now, noisy horses do exist, but they're usually young, hot, or *dramatic*. (Yes, even with horses, attention-seekers exist.) But your average horse communicates nonverbally most of the time.

When I first adopted my horse De Vedras, he freaked out a little and started whinnying because he couldn't find his friend. (Spoiler: His buddy was napping in the barn, totally ignoring De Vedras.) But that's about it. He makes noise once or twice a year now.

His buddies give faint "We're starving" nickers at dinnertime, but otherwise . . . *shrug*

So, when are most horses noisy?

1. Mares in heat might call out.

2. Scared or angry horses neigh or scream.

3. Horses in a fight or play-fight might squeal at each other.

4. Lonely horses whinny for a friend.

Otherwise, snorts and hoof stomping are the main noises you'll hear. And "We're starving" nickers if they're spoiled babies.

7. Riding Gear

Movie Myth: You can ride a horse in whatever you happen to be wearing!

Reality: Upper-body clothing differs widely, but almost every rider wears pants and boots. Shorts and bare feet are an invitation to injury.

If your character isn't wearing leg protection (pants, jodhpurs, chaps, etc.), they won't be risking major injury, but they'd best be prepared for pain. Imagine bare skin rubbing against leather over and over and over . . . yep, you guessed it. Awful chafing. Even worse, bare calves can get pinched by stirrup leathers, badly enough to leave scars in some cases.

Now, riding without proper footwear is a different matter entirely. Put bare feet in stirrups, and your character isn't looking at a little chafing. They're risking serious injury. A damaged foot, wrecked ankle, broken leg—all are risks of inadequate footwear.

Why? If a horse spooks, bolts, jumps, or does anything out of the ordinary, the rider can come out of the saddle. They aren't wearing a shoe with a heel? Their foot slips right through. The ankle gets caught in the stirrup, and they're dragged beside the horse as they bolt. Even experienced riders, like Seabiscuit's jockey, get injured if their foot gets caught when a horse bolts. Having your character ride in stirrups barefoot increases the risk exponentially and is a big red flag.

Obviously, these issues don't apply to riding bareback. But bareback riding isn't half as easy as Gandalf makes it look on Shadowfax!

8. Terminology

Not a myth so much as a mishap, but watch for errors in terminology. They show up occasionally in fiction and are a surefire sign of writing horses wrong. A couple of terms to watch out for are:

1. "Rein" versus "reign": The piece of leather attached to the bit to control your horse is a "rein." Unless your horse is ruling a kingdom, no "reign" is involved.

2. "Halter" versus "bridle": The halter buckles behind the horse's ears and around the nose. A lead line clips to the halter, and people use halters to lead horses around. The bridle also buckles behind the horse's ears and typically has a noseband. In addition, the bridle includes a bit and reins.

Final Note

By no means is this an exhaustive list of movie myths and horse mistakes, but if you avoid the eight red flags in this chapter, you'll avoid throwing horse-knowledgeable readers out of your story. There's no 100 percent correct way to write horses. Like any other animal, every horse has their own personality and unique reactions, but some aspects of horse care transcend discipline, region, and breed.

Your horses don't have to be perfectly realistic. It's called "fiction," after all. But if you pay attention to the big issues, horse-knowledgeable readers can ignore little missteps.

But please don't have your horse jump a canyon. *side-eyes *Spirit: Stallion of the Cimarron**

MATCHING HORSES TO USE, SETTING, AND CHARACTER

ᴄ⁓ᴐ

BY RACHEL ANNELISE CHANEY

If you're reading this, you care about getting your fictional horses right. Congrats! This puts you ahead of 90 percent of Hollywood.

Here's the deal: Most writers get horse *terminology* (gaits, colors, tack, etc.) right. These are universal facts. Unchanging truths. Correct regardless of breed or world-building.

Matching your mount to your world and/or character is a trickier business, and Hollywood will steer you wrong every time. Using the wrong horse may *seem* like a little thing, but it will rip horse-knowledgeable readers right out of your story. Three key issues to consider when writing your fantasy-land horses are:

1. Use

2. Climate

3. Experience of your character

Let's match your mount!

Match Breed to Use

Misconception: Horses are all-purpose.

Reality: Um, no. Humans have developed horse breeds, like dog breeds, over centuries of selective mating. Each breed was created for a specific purpose.

The first thing you should do is pinpoint your horse's purpose. Are they a knight's mount? An over-rough-terrain horse to take your character on a trek? A nobleman's hunter or a cavalry steed?

Each purpose takes a different kind of horse.

Knight's Mount: So, you're writing a medieval fantasy and have armored warriors that need to charge into battle. You might be thinking they need a big horse, tough and muscled. Something like the Budweiser Clydesdales, perhaps?

Sorry, but no. Contrary to popular belief, most armored knights did not use giant, heavy draft horses. Based on recovered equine armor and illustrations, knights' mounts (known as "chargers" or "destriers") tended to be short-to-average height at fourteen to sixteen hands and stocky.

Reason: If unhorsed, an armored warrior needed to be able to leap back on his mount. Those eighteen-hand drafts? Not happening! A fifteen-hand horse? Absolutely!

The smaller, stocky build is also better for sharp turns, kicks, rears, and charges in the heat of battle. Most draft horses are known as Gentle Giants. The fire needed for battle? Not their thing.

The closest modern equivalent to the medieval charger is the Irish Draught.

Trek Horse: The most common mistake I see in books, movies, and TV shows is the use of fine-boned horses on long treks, frequently Thoroughbreds. When most people think of horses, the Thoroughbred tends to be the default view of how they look, move, and act. Thoroughbreds are great. I own them. I adore them. I harbor no illusions about them.

Like most Thoroughbreds, my gelding, De Vedras, and his buddies have lots of heart, so they would go on that long trek over the mountains and through the woods if asked. But they would drop weight, probably get injured or dehydrated, and definitely suffer from fatigue.

If your character is going on a long trip, give them a sturdy mount, like the hardy Mongol horse. Or Napoleon's small but intrepid Marengo, an Egyptian Arabian, who carried the French dictator through the Alps. The smaller horses may not be able to whisk your character away from danger or magnificently rear, but they'd laugh in the face of exhaustion or hazardous conditions.

Hunter/Cavalry Horse: Still love Thoroughbreds? Rejoice! Here's their optimal placement.

Hunting horses and post-medieval cavalry horses shared similar job descriptions and necessary skills, so I'm lumping them together. For hunting, a horse needed to be energetic enough to leap obstacles, fast enough to keep up with prey, and cool-headed enough to listen to its rider.

After the rise of gunpowder weapons and the fall of armor, the physical conformation of cavalry horses shifted. Instead of short, stocky chargers, cavalry mounts got taller and leaner. They had to be fiery enough to charge into the fray, nimble enough to get their riders out of lethal situations, yet calm enough to obey commands immediately.

The closest modern equivalents to these horses are Thoroughbreds and warmbloods—the same breeds that compete in the equestrian sports that evolved from cavalry training.

Fastest of the horse breeds, Thoroughbreds are primarily bred for racing but are highly versatile. Sturdier but slower than Thoroughbreds, warmbloods were developed by crossing "hot breeds" with European heavy horses.

If you're writing a nobleman's hunter (from any era) or a for-pleasure mount or a flintlock fantasy, stick to Thoroughbreds and warmbloods. They're tall (15.2 to 18 hands), muscular, fast, and agile.

What You Learned from Hollywood: Throw a Friesian in it. When a Friesian stole the show in *Ladyhawke* (1985), movie producers decided Friesians were the best thing since peanut butter. So now they cast them. In. Everything.

No, no, no, no.

If you find yourself describing your character's horse as big and black with a flowing mane and tail and feathered feet: Stop and listen. Friesians are *extremely* costly. Always have been. They're amazing animals, but they are *not* cart, commoner, or insane asylum carriage horses. Looking at you, *Beauty and the Beast* (2017).

Bottom lines:

1. Does your horse have a specific use? Keep descriptions in line with the breeds intended for that.

2. Do *not* give your commoner a Friesian. Don't give anyone a Friesian unless they're (a) rich or (b) need a warmblood.

Match Horse to Climate

Misconception: Horses are hardy and can weather harsh climates.

Reality: Horses are both surprisingly tough and exceptionally fragile. If your world features harsh or unusual climates, match your horses to that world.

Hot and Dry: Are your characters moving through a desert, rocky wasteland, or otherwise hot and arid world? Don't pull a *Game of Thrones* and put heavy horses in there. You wouldn't stick a Siberian husky in the desert, would you?

Big, muscly horses need lots, lots, *lots* of water, food, and forage to maintain that size.

If you're writing a desert-esque world, go for a breed that snorts in the face of extreme heat and lack of vegetation—like Arabians, Akhal-Tekes, or Marwaris. Like these breeds, your mount should be lean, compact, and light on their feet. On the shorter side (fourteen to sixteen hands), the desert breeds are masters of endurance. Need to go a couple thousand miles? They've got you covered!

These smaller, leaner equines can take you for longer distances, with less food, than a heavy mount!

Cold and Snowy: On the flip side, don't put that Arabian in a wintry climate! You wouldn't put a husky in the Sahara, so don't put a greyhound on the Alaskan sled team.

Most horses can weather cold temperatures with blanketing and care by their owners. But if your setting features below-zero temperatures, snowstorms, or persistent wintry conditions, you may need to consider going with a horse breed designed to live in freezing climates.

Cold-weather horses tend to be heavier than the average riding horse and grow out a thick, fuzzy coat in the winter. While a big draft horse fits the bill, smaller breeds like the Icelandic horse or the Fjord are great examples of a horse designed for cold winters and mountainous terrain.

If your setting is mountainous, icy, or subject to freezing temperatures, the best match for your world is a horse with strong hooves, thick muscles, and a super-fuzzy winter coat. How tall or short they should be depends on their purpose.

Temperate Climate: If your setting doesn't have extreme weather or unique terrain conditions, refer to the prior section on matching your mount to its purpose. Nearly all breeds can survive just fine anywhere that doesn't have extreme hot or cold.

Bottom line: If you have an unusual setting or climate, pick a breed that matches.

Match Character to Mount

Misconception: Horses are living bicycles. If you learn how to ride, you can ride any horse.

Reality: Every horse has a will, emotions, personality, and quirks. They think, feel, act, and react.

Matching your specific character to a complementary horse is a case-by-case issue, and not necessarily important unless horses are a vital part of your narrative. There are, however, a couple of big issues you should avoid.

Stallion: If your character is not an experienced rider, do *not* put them on a stallion! Don't put anyone on a stallion without a solid reason.

As much as Hollywood likes Friesians, books and movies like stallions even more. Most stallions are much more temperamental than their gelded counterparts. Calm, attentive stallions do exist, but they're the exception to the rule. When in doubt, go with a gelding or mare.

Temperament: On a similar note, don't give your character a cool, spirited horse if they're a nervous or excitable type. Horses are incredibly perceptive, and however a rider is feeling translates through their body and language and down the reins to the horse.

Is your character a confident, skilled rider? Sure, throw them on that fiery steed! Otherwise, I wouldn't recommend it.

Final Note

Horses are strange and frustrating creatures. Even horses of the same breed, sex, and age can behave like totally different animals.

So, there are no rules that are true 100 percent of the time. Ultimately, you know what's best for your story, including your equine characters. But remember this good rule of thumb: Learn the rules like a pro, so you can break them like an artist.

HOW TO INJURE HORSES REALISTICALLY

⤮

BY RACHEL ANNELISE CHANEY

It is a truth universally acknowledged that a main character in possession of a compelling narrative is going to have a bad time. If nothing goes wrong for your MC, how can they prove they're the best?

If your work features horses, great news! There's no end to the number of things that can go wrong for your character. Horses hold the ironic position of being some of the toughest *and* the most fragile animals on earth. Nature finds a way.

Want to fact-check your fictional horse's mishaps? Need a new way to make your main character's life more awful? You've come to the right place. For a quick and dirty reference, think H2G:

- Hooves
- Heart
- Gut

Hooves—High Likelihood, Low Fatality

On the most basic level, horse hooves are just thicker, stronger finger-nails. The difference? Horses have to support half a ton (or more!) on four tough fingernails. With every mile your horse walks, they risk damaging that fragile payload.

So let's dig into those health risks!

Abscess

Have you ever had a blister form *under* your fingernail? If you haven't, picture a pocket of infection trapped under the nail, trying to break through to the surface. (Ew. I know.) That's a hoof abscess.

Hoof abscesses are fairly common and can be triggered by every-thing from stress to an infected cut to a sudden change in diet. An infection forms in the hoof, works its way through the tissue, and bursts out the hoof wall. Just like the *Alien* scene!

Because the infection forms *inside* the hoof, it's almost impossible to detect unless the horse shows pain. But horses are tough customers. Many horses show no signs of distress, so you only know there's a prob-lem when the infection breaks through or the horse is suddenly lame. Depending on the size of the abscess, it can take days, weeks, or even months for a horse to get back to normal speed—even with rest and proper treatment.

Puncture

If you've never seen the bottom of a hoof, you might think the whole thing is a hard, impenetrable structure. Not so! A vital part of the hoof is the frog. (Don't forget this. We'll come back to it.)

The frog is a softer, V-shaped pad of flesh in the center of the hoof. Kind of like the pads on a dog's paw, the frog feels rough and calloused but can be punctured by sharp objects.

Puncturing the hoof frog can lead to soreness, limping, or even an abscess.

Lameness

A catchall term, lameness encompasses all health issues that lead to sore feet, including but not limited to abscesses and punctures.

Making those hooves cover rough ground all day, every day? High chance of lameness!

Sloppy horseshoeing? You'll probably shove a nail into the soft part of the hoof or crack the hoof wall. High chance of lameness!

Lameness of all types is common. If your character continues to push a lame horse, they're in for a bad time! Like, you know, equine death.

Bottom Line

Hoof injuries are minibosses. They're annoying, painful, and slow your progress, but are generally nonfatal. They can be deadly if they get infected or go untreated, but they are not meant to kill. Only to maim or seriously injure. If you need your character stranded or delayed, throw them a hoof issue!

Heart—Moderate Likelihood, High Fatality

In my experience, the 100 percent most misunderstood part of horse health is the seriousness of leg breaks. Raise your hand if you've ever said or heard something like this:

"When a human breaks their leg, we don't put them down. Why do people do it to horses?"

Here's the deal: Horse physiology is different than a human's. (Please. Hold your applause at my brilliance.) I know what you might be thinking. That heading says, "Heart." Why am I talking about leg breaks? Because horses are weird.

Remember that hoof frog? It's a vital part of the circulatory system. When a horse puts force on the hoof and presses the frog down into the ground, it pushes blood up the leg to travel back to the heart.

Without consistent pressure placed on the frog, the heart cannot pump blood up and down a horse's legs. The result? A nasty inflammatory disease that sets into a horse's hoof: laminitis. Laminitis is aggressive, painful, and destructive. Even today, there is *no* cure for laminitis. The pain can be mitigated with heavy drugs. Mild cases can be treated to the point that it no longer poses an issue.

But it cannot be cured.

If your fictional horse breaks their leg so badly they cannot put pressure on the hoof, do *not* have your characters spare them, wrap their leg up like you would a human's, and *voilà*, they return to perfect health. I'll repeat: *Do not do this.* Not only is it medically inaccurate, it's insulting to everyone who's had to choose between putting their horse down or watching them suffer from an incurable disease.

Laminitis can also develop if those pesky abscesses or puncture wounds keep a horse from walking on the injured hoof. An illness can also lead to laminitis if the horse cannot stand for an extended period of time.

I cannot stress this enough. If your fictional horse is injured so badly that they cannot put weight on all four hooves or, worse, can't stand at all, the chances that they'd develop laminitis are high. Insanely high. Snoop Dogg on top of Mount Everest high. Horses just don't survive that in real life.

Bonus fact: Horses are also susceptible to heart attacks. While not as common as laminitis, it's not unheard-of for a horse to collapse during intense work. Survival is *rare.*

Bottom Line

Heart-based conditions are side-quest bosses. Not inevitable, but extremely difficult. Except in rare cases, they're fatal.

Gut—High Likelihood/High Fatality

Welcome to the number one medical cause of equine death. Forget battle wounds. Forget heart attacks. Forget exhaustion or falling over a cliff or any number of creative injuries. The most common, most effective cause of death in horses is simple digestive distress: colic. (No, not baby colic.)

You know how I said horses were weird? It's about to get weirder.

Unlike nearly every animal on earth, horses cannot throw up. Seriously.

Things that make humans vomit (stress, poison, sickness, eating too much/too little, extreme exercise, rapid body temperature changes) make horses colic. So, what happens when a horse colics? It is a mild form of bloating, which may or may not work itself out. In deadly cases, the horse's intestines twist around themselves and kink, either as an involuntary reaction or because the horse rolls in distress.

So how could your fictional horse colic? Ingesting poison, being pushed to extreme lengths, or being forced to trek through a climate it wasn't bred for can result in colic. The most likely culprit? Lack of forage.

Horses can't exist on a scoop of grain. They need ten to twenty pounds of forage (grass, hay, etc.) every day to stay healthy. Without forage, they'll get a stomachache. Stomachache = colic. So, if your horses are traveling hither and yon without any forage and they *don't* colic . . . yeah, horse-knowledgeable readers are going to side-eye that.

But good news! You can improvise forage. My crazy horse suggests leaves.

Bottom Line

Gut issues are final bosses. It's almost impossible to completely avoid them and the fatality rate is no joke. Good luck.

Final Note

Obviously, lots of things can kill or injure a horse. On the flip side, remember that I said horses can be some of the toughest animals? It's true. Horses shake off stuff like cuts, abrasions, heavy hits, and puncture wounds all the time!

Horses are vicious with each other, even in play; it's where we get "horseplay," after all. They kick, body slam, and rake their teeth down each other. They're used to surface injuries.

So, if your character gets in a scrape and their horse takes a few hits, don't sweat it. Those are just enemy minions. Clean those cuts, get some rest, and keep moving.

Your character has bigger bosses to worry about.

HORSE PSYCHOLOGY 101

⤳

BY DEBBY LUSH

Are the horses in your fantasy novels nothing more than a mode of transport?

Any character who keeps the same horse for a long time will form a relationship with it, even if only to preserve its health and usefulness. Many will take it further. Even if your characters change horses regularly, you can add a layer of authenticity to your work by deepening your knowledge of how riders interact with their horses. This is important, especially if you've never ridden yourself, because you will undoubtedly have readers who are riders.

Horse Psychology

One of the most annoying traits of many writers (and plenty of the general public) is anthropomorphizing animals. Horses do not, and never will, think like human beings. (Unless, of course, your fantasy horses are really people in disguise—looking at you, Mercedes Lackey.)

To understand equine behavior and how it influences the way we handle and train them, it's useful to have some understanding of horse psychology and the ways horses interact with one another in a natural situation, which can inform how they will interact with us.

1. Horses are herd animals; they always feel more comfortable in company.

2. Horses are prey animals; everything might be out to eat them.

3. A horse is not a machine. They are all individuals with character, and although you can beat them into a terrified submission, if you train them that way, you will never have anything more than a dull means of transportation that might react unpredictably to danger.

In the wild, horses live in large herds with a clearly defined hierarchical structure. Contrary to popular belief, the herd is not led by the stallion but by the dominant, or lead, mare. She leads the herd between grazing grounds while the herd stallion drives from behind, keeping all his herd together and seeing off other stallions seeking to steal his mares.

Apart from these two, hierarchy within the herd is determined by position and attention, and not, as was once believed, by aggression, or "pecking order." The nearer to the center of the herd, the safer the horse is from predators. The ones on the outside are most likely to be eaten.

Gaining a safer, inside space is achieved by either moving in when a previously more dominant horse isn't paying attention, or by jostling—shoving the weaker-willed horses to the outside of the herd, using those big shoulders they have.

To relate this to horse training, gaining a cooperative and safe equine partner means two major things:

1. You need their attention.

2. You must gain control of their shoulders. Not their heads—
   their shoulders.

Novice riders make the mistake of trying to turn a horse by pulling
on the rein on the side they want to turn toward. All this does is to turn
the head that way, while the shoulders can go in the opposite direction!

How Do You Gain Their Attention?

This is a matter of training—at its best, achieved with a reward-based
system. At worst, by the use of punishment, or by equipment that keeps
the horse's head down in a submissive posture.

Head height denotes dominance—the more dominant the animal, the
higher the head carriage.

The dominant horses in a herd have responsibility for keeping
watch for predators, so their heads are held high for a clear view. Submissive horses have their heads right down on the ground, grazing. If
your horse is startled, his head will shoot up as he gazes around, looking out for danger. If his head is up all the time, you don't have his attention, or a submissive ride.

When we talk about submission to a rider, the most desirable result is
a sublime cooperation where communication is so subtle, horse and rider
appear to be one creature. This is only possible if the horse trusts their
rider to be the one responsible for watching for threats (i.e., the dominant
one), and this can never be achieved by force. Gadgets that keep the horse's
head down artificially only create an illusion of control, not the real deal.

An additional factor in attention is *balance*.

An unbalanced horse will always be nervous, because it is in danger
of falling over and getting eaten!

As soon as you climb onto a horse's back, you compromise its natural balance. We sit toward the front of the horse, overloading that end
and making it more likely to stumble. Training a horse to carry the rider

The real deal, English-style: a relaxed horse totally focused on his rider (Credit: Rui Pedro Godinho, courtesy of Debby Lush)

in a biomechanically functional manner is the only way to ameliorate this situation, and is limited by how fast a horse learns and by the development of the muscles needed to cope with this artificial situation.

Only when a horse feels confident in its balance with a rider on board will it be able to pay full attention to its rider. Before that, its natural instincts will keep it outwardly focused, watching for predators.

This also demands that the *rider* is balanced in the saddle! An unbalanced rider will raise a horse's anxiety levels, causing distraction and a lack of attention to the rider's demands.

Controlling the Shoulders

Shoulder control, and consequently steering, is a matter of training, but also of riding technique. While it seems counterintuitive, the rein on the outside of the turn must be the dominant one.

A horse's neck is very bendy. Not so much the rest of its body. Turning the neck does not turn the body. Conversely, keeping the neck fairly straight makes it more possible to turn the entire unit. This is done by pressing the outside rein against the horse's neck.

In English riding, we do this with a small inside bend in the horse's neck. This means allowing a tiny bit forward with the outside hand to permit the bend, but maintaining the contact to the bit, so the outside rein pushes the shoulder in the direction you want to turn.

Riding English-style: You can clearly see the outside (right) rein pressed against the neck to turn the horse toward the left in this canter pirouette (Credit: Mick Green Photography, courtesy of Debby Lush)

In Western riding, it's done by neck reining, where you take both reins to the direction you want to turn, usually with both reins in the one hand. This results in the horse turning its head away from the direction you want to go while turning the shoulders efficiently, so the entire animal will go where you want.

How Do Horses Learn?

One other useful aspect of equine psychology to understand is how horses learn.

Horses learn by memory.

They have no ability to synthesize ideas or to connect concepts (unless the trainer's response/reward is immediate).

A horse does not spend time thinking. Their only occupation is eating, or reproducing at the appropriate season.

This must be taken into account when training: Only if the trainer/ rider is 100 percent consistent in how they interact with the horse will training be fast and successful.

If, for example, you teach your horse to go in a particular way one day, then the next you are too tired to be bothered, you have only a fifty-fifty chance of the lesson sticking. It's a numbers game. Horses have excellent memories, so if you are not consistent, their response won't be, either.

This is why purchasing a well-trained horse doesn't always work for the inexperienced rider. For one thing, the horse is used to consistent signals from its trainer and can become confused by the erratic movements of the less experienced rider, causing anxiety and—guess what?—distracted and unpredictable behavior. For another, that excellent training may well begin to unravel as the new rider's demands do not conform to the consistency of the professional. Plenty of scope here for adding humor to your stories!

Gender Differences in Character

There is a relevant saying among horse people: "Tell a gelding, ask a mare, negotiate with a stallion."

Stallions are by nature more aggressive and don't take well to being told. You need an experienced rider to handle a stallion. Impressive though they seem, don't mount your character on a stallion unless there's a damned good reason. Even then, make sure it's an experienced rider.

A stallion is alternately called an "entire" (unlike a gelding, he still has all his "bits"). What might not be so obvious is that mares are also entires, and some may be as difficult to handle as a stallion. If you want an easy ride, pick a gelding.

I hope you found this short insight into horse psychology of interest, and hopefully some of you will find it of use in adding a more authentic layer to the horses in your fantasy worlds. Let's face it, most of us have horses in our worlds, so why not use them to add more flavor!

PART 6

✦

SO YOU'RE GOING ON AN ADVENTURE

THREE WAYS TO WRITE
A BETTER HIKE

༄

BY VICTORIA SANDBROOK

From Dorothy's journey through Oz to the walk to Mordor, on-foot journeys are a staple of fantasy fiction. Wide-eyed young heroes tread jauntily between adventures with rucksacks and minimal provisions. Bands of travelers opt to take shortcuts through treacherous mountain passes. Distance, day length, and weather often seem to have little bearing on anyone's rate of progress. In reality, the difficulty of the terrain, the availability of food and water, the weight and design of a pack, and unpredictable forces of nature all impact the stamina and well-being of travelers on foot.

But you don't have to assume every character will be a Cheryl Strayed or a Bill Bryson, bumbling through your fantastic wilderness with the know-how of a mundane city slicker. If you want your characters' journey to ring true, consider how these variables can play into your world-building and plot. In reality, "one does not simply walk into Mordor"; one has to plan the trip first.

1. Troublesome Terrain

Will your characters traverse the Misty Mountains or frolic down the yellow brick road? Follow a clear path or force their way through dense jungle brush? Different terrains require vastly different travel times and skills. A delivery boy able to run all day may have trouble hoofing it over a trail-less mountain without great effort, magical intervention, and/or lots of scrapes and blisters. Tolkien's scene on mount Caradhras—especially as represented in Peter Jackson's *Fellowship of the Ring*—gives me great pause: How on Middle-earth did they get up there, much less down again? As a hiker, I want a better explanation than just "magic."

In the real world, the Yosemite Decimal System (YDS) categorizes terrain into six classes, from walkable to requiring equipment for more than just safety. Each class has its own concerns, but the first three are generally hiking-related, covering everything from a sidewalk to mountainous, hand-over-foot scrambles. Classes 4, 5, and 6 cover increasingly technical rock climbing, which (in the real world) is most often tackled for recreation and not travel.

Besides the type of path, you also have to consider grade, altitude, and season. On flat Class 1 terrain (think the yellow brick road), an average human walking pace is around four miles per hour (a fifteen-minute mile). On steep Class 3 terrain, gaining a thousand to two thousand feet of elevation per mile (arguably entering Misty Mountain territory), an experienced and fit hiker can hit a two-to-three-mile-per-hour pace in good conditions. Your characters' level of fitness and familiarity with the terrain will definitely affect how long this pace can be maintained. Other surfaces—sand, ice, snow, gravel—will all affect speed and stamina as well.

For someone used to living at sea level, altitude sickness can set in at eight thousand feet elevation. Supplemental oxygen is needed above 12,500 feet. Remember, though, that rough terrain can be found below these limits: Mount Washington is only 6,289 feet versus Mount Everest's 29,029 feet, and the former's grueling paths are often used to train for the latter.

Finally, winter weather can drastically change terrain. Some rough paths become smooth sailing for snowshoers and cross-country skiers. Others become treacherous ice chutes or avalanche-prone fields. Crossing a large backyard in hip-deep snow can feel like you've hiked a mile (ahem, Tolkien . . . again). Unless your characters are well provisioned and acclimated, setting the journey in winter is a great way to put them in immediate jeopardy.

2. What's on the Menu?

Got lembas? Great! Near a clean water source at all times? Perfect! Your characters are all set for staying well fed and hydrated over their journey. Even in the real world, it's not unrealistic to find a path where food and water are readily available at a village or through hunting and foraging. But even in lands of plenty, your characters may not be able to find everything they need every day, and it's likely they'll carry some provisions.

How much your characters carry may depend on how much they need. Long-distance hikers in temperate weather burn three thousand to five thousand calories every day; in winter, human bodies burn calories even faster (approximately one thousand calories for every hour spent gaining a thousand feet in elevation). Calorie-dense foods are a traveler's best friend. Assuming that lembas has the caloric density of Fritos (160 calories per ounce), your human characters would only need twenty to thirty ounces per day.

A steady diet of beef jerky would require twice that amount; it isn't much weight-wise, but it wouldn't take long to feel pretty awful. On the other hand, you'd need to eat about seventeen pounds of apples to meet the same caloric need. Not only is that rather outrageous if your character is carrying a few days' worth, but that's a *lot* of apples. Still, some characters (your scarecrows and tin woodsmen, for example) may not need to eat at all.

Water needs will vary based on exertion, environment, weight, and more. You can use an online calculator for an exact volume. When it comes to writing, though, access may be more important. If your characters aren't drinking frequently from a source, water gets heavy: Every liter weighs 2.2 pounds. And if they're not filtering or boiling water before they drink it, they'll likely catch something. *Giardia* is in almost every body of fresh water on Earth, no matter how seemingly pristine.

All this talk of weight leads right into the next area of concern.

3. That Knapsack on Your Back

Is your expedition equipped with Bags of Holding™®? If not, there is likely a limit to what your characters can carry due to both the packs' design and the weight carried.

There's a good reason why modern hiking packs are built as they are. The belt is key: A well-fit pack puts most of the weight on the hips, and the shoulder straps are primarily for load balance. This saves the back a lot of strain. External frame packs are inherently heavier and less stable but allow weight to be more effectively placed on the hips and keep the traveler walking upright. Internal packs give hikers a better center of balance, trading a bit of comfort and good posture for a more streamlined profile. I shudder to think of how uncomfortable Dorothy's picnic basket would have been after a few hours, much less days on the road.

This is where pack weight becomes important. If your characters are carrying old-style rucksacks, there's going to be a lot of weight-shifting, back strain, and fatigue. Even if your characters are using well-designed packs, it takes only twenty pounds or so to throw someone off their game if they haven't been training while carrying weight.

If you're sending characters into an unexpected journey, it will take them some time to get used to lugging their packs around, even if the weight carried is reasonable.

So how much is reasonable? For safety, a pack should not weigh more than 33 percent of a hiker's body weight; ultralight packs can be lower than 20 percent, depending on season and needs. But some take the concept of "ultralight" to an extreme known as "stupid light" and choose to leave basic safety gear at home. HikeSafe.com provides a list recommended for the responsible hiker in New England; other climates would require different considerations, but it's a good start. Know what you want your travelers to have when the going gets rough and how they'll manage if they don't have what they need.

Tools to Help

So what does your world demand of your characters? What issues are solved by your tech or magic, and where are your characters more at risk? And where do you want fact to end and fiction to begin?

If you start with an analogous real-world terrain, turn to local hiking clubs and guidebooks to get an idea of the skills required and the standard travel times anticipated. If you're setting your journey in a less modern world, read first-ascent stories in the archives of old climbing journals like *Appalachia*. Go to your local outdoor store and read up on old-fashioned gear to back-engineer devices to which your characters may have access. Plus, there are loads of great blogs dedicated to every aspect of hiking, climbing, and survival.

So just how real should your journey feel? Well, it's up to you. But depending on what you throw at your characters, whether fact or fiction, their mileage may vary.

WILDERNESS SURVIVAL

❧

BY REBECCA MOWRY

Being a wildlife biologist typically means spending a significant amount of time traveling around, working various short-term jobs to gain experience in the field. I've finally landed in western Montana more or less permanently, but it's been a wild ride: I've hiked and back-packed in a wide variety of ecosystems, from the remote desert of Texas's Chihuahuan Desert, to the high elevations of central Colorado, Yellowstone National Park, and eastern Arizona (yes, there are high, snowy mountains in Arizona!), to the hardwood forests and clear rivers of the Missouri Ozarks.

In this field, wilderness safety is something to take very, very seriously: Not only are we spending the majority of our time in wildlife habitat—usually alone—and far from cell phone towers, we're also in-tentionally seeking out critters that could very easily and seriously harm us if we're not careful enough. And I've been fortunate to have sampled enough various habitats that I can hopefully provide some insight into myths, tips, and tricks that could help you (and your characters) survive (or not) in whatever wilderness you've stuck them in!

1. Myth: The Desert Is a Wasteland

It's easy to look at a desert ecosystem and see nothing more than a hot, barren, brown terrestrial hell. But most deserts are full of life.

During the heat of the day, yes, there's not much there. But just wait for the sun to set and the desert comes alive with insects, arachnids, reptiles, amphibians, even large mammals. Granted, most of them want to bite, stick, or sting you, and many are venomous, which makes sense when you think about it—if you've gone through the trouble of adapting to so harsh an environment, you're not going to give up your place in it without a fight.

And if you want to see an even more dramatic change than day to night, go to the desert just after it rains. The Southwestern deserts—including the Chihuahuan Desert in West Texas, where I lived—usually get most of their precipitation in the form of summer monsoons. And let me tell you, the desert really comes alive. This year, West Texas had a crazy wet winter, resulting in a spring of green plants and colorful wildflowers that, in my opinion, rivals any other ecosystem any day of the year.

The point of all this is: If your characters get lost in the desert with no hope of escape, all is not lost. If they're truly desperate and not completely incapable, they can hunt mule deer, pronghorn antelope, jackrabbits, and any number of meaty birds like doves and quail. They must watch out for rattlesnakes and scorpions and the occasional mountain lion, and they must, of course, find water. I'll get to that in a moment. They will probably need to travel at night and rest under shelter during the day, or the sun will scorch them. If you really are interested in learning about all the ways a desert can kill you—and how you can avoid it—go read *Death in Big Bend* by Laurence Parent.

2. Myth: If You're Dehydrated, You'll Know It

When I lived in West Texas, I spent four days hiking a thirty-seven-mile loop through Big Bend National Park. Each day of that trip, I spent upward of fourteen hours without urinating a single time. I didn't feel sick, and I rather liked not having to worry about doing my business around three guys—but it was almost certainly not good for my kidneys. In Big Bend, rangers recommend drinking two gallons of water each day. I was probably draining my three-liter CamelBak and one-liter Nalgene bottle, and no more—that's just over one gallon. If you're drinking enough water, you should be going to the bathroom, and your urine should be clear or pale yellow.

Dehydration is serious business. One of the guys on my trip had gotten lost on that trail a few years previously and got so dehydrated that he almost certainly would have died if another hiking group hadn't seen him wandering aimlessly in the scrub. Dehydration doesn't just happen in the desert, either; the Rocky Mountains can be scorching on a midsummer day, and, depending on the time of year, water may be hard to find. Many a time, I have spent a full day hiking and come home to realize I hadn't urinated a single time. Especially when it's cold or cloudy, it's hard to remember that you're still sweating, you're still expending energy, and you still need to drink water.

In the desert, water can be found in springs (there are a good many of them in Big Bend Ranch State Park, for example), tinajas or huecos (little eroded pools in the rocks that hold precipitation and can sustain life for miles around), and ephemeral creeks and washes. But if you (or your characters) are purposely taking a trip to the desert, the biggest priority should be making sure you bring enough water. (On our thirty-seven-mile trip, we cached ten gallons beforehand.) It's a myth that you can eat cactus to survive; most of the time, the acidity will make you very sick and probably dehydrate you further. So if you eat some, don't eat too much.

In the forest, it's a lot easier to find water. You should still bring a filter, though. *Giardia* is a serious and very unpleasant protozoan parasite found in most water bodies, rivers, and creeks, even in the backcountry. Getting *Giardia* is probably better than dying of dehydration, though.

3. Myth: If You're Lost, Don't Worry. Rescue Planes Can Easily See You

I wouldn't count on that. For both Southwestern deserts and woodlands.

I've been on enough aerial wolf, elk, and deer surveys by now to be able to tell you that it is *really* hard to spot stuff among the trees. Biologists usually try to do their surveys in the early morning and late evening in order to maximize the likelihood that the wildlife will be standing out in the open, feeding. I've counted an elk herd only to fly over it ten minutes later, after the animals had taken cover in the trees, and—*presto chango!*—the elk were *invisible*. And trying to find wolves without the help of tracking collars? Forget about it.

The problem with deserts is that (a) during the day, you'd better be taking cover to keep the sun from killing you, and (b) there are a lot of yuccas and shrubs and bushes scattered haphazardly about that would make it very difficult to find a human. We surveyed pronghorn in those environments and counted a lot of "yucca-lopes," and missed who knows how many pronghorn because we thought they were yuccas.

And these animals were literally *right below us*. Try searching an enormous area for a single lost human.

So if you're lost and hoping for rescue from above, your best bet would be to get out in the open and find some way to attract attention. Bright clothing, fire, spelling a message in white rocks, waving your arms around—whatever it takes. That's where the mirror comes in handy—flash the sun's reflection in the pilot's eyes and he's bound to notice eventually.

Better yet, carry a SPOT or inReach satellite communicator unit.* Every Montana FWP pilot uses one in case they're forced to land in the backcountry, and more and more field biologists carry them every time they venture into the woods.

A friend of mine was mauled by a grizzly bear while doing field work in the Montana backcountry a few years ago. Her inReach helped save her life. You'll notice I haven't covered wildlife attacks in this chapter, because what you should do to prevent or stop an animal attack varies widely depending on the species and the circumstances. All I'll say for now is: Carry bear spray, know how to use it, and get a satellite communicator if you can.

By the way, here's a hint I learned from author Jon Krakauer: Remember that lots of people "get lost" for fun, on purpose, and don't need help to get back. If a plane flies over you, waving one arm means *I'm okay*. Waving two means *I need help*.

4. Bonus Myth: Cotton Is Nice and Warm and Great for Wilderness Trips

No, no, no! Remember this: Cotton is rotten!

The thing about cotton is that, yes, it's nice and warm and dry—but only when it's nice and warm and dry outside. When cotton gets wet and cold, you better hope you've got a fire or a warm shelter to get back to. Go for wool for your socks and underclothes. Wool is slower to dry, it's true, but if it gets wet, it holds on to your body heat. So you'll be wet, but warm.

Cotton does dry quickly, so it can be good for hot days when you're sweating a lot, but I always recommend keeping a set of wool thermals and socks in case bad weather or an unexpected temperature drop comes your way. Most people know the experience of getting all hot

---

* See findmespot.com/en-us.

and sweaty in a cotton shirt on a cold day, then freezing their butt off once they've rested because their clothes are wet.

I usually wear a quick-dry outer shell (pants, shirt, and/or jacket) with warm wool underclothes. And I *never* wear cotton socks when I'm hiking, not ever.

Wilderness Survival, in Conclusion

Your best insurance against getting in trouble in the wilderness is to be prepared, always tell someone where you're going and when you plan to get back, and remember that you are *never* in control.

Overpack. Bring too many clothes. Bring too much water. Bring stuff you might not need. Within reason, of course, but it's better to have something and not need it than the other way around.

National parks require all backcountry hikers to get a permit, which usually includes information on where you're going and when you expect to be back. This permit may save your life if you get lost. This type of thing is good to do wherever you're going, not just in a national park.

And you're not in control, no matter how much preparation you've done. But the more you prepare, the more likely you can handle whatever Mother Nature may throw at you. I'm a biologist; I love Mother Nature, as do many of my fellow outdoor enthusiasts. But no matter where we go, that love *must always* be accompanied by a healthy dose of respect. For our own sake.

HOW TO WRITE ROCK CLIMBING WRONG

❧

BY MICHELLE HAZEN

So, you have a killer book idea, and it involves a badass rock-climbing scene, but you've never been climbing. No sweat—I've got you covered.

Before we jump into the specifics, remember that in fiction, when you introduce a specialized sport, you need to do two things: (1) do not confuse your audience, and (2) convince them your character knows what they're doing. Sometimes having your character drop just the right lingo is enough to establish legitimacy to the audience, and past that, you want to choose the simplest motions, so you don't have to bog your pacing down in technical descriptions. Nobody wants to know about every chicken-head you clove-hitched off to.

Of course, if you want to write rock climbing *wrong*, the best way to do it is to copy anything you've seen in a movie. Especially *Cliffhanger*. Documentaries are good, but feature films are often horrendous. The *best* thing to do is to go to your local rock-climbing gym, because you'll be able to picture everything much more clearly once you see it in action. Plus, you can go up to people and ask, "What's the name of that thingy?"

Speaking of which . . .

What's the Name of That Thingy?

Carabiner—The oval-shaped metal clips that are used as joiners for everything in climbing. If you rub a rope across a rope, the friction cuts it, so everything must be joined by carabiners.

Lead climbing—The action of being the first person up a cliff, a.k.a. the lead climber. "I'm going to lead this pitch." More on this below!

Belay—When you belay someone up a climb, it means that the nonclimber end of the rope goes down to you. You pay out more slack as they climb and use a "belay device" to arrest the movement if they fall. It holds more weight than grabbing it with your hands and gets you less rope burn! "I can belay you on this route." "Let me grab my belay device." When you're climbing, you usually need a team of at least two: the climber and the belayer.

Free climbing—When you're climbing with your hands and feet *and a rope*. You don't climb the rope, and it doesn't hold your weight; it's just there to catch you if you fall. Not to be confused with . . .

Free soloing—When you're climbing with your hands and feet and *no rope*, too high up to be considered bouldering. Falls would lead to serious injuries or death. The documentary *Free Solo* is a great place to see this in action. And, yes, I do realize that it would have been less confusing to name free climbing and free soloing something more intuitive. When I'm Dictator of the Universe, we'll rename them Roped Climbing and Un-Roped Climbing, respectively.

Harness—This is how the rope attaches to you. The harness goes around your waist and the tops of both legs, and the rope attaches in front of you, roughly where the fly of your jeans is. Google a picture, because it's different than the full-body, over-the-shoulder harnesses you often see utility workers using. Pro tip: You can tie the rope directly to the harness without using a carabiner in between, though you can use a carabiner as well. If your character is going on an unplanned climb and has to improvise, they can tie into their belt, but make sure you highlight how unsafe this is. If you need more action, you can always have the belt buckle break!

Bouldering—Climbing on boulders, where you don't go high enough to need a rope, and you can just hop down at the end. Sometimes people use a "bouldering pad" to cushion the landing. It is exactly what it sounds like, but firmer than you're thinking.

Bolt—A piece of metal permanently bolted into a drilled hole in the rock, with a stiff metal loop to clip carabiners/quickdraws into. Usually used on "face climbs," which mean solid rock where there are no cracks to place protection. "He stretched to clip the last bolt."

Quickdraws—Two carabiners connected by a few inches of webbing. One carabiner clips into the bolt; the rope runs through the other carabiner.

Protection—A catchall word for anything you run your rope through so that it will catch you if you fall. Can mean bolts, cams, nuts, quickdraws attached to bolts, or carabiners clipped to balcony railings in your suspense sequence.

Trad climbing (traditional climbing)—Climbing while placing cams, nuts, hexes, or other kinds of gear into cracks in the rock. Yes, basically you're just jamming stuff into cracks, clipping a carabiner into that, running your rope through the carabiner, and hoping that if you fall, the stuff jammed in the crack will stick well enough to hold your body weight. There's a good explanation of this about twenty minutes into the documentary *The Dawn Wall*.

Sport climbing—This is climbing with bolts and quickdraws. It's for when you want to climb a solid piece of rock with no cracks, or if you're too sane to want to trust your safety to a bunch of temporary stuff crammed in cracks.

Cams—This is a nifty piece of gear invented by climbers who wanted to jam better stuff in cracks. It's a spring-loaded doohickey where you pull back the trigger, the lobes fold up, then you stick it in a crack, and it opens to the size of the crack. Then, if you fall on it, it opens up even farther to jam hard into place. You can google a picture for reference, but it's often best not to write these in because they confuse readers.

Grappling hook—No. Not a thing. Unless you're Batman, just no.

How Does the Rope Get Up There?

This is the number one question people ask me about climbing, and the first thing people get wrong in fiction. Unfortunately, when your character is ready to climb a cliff, there's rarely a safety rope already hanging on it. And if there is, they shouldn't use it, because that sucker's been hanging out in the sun way too long and will likely snap as fast as the Hulk's temper.

Since you want a rope to catch you when you fall, you can lead climb or you can top rope. You have to lead climb before you top rope, because *that's* how the rope gets up there. One person climbs up, clipping quickdraws or carabiners to pieces of protection and running the rope through the carabiners until they get to the top. If they fall, they fall down past their last piece of protection until the rope catches them. So if they're five feet above their last piece of protection, they'll take at least a ten-foot fall.

At the top, they run the rope through carabiners attached to the anchors. The anchors can be permanently bolted in or made of trad gear that's removable. Anybody who top ropes the climb after the leader will be caught immediately by the rope, no fall necessary.

Pro tip: The rope slides *through* the carabiners; it doesn't tie off to them. If it did, you'd be like a dog hitting the end of its leash as soon as you climbed past.

Question: How Do I Make My Character Talk Like a Rock Climber?

Biner—This is common shorthand for carabiner. "Hand me that biner."

Crimper—A very small hold. "That climb looks crazy crimpy." "I ripped my fingernail off on that crimper."

Jug/juggy—A way to say a climb has big holds and looks easy. "Let's do the 5.6; it's juggy as hell."

Crag—A way to say a climbing area. "I've been mostly climbing at the local crag."

Pro—Common shorthand for pieces of protection. "This climb doesn't have much pro." This can include bolts but usually refers to pieces of trad climbing gear.

Rappelling/rap—Rappelling is using the rope to lower yourself to the ground at the end of a climb. It's how you get *down*, not up. "Time to rap the route."

What Do You Call a Hard Climb?

The Yosemite Decimal System is how climbs are rated in difficulty in America. For rock climbing, it starts at Class 5. Classes 1–4 are various types of hiking to scrambling, using your hands more as it gets steeper.

5.6 is about as easy as any actual climbs are graded.

5.7 still easy.

5.8 standard beginner fare.

5.9 intermediate.

5.10 intermediate. Once you get to 5.10 and above, it also divides into 5.10a, 5.10b, 5.10c, and 5.10d (because it's America, and our measurement systems never make sense).

5.11 is a hard grade for a recreational or weekend climber.

5.12–5.13 are *really* hard. Bordering on you'd have to be a professional and climb all the time to do these.

5.14 looks practically impossible.

5.15 can only be done by a handful of people in the world.

How Can I Learn More?

Head out to your local gym or crag! It's the fastest, most fun way to learn how to write the rock climbing in your book.

CASTLES AND RUINS

৶৹

BY CHEYENNE L. CAMPBELL

Castles: The Fantasy Fundamental

What's a fantasy world without a castle? I bet that if you, like me, obsessed over this intrinsic ingredient of the genre as a child, you have in your head a sprawling stone behemoth of turrets, towers, parapets, spires bedecked with banners whipping in the magical winds of the realm, and a creaky drawbridge over a monster-infested moat.

Standard fantasy castles likely fit into one of two categories: a residence bustling with servants, knights, and royal ceremonies, or the sort that featured in a classic Macintosh computer game—*Dark Castle*—filled with plague rats, booby traps, and a Big Bad waiting to slay your adventurer.

Or if you—also like me—spent your childhood rewatching *Monty Python and the Holy Grail*, you might also hold Castle Anthrax or Swamp Castle as your predominant mental image (both of which, incidentally, were filmed at Doune Castle in Scotland, which also doubled as Castle Leoch in *Outlander*).

Until my move to the United Kingdom, where I've spent fourteen years staring at a hilltop castle outside my bedroom window and hiking through prehistoric ruins before teatime, I was guilty of assuming castles fell into the category of "If you've seen one [in *Monty Python/The Princess Bride*/enter pop-culture juggernaut here], you've seen them all." A problem arises when you then *write* castles based on a single mental image, denying yourself the opportunity to make this fantasy story staple mean something unique to your world. And every fantasy story deserves settings that breathe, vary, and become characters in their own right.

The Basics

Let's start with what a castle is in our world. In general, we're talking about structures to house and defend nobility, built between the fifth and fifteenth centuries. One archetypal example is Caerphilly Castle in Wales, with its square shape, gatehouses, concentric curtain (outer) walls, and surrounding moat. "Palace" and "fortress" are often used interchangeably with "castle," though palaces tend not to be fortified, and fortresses don't necessarily house nobility. Towers are just one part of a castle, usually, but Tolkien himself rarely used the word "castle," choosing instead his Elvish terms for tower like "minas" and "barad."

Then there are the world-building basics to ask: Did natural resources dictate its design and materials—and were they local or imported? What's the reason for its location—trading on a seaport, defending with long-range artillery on a hilltop? Who lives and works inside, or who died inside, rendering their wizard lover a hermit who turns intruders into talking animals?

It's also helpful to think logistics. The thing that shocked me most about my initial castle explorations was how tiny many of the bedrooms and staircases are, often in narrow, twisting, cramped towers where you're lucky to pass someone coming the other way without one of you tumbling to your death. Were people generally smaller when the castle was built, causing issues for current residents? What if larger invaders from across the sea were to capture it—would they need renovations to even access the upper levels?

And as for the one castle room you don't often see described in fantasy, toilets in British castles tend to be holes in exterior walls that projected waste into the moat below, adding a whole new dimension to the disposition of any potential moat-dwelling creature.

Speaking of design, while Caerphilly might have the classic stone-keep-and-concentric look that's easily dropped into a story, castle architecture around our world varies widely, from the Alcázar Castle in Segovia, Spain, shaped like the bow of a ship, to Bavaria's fairy-tale-ish Neuschwanstein, to grand residences like the Château de Chambord in France, to the Mediterranean paradise of Castello Aragonese off the coast of Naples. What works in one climate or culture might make little sense in another.

More Than a Setting

When I began exploring Britain, I paid entry fees at sites like Alnwick Castle in Northumberland, famously used in Harry Potter, or Eilean Donan in the Scottish Highlands, peering at exhibits of weapons used to behead convicted criminals, or a hairbrush abandoned by Bonnie Prince Charlie. Most offer tours by guides in period garb, sharing accounts of historically significant battles, or the daily grind of castle inhabitants. Take Edinburgh Castle. You can have no better intro to castle artillery because it was the most besieged location in the UK. It's even home to a restored medieval cannon, Mons Meg, one of the largest in the world. All of this presents valuable intel on how a working castle, well, *worked*.

But if the guides are costumed, if the bedrooms are re-created down to the tapestry design, and if the reenactments demonstrate the amount of work required by kitchen staff waking at two a.m. to cook breakfast for two hundred people, for example, you're being told a story already. For inspiration that goes deeper than helping sketch out a setting for your own story—to unearth, say, what your story might *be*—I recommend looking at not just reenactments and reconstructions but ruins.

On my last visit to Edinburgh Castle, I didn't photograph the cannons pointing off Half Moon Battery, or the crown jewels, or the impressive Great Hall—a setting worthy of an epic fantasy banquet. I photographed a piece of wood.

Tucked away in the castle vaults are three wooden prison doors that I hadn't noticed previously. And we're not even talking medieval prisons—these held prisoners from the War of American Independence and the Napoleonic Wars. But it wasn't their historical significance that triggered my imagination. It was their graffiti.

Names and thoughts carved by prisoners' hands into the wood kindled an entire plot. Viewing this display in a cold, dark chamber helped me envision the living conditions, giving a sense of temperature, travel distance of sound, echoes, light (or lack thereof), and other ambient factors. But one small detail such as a name gouged in wood, even buried as it was in the mountain of story fodder that is Edinburgh, can unleash a reason to *have* a castle in your story in the first place.

The Beauty in Ruins

Castles ranging from those mentioned earlier to the Tower of London (despite its name, a castle with multiple towers) and even St. Michael's Mount off the coast of Penzance in Cornwall—accessible by foot only at low tide—can inform the functional and aesthetic aspects of your story's largest structure. But what about the buildings left in ruins, such as Whitby Abbey in North Yorkshire, built in the seventh century, likely raided by Vikings, and used as a setting in Bram Stoker's *Dracula*? Or Urquhart Castle's ruins beside Loch Ness, "slighted," or deliberately damaged, to prevent Jacobite occupation?

Like a slab of wood in a dusty dungeon, these are not restored to the appearance of their glory days but left showing the aftermath of battles, bombs, or simply the passage of time. And this lack can leave greater room for imagination.

Cornwall and West Devon in South West England are full of ruins—castles such as the circular Restormel, Falmouth's hilltop Pendennis defending the mouth of the river Fal, and Tintagel, linked to Arthurian legends. But what this area simply overflows with in terms of ruins is mines, and their iconic features: engine houses and chimneys.

All part of a UNESCO World Heritage Site, these stone structures appear around bends in the road and jut out of the hills and moors on a misty walk, without obvious purpose to the uninitiated. Because as with many prehistoric stone monuments—also numerous in the South West of England—there are no entry fees, no queues of bus tours, and no souvenir shops. This is what makes these types of neglected structures so informative to world-building: The true history must be researched on your own time. Without a guide telling you what you're looking at, the magic is in what you *don't* know. Derelict circular chimneys perched on seaside cliffs become portals, or prisons, or silos for storing illegally harvested mermaid hair.

Going back to Tolkien, his Middle-earth locations were famously inspired by places he'd visited throughout his life. Helm's Deep, the fortress held by Aragorn and company, is a fortified mountain ravine based on Cheddar Gorge, a four-hundred-foot gorge outside Bristol, England, whose caves and crags inspired a honeymooning Tolkien. Cheddar is a beautiful natural wonder (and, of course, the home of Cheddar cheese), but I marvel when I visit that, from this thin, winding road between clifftops, Tolkien conjured such a monumental set piece for some of the most pivotal scenes in *The Two Towers*. There is value in looking beyond actual *castles* to inspire your castles.

Whether your action takes place in castles, forts, towers, mines, or a labyrinth carved into a hillside, what's vital is assigning your setting its own history and purpose—to make it feel integral, not tacked on. Inspiration for this can come from anywhere you visit—whether in person or through research. But remember, don't be afraid to forgo the glossy brochure and gift shop and go off-map. The more unexplained, the better.

THINGS AUTHORS DON'T KNOW ABOUT THE WOODS

༄

BY DAN KOBOLDT

It's hard to put a number on how many books I've read that feature characters in the woods. Sometimes they're fleeing, sometimes chasing, sometimes just looking for something to eat. As someone who spends a lot of time in the woods, I should tell you that most authors get it wrong. Here are some realities about the woods that every writer should know.

A Forest Has More Than Trees

When writing about the woods, many authors focus on just one thing: the type of trees and how many there are. In a mature deciduous forest, there are typically at least four layers of plants:

- The top canopy, formed by the tall trees, begins twenty or thirty feet overhead and goes much higher.

- Below that, you'll often have a second canopy from saplings and smaller trees, like dogwoods and cedars.
- The third layer, called the understory, comprises shrubs and bushes, like honeysuckle.
- Lastly, there's the ground cover of forest herbs: weeds, wildflowers, and other things that grow quickly in spring before the deciduous trees get their leaves.

All of this must be negotiated by someone on the ground. Which leads me to my next point.

Running Often Isn't Possible

Nothing throws me out of a book faster than a character running (or worse, galloping) full-tilt through a dense forest. If you only had the big tree trunks to worry about, you'd be fine. It's the understory that's the problem: Dense, shoulder-high thickets are almost impossible to traverse quickly. And if it's a patch of evergreens, forget it. They're hard to even walk through, because they can grow so closely together with branches that hang almost to the ground.

Running or riding a horse at top speed is also pretty much begging for a broken ankle. Holes, stumps, and fallen logs all lurk beneath a deceptively placid layer of fallen leaves. I admit that there's a scene in *The Rogue Retrieval* where the main character rides a horse at full speed through the woods, but it's on a clear trail (and he's kind of being chased by a dragon).

Move Quickly or Move Quietly, but Not Both

Having stalked many animals in the woods, I can tell you that most of them are pretty quiet. They have to be in order to survive. The loudest thing in the woods by far is a human being. Most hunters sneak into the woods well before the animals are moving about, and they find a place to sit very, very still. We don't walk around, because it's nearly impossible to sneak up on game. Moving quietly is possible in many areas—the best-case scenario being a cleared trail shortly after rainfall— but, generally speaking, one has to slow way down to move without making significant noise. I'm talking five to ten seconds to place each step. The faster you go, the more noise you're likely to produce.

What this means for any kind of a forest chase is that a person running through the woods would be easy to hear coming from a long way off, and easy to follow, too. There's one time when a person can move through the forest both quietly and at a decent speed: when the ground is wet, either from heavy dew or recent rainfall. You still have to avoid snapping twigs and kicking branches, but otherwise you can find stealth.

Visibility Varies from Negligible to Decent

The visibility in a forest depends on a few factors, the most important of which is the season. Visibility is poorest in late spring and summer. Because of the undergrowth and the greenery, you usually won't be able to see more than twenty or thirty yards in any direction. Also, someone on the ground usually can't see the sky, the clouds, or the stars at night because of the top canopy. So yeah, that whole navigating-by-the-stars thing won't happen in a dense forest.

Visibility is strikingly different after the leaves fall. The woods are a very different place then. You might be able to see fifty or a hundred yards, depending on the terrain. Snow on the ground makes a difference, too: The contrast makes animals and people stand out at a distance, especially when they're moving.

Ironically, better visibility doesn't always help the hunter, because it works just as well for the animals.

Getting Lost Is Easy

It is very, very easy to become disoriented in the forest. Here are some of the reasons:

- You don't walk in a straight line. There are thickets and fallen trees to skirt around, ridges to cross, and game trails to follow.
- You can't count on the sun or moon, because they're often hard to see through the canopy or when it's cloudy.
- Deep in the woods, everything starts to look the same. You think you know where you are, but you might be wrong.

Even when I'm hunting an area I know well, I never enter the woods without my GPS and an extra set of batteries for it.

The Best Way to Hide

Humans (as well as predators and many bird species) have excellent perceptive vision, meaning that they can easily spot movement. Thus, the best way for anyone or anything to hide in the forest is to keep absolutely still. Movement, even swatting mosquitoes (which are voracious in the forest, by the way), will give you away.

Wearing the right colors helps, too. Blue, red, and bright orange are colors you won't often see in the woods, so they stand out like neon signs. A hunter in full camouflage, sitting still with their back to something that breaks up their outline (like a wide tree), is virtually invisible. That same hunter walking back to the truck is easy to spot.

If I were fleeing someone in the woods, I'd go to ground as quickly as possible and lie still.

The Truth About Tracking

The concept of "tracking people" in the woods in fantasy literature has always bothered me. You know, the old "Aha! This twig is snapped here, so they went in this direction." Most of the time, unless someone is in view, you'll have little idea which way they went. The ground is hard and strewn with fallen leaves. Twenty people might have walked through the same stretch of woods half an hour before me, and I wouldn't be able to tell.

Following someone on a trail will help, though, since it may have been worn down to mud that can hold a footprint. Other things that would help:

1. If the quarry is bleeding. Blood stands out on the forest floor and falls in a pattern that usually indicates direction.

2. If there's snow on the ground. Nothing reveals tracks better than half an inch or more of snow on the ground. Not only are all tracks visible, but you can tell old ones from new ones.

Tracking someone/something that's bleeding through snow-covered woods represents the best-case scenario. Of course, clever quarry might think of ways to turn that against would-be pursuers.

I have tracked wounded deer through the woods on a few occasions. When fleeing danger, animals (including humans) have certain tendencies. They prefer to flee downhill and via the path of least resistance. They run largely in one direction. And they avoid open areas whenever possible.

Expect Strange Noises

Often when I'm sitting in the woods, there's not much to look at (even with my hunting binoculars), so I use my ears instead. Sound usually travels farther than I can see. There are many familiar noises: crows, woodpeckers, crickets, that sort of thing. And let me tell you, I have heard some strange noises. One that I hear somewhat often is a squeaky-squeaky kind of creaking noise; I suspect it's some kind of bird. Other noises are less common, yet more puzzling.

Here's a good example. Once while hunting on a wooded island along the river, I heard this whooshing sound. It would happen once every fifteen or twenty minutes. It almost sounded like a bellows, but I was five miles from any hint of civilization. Then I came to an open patch of sky and I saw what it was: a flock of small birds flying in unison. I think they were teal, and they flew like little stunt planes. The whooshing sound happened when they all made a sharp turn at the same time. I wouldn't have guessed that in a hundred years.

Other strange noises I've heard remain mysteries. Once I heard something that sounded like a baby crying in long, plaintive wails. That one still haunts me.

The Woods Are Beautiful, if You're into That Sort of Thing

Despite all the bugs and tripping hazards and briar patches (and poison ivy!), the woods tend to be a peaceful place. I might spend eight hours without seeing another person. Away from the rush and noise of modern life, time passes more slowly, and twilight seems to last longer. The tranquility of the deep woods, with the sigh of wind through the treetops, is something we outdoorsmen (and outdoorswomen) cherish.

There Are Exceptions to Challenges of the Woods

Some of the difficulties I've described here can be addressed, in part, by preparation. For example, a character wearing heavy clothing, solid boots, and wielding a stout stick or machete can barge through fairly thick ground cover. Also, familiarity with the terrain can be a huge advantage. Someone who knows an area well is more likely to know where the trails are, move quickly, and avoid getting lost than someone passing through for the first time.

And obviously, none of these problems (stealth, visibility, and getting lost) apply to elvenkind. Or the Dúnedain.

WRITING REALISTIC FORESTS

ꙮ

BY TERRY NEWMAN

Trees are great. Most people like trees. I wouldn't trust anybody who didn't. Trees are, of course, a staple of fantasy writing—how much more "fantasy" can you get than a "sylvan glade" in an enchanted forest? However, it's surprising how often trees and woods are used as nothing more than "scenery" in a story, when they could contribute so much more. Trees can help create a unique atmosphere in any tale.

Basically, there is a lot of ignorance about trees and probably even more so about the assemblages of trees that we call "woods" and "forests." The last two terms are not just defined by the number of trees present—although forests are usually larger than woods—but also by the density of tree growth and hence how open or closed the canopy may be. A closed canopy usually demarcates a forest, if you're wondering. The words came into the English language from different sources. "Wood" comes directly from English's Germanic root, from the Middle English "wode," and before that the Old English word "widu." "Forest" came into Britain with the invading Normans, but unlike much French, which has a Latin root, the word was also derived from the Germanic, in this case for a pine or fir tree.

This chapter is intended to help give writers a basic understanding of trees and woods in what one would (mostly) call the more temperate of wooded lands.

Ancient Seminatural Woodlands and Primary Forest

The term "ancient woodland" is used in the UK to refer to any wooded land that has existed for the last four hundred years and that may well have also existed for thousands of years, since the last ice age—some eleven thousand years ago. If you live somewhere that doesn't have a handy ice age to count from, you might well be using terms like "primary forest," "virgin forest," or "old-growth forest" instead. The emphasis here is on an ecosystem that can be considered a climax community. That is a biological community of plants, animals, and, of course, fungi, which, through the process of ecological succession in a location over generations, has reached a steady state.

A major preoccupation of the general population, with regard to a largish collection of trees, is whether it is "natural." Obviously, it depends on your location, but if you are in a reasonably well-populated area with a basic level of technology (even in your fantasy world), a "wood" will be managed to some degree.

Trees are a resource; wood is a valuable crop, and there is not a wooded place in a country like England (should your world be something like England) where the woods are really natural. The phrase usually used, then, is "ancient and seminatural woodlands." The evidence for such management is not necessarily seen in whole-scale clearances and tree felling. But one of the most common methods of tree management involves coppicing and pollarding. These are two cutting and pruning techniques used to produce useful wooden hurdles or poles, taking advantage of the ability of some trees to naturally regenerate from the cut base, or stool, to produce lots of long shoots. Coppicing involves cutting low (fifteen centimeters) to the ground, while pollarding involves cutting higher from the ground (1.5–2.5 meters) so that deer and cattle can't eat the new growth. Coppicing, by preventing a tree from maturing, also increases the longevity of a tree—in the case of one English lime tree, to something like two thousand years. Pollarding produces the sort of trunks that have swollen areas that sometimes really can look like the faces of woodland spirits— but actually (apart from natural accidents) they are more likely to be evidence of human activity. Pollarded trees are more often found in wooded pasture and at boundary sites than in woodlands.

Coppicing and pollarding help characterize woodlands. They are old techniques—in some places dating back to the Bronze Age. Different trees tend to be used for different functions—both then and now. Willow, being so flexible, makes excellent baskets and even some furniture. Ash produces strong, straight poles excellent for tool handles and brooms. Sweet chestnut is ideal for fence posts and sheep pens. Hazel is most likely to be used for thatching, spars for hedge laying and hurdle making. The very hard broadleaf tree, hornbeam, was used for charcoal making. If that sounds strange, you have to remember that another primary use of coppicing and pollarding was to provide firewood. It is far easier to cut coppicing poles than to fell an entire tree and then divide that into logs. Bundles of branches are not just suitable for burning; they can also produce a winter fodder crop sometimes known as tree hay.

What Kind of Tree Is It?

Trees come in all different shapes and sizes. It's part of the reason why trees are such fun. They include some of the oldest organisms on earth and some of the largest.

The Great Basin bristlecone pine is a species of pine tree found in the American West, mostly in Utah, Nevada, and California. One of these trees is calculated to be 5,065 years old! Yes, there are older organisms in the world, but they tend to be colonial. So the bristlecone pine is the longest-living noncolonial organism on Earth (probably).

In terms of large organisms, we know about blue whales and giant squid. There is also a honey fungus that measures 2.4 miles (3.8 kilometers) across, living in the Blue Mountains of Oregon, that probably qualifies as the largest of organisms. But growing underground doesn't really impress like a 379.7-foot-tall giant redwood or the group of genetically identical trees that stretches across more than a hundred acres of Utah's Fishlake National Forest. These quaking aspens, also considered one of the most massive living organisms on earth, grow in groups called stands. Within these stands, a single tree will spread by sprouting new stems from its roots, often several feet from the original trunk. That is a lot of tree.

This brings us to an interesting idea that really does seem to be straight out of James Cameron's *Avatar*. Trees probably talk to each other. After laboratory experiments showed that pine trees can share nutrients, more extensive ecological experiments indicated that different species of trees might be in contact with each other. Mother trees might be able to help "feed" their young, even reducing their own root growth to allow their babies more room. This ability appears to be linked to mycelia, the massive web of hairlike mushroom threads that grow underground throughout forests. Many of these fungal threads form a symbiotic association with the roots of a vascular host plant. These mycorrhizal fungi can, it seems, transmit messages between trees, triggering them to share nutrients and water with those in need. The forest is perhaps just one giant superorganism, or at least a very interlinked ecosystem.

In considering tree classifications, we are mostly concerned with simple definitions. Distinctions like "evergreen" and "deciduous" and "broadleaf" and "needle-bearing" seem quite straightforward, but don't be confused into thinking that "evergreen" = "needle-bearing." The needle-bearing European larch is deciduous, dropping all of its needles in the autumn and going yellow, but this larch retains its cones! Some broadleaf trees, however, are evergreen rather than deciduous—the holly being the most famous, along with the hedge-forming box.

Softwoods and hardwoods are another easy-to-recognize classification. In general, softwood comes from conifers, which usually remain evergreen, while hardwood comes from deciduous trees that lose their leaves annually. Hardwoods tend to be slower growing and denser. They can also be monocotyledons and angiosperms. Although monocots differ from dicots in four distinct structural ways—leaves, stems, roots, and flowers—the main difference, which they are named from, is in the so-called seed leaf. Monocot trees—including palms, bamboo, and coconut timber—have one leaf, while dicots (alders to zebrawood) have two such leaves.

Burning Trees

"I'll just go collect some wood for the fire" is a book and film cliché. Good luck with that. A lot of wood isn't too keen on burning. Anything wet would probably rather not, and wood does get wet rather quickly. New wood doesn't like burning very much, either, which is one of the reasons why logs get seasoned. Of course, logs aren't easy to find in a forest (they don't grow on trees, ha), and that means finding some branches small enough to transport, yet large enough to produce a reasonable amount of heat and thus not require constant topping up. Who wants to go into the wood at night? People do—but mostly when writers want them dead. When somebody goes to get wood for a fire—

everybody should go get the wood! Then, once you have what looks like enough, go get the same again. A useful rule of thumb is that usually you need twice as much wood as you would imagine.

All good Boy Scouts know that wood that doesn't snap isn't good to burn and that you can break some dead twig off a tree to help get a fire started. This is true. These will last about five minutes and not warm you much, let alone heat a pot. You can see why coppicing is such a good idea to produce some good, evenly sized bundles of sticks. Oh, and if you have experience with a nice indoor wood-burning stove, remember that an open fire will need around five times more wood than a wood-burning stove. It's also harder to start a fire in the cold.

The Wind in the Willows

I live in a village that has had a prominent role in the development of the game of cricket. I happened to be walking the dog one morning in late summer when I was suddenly aware of something. This something was the sound of the wind. More specifically, I was actually listening to "the wind in the willows." Willow is used to make cricket bats (as you should know). This rather blew my mind—the actual *wind* in the *willows*—the hairs rose on my neck. It was so evocative, a sort of rustling, and it transported me immediately to my favorite childhood book.

On another occasion, halfway around the world, I was standing in the Vallée de Mai Nature Reserve on the island of Praslin in the Seychelles. The reserve consists of a unique palm forest, made up principally of the island's endemic coco de mer palm, which has the world's largest nut. This forest, with its primitive plants and unique animal species, is a relic from the time when the supercontinent of Gondwana was dividing into smaller parts, leaving the Seychelles islands between Madagascar and India. I realized as I was listening to the wind blow through this unique forest, with its large-leafed palms flapping together, that I was hearing what dinosaurs heard.

The hairs on the back of my neck really did rise—again.

Trees can do that to you. On a simple walk on an autumn's day or while contemplating flesh-eating sauropods. Trees are rather magical and, when used well, can add magic to whatever you are writing.

ABOUT THE CONTRIBUTORS

Olaseni Ajibade is a Nigerian MD currently working as a hospital-based physician in Augusta, Georgia.

Marie Brennan is a World Fantasy Award–nominated novelist with a background in anthropology and folklore. She doesn't speak any language fluently apart from English, but she's dabbled in Spanish, Latin, Japanese, Irish Gaelic, Old Norse, Finnish, and Navajo.

Carrie Callaghan is a senior political analyst at the US Department of State. She is the author of the novels *Salt the Snow* and *A Light of Her Own* (both from CRP/Amberjack). She lives in Maryland with her family and three ridiculous cats.

Cheyenne L. Campbell is a Native American (Iroquois) from Grand Island, New York, who holds dual UK/USA citizenship and graduated with a first-class film BA from Cornwall's Falmouth University. She has edited and written for *ONSCREEN* magazine. Her writing is inspired by her travels around the Cornish coast, the Scottish Highlands, the English countryside, Venetian canals, Greek islands, and Alpine villages.

Rachel Annelise Chaney spent her childhood inhaling every scrap of horse information she could find and riding every equine she could climb on. Since adopting an ex-racehorse, she's ridden, trained, or cared for everything from Thoroughbreds to quarter horses, drafts to Arabians, warmblood jumpers to paint barrel racers.

Christina Dalcher, PhD, is a theoretical linguist specializing in the phonetics and phonology of sound change. Her research covers the physical, cognitive, and social forces contributing to variation in Italian and British English, and she has held faculty positions in the US, UK, and UAE.

Spencer Ellsworth is the author of the Starfire space opera trilogy from Tor and *The Great Faerie Strike* from Broken Eye Books. He lives in Bellingham, Washington, USA, with his wife and three children, and he's . . . still working on the Crusades book.

Hannah Emery has a PhD in sociology from UC Berkeley. She wrote her dissertation on the social construction of identity, looking at how parents choose names for their children. She's taught courses on sociology, identity, and family. Though a sociologist by training, she has pivoted to community-building work for families in her local area and working to connect kids and families with nature.

Dustin Fife is a biostatistician with a PhD in quantitative psychology from the University of Oklahoma. He's also a serious woodworker with a decade of experience at woodcrafting.

Jen Finelli is a screenwriter and world-traveling science fiction writer with real-world experience as a doctor, autism therapist, reporter, and ghost and nunnery escapist.

Colleen Halverson earned her PhD in Irish literature from UW-Milwaukee and her master's degree at Northern Arizona University. A *USA Today* bestselling author, she writes fantasy and historical romance, often infusing her books with Celtic mythology and history. She currently resides in the Driftless area of Wisconsin with her husband and two children.

Michelle Hazen is an author, book coach, and freelance editor who has been rock climbing for seventeen years and has been annoyed by Hollywood's misportrayal of the sport for nearly as long.

Kate Heartfield has an honors degree in political science as well as a master's degree in journalism from Carleton University. She served for more than a decade on the editorial board of the daily newspaper *Ottawa Citizen*.

Wanda S. Henry holds a PhD in history from Brown University and is a visiting assistant professor in history at Wheaton College, where she teaches about the social history of death.

Crystal King is a culinary enthusiast, marketing expert, and the author of the food-laden novels *The Chef's Secret* and *Feast of Sorrow*. She has taught classes in writing, creativity, and social media at several universities, including Harvard Extension School and Boston University, as well as at GrubStreet. She resides in Boston.

Dan Koboldt is a genetics researcher as well as an author of fantasy and science fiction. He is also an avid bowhunter and outdoorsman. Every October he disappears into Ohio's hardwood forests to pursue whitetail deer and turkey with bow and arrow. He lives with his wife and children in Ohio, where the deer take their revenge by eating all of the plants in his backyard.

J. R. H. Lawless is a Newfoundland-born lawyer who grew up, lives, and practices in Saint Pierre and Miquelon, a set of tiny islands belonging to France but located off the east coast of Canada. After earning dual master's degrees in political science and law from the elite French public administration schools Sciences Po Bordeaux and Sciences Po Paris, he worked for years as secretary-general of a parliamentary group at the French National Assembly.

A. R. Lucas is a decision scientist, origami enthusiast, and science fiction and fantasy writer with degrees in cultural anthropology, psychology, and business. She's worked around the world in jobs ranging from archaeology to economics.

Debby Lush is a United Kingdom–based professional trainer of dressage horses and riders. A former international competitor, she has published two books on the subject.

Michael Mammay is a science fiction writer and the author of the Planetside series, published by Harper Voyager. He graduated from the United States Military Academy and served as an Army officer for twenty-seven years. He holds a master's degree in military history and is a veteran of Desert Storm, Somalia, and the wars in Iraq and Afghanistan. He is now a full-time writer living with his wife in Georgia.

Rebecca Mowry is a big-game biologist with work experience in Montana, Idaho, Missouri, Texas, and Colorado. Over the past fifteen years, she's spent countless hours in the field with wolves, woodpeckers, mountain lions, river otters, and a big salamander called a hellbender.

Terry Newman's scientific career, which involved a lot of looking down electron microscopes, started with the classification of ancient and seminatural woodland in his native Hertfordshire. He then moved on to investigating the endodermis of plant roots before becoming caught up in all things cellular. Although now happily writing fantasy in one of the most wooded areas of the UK, he was probably never happier than when staring up at wonderful trees.

Amy Perkins-McKenna is a biological scientist by training and is here to share some of her horse expertise. She's been riding for twenty years and has been dipping her toes into everything from endurance to eventing to natural horsemanship.

Diana Pinguicha is a computer engineer, writer, and artist who was born in the sunny lands of Portugal and currently calls Lisbon home. She can usually be found writing, painting, devouring extraordinary quantities of books, or walking around with her bearded dragon, Norberta. She also has two cats, Sushi and Jubas, who would never forgive her if she didn't mention them.

Eric Primm is an engineer for Boeing and has spent the past nine years making sure the wings don't fall off various aircraft. He is the club leader of St. Louis Counterpoint Martial Arts and a black belt in both Counterpoint Tactical System and Cacoy Doce Pares. He writes fiction about philosophers and nonfiction about martial arts.

Ember Randall began learning tae kwon do at age fourteen and has been training in various martial arts ever since, earning first-degree black belts in both tae kwon do and Shaolin Kempo. During the day, they're a software engineer, with a focus on accessibility and user-centered design. In their scant free time, they juggle running, climbing, larping, and, of course, writing.

Amber Royer is a small-scale chocolate grower, gardening columnist, and coauthor of the cookbook *There Are Herbs in My Chocolate*. She writes the Chocoverse comic space opera series and the Bean to Bar Mysteries, both of which feature chocolate as a central theme. She has a master of library and information science degree from University of North Texas and teaches creative writing for both the University of Texas at Arlington Continuing Education and Writing Workshops Dallas.

Tahereh Safavi is editor-in-chief of the Ubergroup, an intensive writer's workshop focused on connecting debut authors with verifiable advice from top industry dealmakers. She is an improv actor and circus performer for her day job and spent a decade working Renaissance faires, where she learned to take real history and make it accessible to a general audience. Her big project is *Berserker Queen*, the true story of a Frankish princess who killed Viking kings. You can find more of her articles on history with Brown people at twodrunkhistorynerds.com.

Victoria Sandbrook is a fantasy writer, nonfiction editor, and hiker. In her previous role as the editor at Appalachian Mountain Club Books, Victoria worked closely with authors writing instructional content on hiking, paddling, and other means of outdoor travel. She has also been certified in wilderness first aid, has received training in outdoor leadership, and has logged a few hundred miles on foot in the White Mountains of New Hampshire.

Sarah J. Sover holds a BS in biology with an emphasis in ecology and animal behavior from Georgia Southern University, where she graduated as a Bell Honors' Scholar. She has a background in wildlife rehabilitation and veterinary medicine.

Hayley Stone received a bachelor's degree in history from California State University, Sacramento, and continues to study history in her free time. She is the author of the Last Resistance sci-fi series and the award-winning weird Western *Make Me No Grave*, along with numerous short stories and poems.

Graeme K. Talboys was a teacher in schools and museums before he became a full-time writer. As well as works on museum education, he has written a number of general nonfiction books. He has also written several fantasy novels. His latest series, Shadow in the Storm, is being published by Harper Voyager. He lives in Scotland with his wife and two cats (and five million Scots).

E. B. (Emily Brooksby) Wheeler has an MA in early modern European history with an emphasis on religion and society and an MLA in historic and cultural landscapes. She sometimes teaches history at Utah State University and consults on historic landscape preservation, and she is the author of more than a dozen books of history, historical fiction, and historical fantasy.

Jay S. Willis holds degrees in history and political science as well as law from Capital University. His history studies focused on medieval Europe with independent research on European medieval magic and the Spanish Inquisition. Jay combines his education with both the practice of law as an assistant prosecutor and as a fantasy fiction writer. His epic fantasy series the Sphere Saga was published in fall 2021.